Listen

By the same author:

With the End in Mind

Kathryn Mannix
Listen

*How to find the words for
tender conversations*

WILLIAM
COLLINS

William Collins
An imprint of HarperCollins*Publishers*
1 London Bridge Street
London SE1 9GF

WilliamCollinsBooks.com

HarperCollins*Publishers*
1st Floor, Watermarque Building, Ringsend Road
Dublin 4, Ireland

First published in Great Britain in 2021 by William Collins

1

A catalogue record for this book is available from the British Library

ISBN 978-0-00-843543-1 (hardback)
ISBN 978-0-00-843544-8 (trade paperback)

Thanks for reading this book. It's important to note that it is not a
medical textbook, and its contents are not a substitute for medical advice.
Please always seek the advice of a qualified professional healthcare provider
if you have questions or concerns about your own physical or mental health,
and advise/support others to do so, too.

Typeset in Adobe Garamond Pro by
Palimpsest Book Production Ltd, Falkirk, Stirlingshire

Printed and Bound in the UK using 100% Renewable Electricity
at CPI Group (UK) Ltd

MIX
Paper from
responsible sources
FSC™ C007454

This book is produced from independently certified FSC™ paper
to ensure responsible forest management.

For more information visit: www.harpercollins.co.uk/green

To the patients, families, colleagues
and mentors who shaped my practice.
'Thank you' will never be enough.

Contents

List of Figures

Introduction

'I can't find the words.'

Right now, there is quite likely to be a conversation you are trying to avoid. It is probably one that is important to you, but it has a quality of discomfort to it. Perhaps the conversation requires sharing of a difficult truth; enquiring about information that may be life-changing; proposing something that risks rejection; discussing a topic that will unleash strong emotions; consoling someone experiencing sorrow. There is a push-pull of commitment: the need to act and yet the fear of vulnerability. Not just yet. Soon, but not just yet: I will call, or visit, or make that appointment. We stand on the brink, unsure how to begin.

We all have moments when words fail us. Often this is because the words we need are swirling in a fog of emotions; sometimes leaving them hidden seems more appealing than taking the risk of putting a distressing situation into words.

There are moments when a look, a touch, a shrug, a nod might communicate better than words. A hug, the clasp of a hand, a pat on the arm may speak volumes. Some of us are more comfortable than others with physical gestures; sometimes we might offer a cup of tea, a handkerchief, or a companionable silence.

But eventually there comes a time for words, and then the word-finding difficulty begins. Perhaps we know what we want to convey, but the words feel inadequate. Perhaps we wish we could talk about something important to us, but we fear becoming emotional in speaking of it. We may want to ask a question yet fear it will seem intrusive or insensitive. Maybe it is bad news that needs to be broken, and we dread the distress we will cause in pursuing the task.

This book is about those moments. It offers some ways into finding the words and enabling conversations. It draws on a fascination with the ways we communicate with one another that I have explored throughout my life in social and professional relationships, and it is informed by my work as a doctor, psychotherapist and trainer. Rather than suggesting a script to follow, this book offers stories to think about alongside a discussion of some skills and principles to trust. I hope this combination will give you a handle on the conversations of significance that lie ahead for you, and some ideas to adapt for the situations that you find yourself facing.

A word about stories: throughout this book I have used stories to illustrate the principles of communication. Some of them are my own experiences, some are other people's that they have discussed with me and some are fictional representations of common human experiences. Names and other details of the 'real' people have been changed to protect their identities, and the book does not distinguish the real from the imaginary: all are here simply to provide examples for readers to reflect on, to illustrate or illuminate their own life experiences.

The skills involved in important conversations are nuanced and layered. They are not tools to be used one at a time, but are more like the movements you make to join in a dance: stepping, turning, pausing, changing direction and keeping in time to the music as we move together around the dancefloor. And a bit like salsa dancing, conversations usually need at least two people, for participants to join in and to take turns. Perhaps one person is leading, and yet not forcing. Perhaps one is following, and yet not under pressure. As a dance or a conversation continues, the roles of leader and follower may swap. And in the same way that a dance progresses using steps forwards and backwards, sharing and preserving the space, a conversation includes words and silences, speaking and listening, statements and questions. There is consent, and there is partnership.

There is no right way to hold a conversation about matters that are serious, or sorrowful, or embarrassing, but there are some wrong ways. 'Getting it wrong' is often not about the words themselves, but the dance: insisting on instead of inviting a discussion; speaking lots and listening little if at all; raised voices and too little silence; speaking without consent, or at the wrong time, or to 'get it over with' rather than to explore.

Those occasions when we get it wrong cannot be undone, but we can learn from them. Like dancing: we can understand why we tripped up and know how to tread more gracefully next time; how to keep our balance; how to lean on or support each other as we progress. When to move forwards; when to step backwards; when to trust our hearts and simply follow the music.

This book is an invitation to notice and to expand a skill set that we all possess: our innate ability to join in conversations. Rather than being a textbook or like a dance lesson, it is more of an exhibition or a dance festival where both beginners and accomplished artists can be observed. Instead of training, this book offers encouragement: we will consider ways to open conversations that previously felt too daunting; we will examine how to feel our way into them gently and hold the space there that allows our conversations to flourish.

The style and skills we use will overlap; some we will use all the time, in the same way as dancers move to the rhythm of the music, keep balance and work together. Such skills are like basic steps, while others are turns or twirls that we will use only occasionally. The skills are presented in a roughly sequential order: first, those to engage in a conversation, to get alongside another person and gain their confidence and trust, to begin the process of discovering their current position.

Having looked at those basic skills to open up a conversation, we will observe them again as they are put to use, with only a slightly different emphasis, to explore possibilities for change, or agreement, or resolution. The style remains the same: we are working with, not doing to, the other person, acting as partners, working together to keep in step.

Later chapters show how the same style and skills can be used when the occasion for conversation is particularly challenging. Gradually, we explore together how experienced practitioners of the art of tender conversations use the skill set to hold space and maintain communication in sometimes tricky circumstances. We look at the principles in action: not set scripts, but individual conversations that will offer insights. You may see phrases that feel familiar and comfortable to you; you may see others that you would adapt to your own words as you apply the same principles yourself. The genuine-ness of using our own words cannot be overstated. Even after decades of dealing with complex, sorrowful and deep conversations with sick people and their families, often when I need to speak, I do not know exactly what to say. But I have these principles to follow, and I trust them to guide me as the conversation begins.

We can learn some basic steps together, but whether it's dancing or tender conversations, you will only become accomplished by practising. We can all do this. It only feels daunting until we start.

Storytelling

We explain our world through stories. Whether our life story is a quest or a tragedy, a tale of brave deeds and monsters faced or of changing fortunes and unwelcome plot twists, we live it one unpredictable day at a time. We are both the storyteller and the principal character, and every life is a tale of light and shade, hope and despair, suspense and revelation.

Being able to tell our story helps us to make sense of it. Perhaps we tell it to ourselves, quietly pondering. Perhaps we write it down, recognising in reading back something that we did not recognise at the time. But for most of us, chatting to a friend or reflecting with a confidant is the way we tell our stories. And as we tell them, we hear them anew. Telling helps us to notice and to interpret details, to become aware of the bigger picture or to discern aspects we previously overlooked or denied. Finding a listener who will give our story their full attention, who is prepared to become completely caught up in the tale, is an opportunity to meet ourselves, complete with our noble hopes and miserable failings, and to understand ourselves and the world around us in a truer, more helpful way.

This is a book of stories about people and conversations, about speaking and listening, about the challenges we all face in life. It seems appropriate to start with a story, then. It sets the scene for what will follow.

The tiny woman in the emergency department's quiet room leaps from her seat with a scream, and her fist meets my cheek before

I realise what is happening. As an orange light explodes in my head, I feel myself stagger backwards.

'Liar!' she screams into my face. 'You LIAR! He can't be dead!' Then she collapses backwards into the low seat like an unstrung puppet, her face folded into her lap and her hands clasped over the back of her trembling head. She is wailing, the noise of her overwhelmed howling filling the space around us, and I don't know what to do. My head is spinning with the pain of the blow and the surprise of her actions. I know I must stay, but I also know I am going to fall over. I hear the door open behind me and I turn to see Dorothy, the ED staff nurse, and a hospital porter: our security detail. I shake my head, tears scattering with the movement, and gesture speechlessly to the porter to leave the room. This woman doesn't need a security incident. Her husband has just died in our resuscitation room and I have made a terrible job of telling her. I feel dizzy and sick, but I know I mustn't make this any worse.

'Maybe stay near the door, Ron?' says Dorothy, quietly. She closes the door, leaving the porter outside. She smiles sadly at me and takes a seat beside the weeping woman. 'Avril?' she asks, kindly. 'Are you Avril?' The woman nods without looking up, gulping and shaking. 'Are you Avril de Souza?' asks Dorothy, and the woman looks up.

'Yes . . .' she manages to say from a mouth distorted by a horrified grimace.

'Avril, what's your husband's name?' asks Dorothy.

'Joselo,' moans Avril. 'He's called Joselo. I got called to the hospital. He had a pain in his chest at work. I need to see him. I need to see him now!' The fire is returning to her voice. Dorothy turns to me and says simply, 'Please sit down, doctor, in case Mrs de Souza has any questions while we talk.'

I sink gratefully into a chair on the other side of the coffee table in this sparsely furnished, uncomfortable and too-small room in the emergency department of an old hospital, where I spend time each week talking to the friends, families, partners of people brought into the department, explaining that their loved one's life now hangs by a thread. But never before have I had to tell someone when they arrived that they got here too late, that their dear person has not survived. That job is usually reserved for more senior staff.

The room stops spinning as I watch Dorothy talking to this overwhelmed wife. This new widow. This woman I have shocked so badly that she hit me as an act of denial of a reality she could not bear, could not encompass, injured beyond tolerance by my sudden and unanticipated announcement.

Yet I did it 'by the book'.

Check it's the right person – yes, the right name, and sent here by a phone call from the foreman at the foundry where her husband works. Worked. Until today.

Warning shot – 'I am very sorry that I have terrible news for you.'

Pause.

Tell the news – 'I am so sorry to say that Joselo died a few minutes ago. We were unable to restart his heart . . .'

Pause to let that sink in. And that's when she screamed and hit me, as I stood towering above her in my white coat with my prissy sentences, terrified but trying to sound brave; still sweating from the exertions of prolonged chest compressions that did not revive the unconscious man on the resuscitation-room trolley; still nause-ated by the horror of being asked to agree with the most senior medic present that it was time to 'call' the arrest (meaning to acknowledge that death has occurred); still horrified that instead of being given the task of writing up the resuscitation attempt, I'd been sent to tell his wife who had arrived while chest compres-sions were in progress and who had not been allowed into the resuscitation room. Instead, she'd been sent to sit in the Room of

Doom, as we dubbed this tacky area with its wipe-clean soft furniture and paper-thin walls.

Now Dorothy is giving a masterclass in dealing with unwelcome news. She is sitting down. *Why didn't I sit down?* She has taken Mrs de Souza's hand in hers and she is stroking Mrs de Souza's shoulder with her other hand. I know Dorothy has three patients in the observation unit who are all very sick, and that she can't spend much time here, and yet here she is bending time, extending it by sounding unhurried, making every second count as she focuses her attention on Mrs de Souza.

'This is very shocking, my love,' she purrs to Mrs de Souza. 'Very shocking. Did you know he had a bad heart?'

Mrs de Souza lifts her head and takes a sobbing breath. Dorothy hands her a tissue from the box on the table. Mrs de Souza blows her nose, then says, 'He's had a bad heart for years. He was in here with his first heart attack a couple of years ago and we nearly lost him. He's had more pains recently, that angina pain, and the doctor changed his tablets . . .' She trails off.

'Were you worrying about him?' asks Dorothy, a question I can see reaching to the weeping woman's soul.

'He wouldn't rest,' Mrs de Souza sighs. 'He worked too hard. I told him he was lucky to survive last time.'

'So you thought he might die last time?' asks Dorothy, gently, and Mrs de Souza stares into the middle distance, mopping her eyes and nodding.

'I think we've been on borrowed time,' she whispers. Dorothy waits. 'He wasn't well this morning: stressed by something at work, he looked grey and I told him to stay off, but . . .' and she shakes her head, weeping more quietly now, sorrow instead of shock, sadness in place of anger.

It is fascinating to watch the way Dorothy has used questions to help Mrs de Souza step from her knowledge of her husband's heart disease, past his first heart attack, into her recent worries about his health and to her very specific concern this morning. She has built a bridge for Mrs de Souza to walk across, and in answering Dorothy's questions Mrs de Souza has prepared herself for this unwanted and yet not entirely unexpected moment. She has told Dorothy the Story So Far.

'I am so sorry, my love,' says Dorothy. 'He wasn't conscious when the ambulance arrived, and his heart was beating very slowly at first and then it stopped. The team did all they could . . .' She pauses again, and in that pause I see the path I could have taken: a conversation about the past, the wife's concerns, her worry today. I was so busy making sure I told her the dreadful news that I didn't bring her to a place where she could receive it. Dorothy has wound back the story and then brought her, step by step, to this place: now we can move forward a little further.

'Would you like to come with me to see him?' asks Dorothy. 'He's lying on a bed around the corner, and you can sit with him there if you would like to.

'Would you like us to contact somebody for you? Your family? A priest? Anyone who can support you here?'

Mrs de Souza says she would like a Catholic priest to be called, and Dorothy takes her by the hand to lead her from the room. As they pass me, Dorothy says, 'Make us a cup of tea, we'll be in cubicle three. Bring one for yourself, too.'

Then Dorothy takes Mrs de Souza to sit with her dead husband. When I deliver the tea, Mrs de Souza thanks me like a long-lost friend. I suspect she has no memory of hitting me. Dorothy has reconstructed the whole transaction, skilfully yet simply, by using gentle questions about what Mrs de Souza knew, to help her to recognise that she was already expecting bad news. Dorothy has helped Mrs de Souza to tell herself the story of her husband's ill-health so that both the listener and the storyteller herself could hear it. She didn't use prepared phrases or a careful script: she asked questions, went where the answers took her and offered her complete attention with graceful kindness.

By the book clearly isn't good enough, I will reflect later. We need a new book: a book about how to listen, instead of what to say. Perhaps Dorothy should write it.

Dorothy leads me out of the cubicle where Mrs de Souza is sitting with her dead soulmate and takes me to the consultant's office. I feel sick. I don't want to talk about this any more. I feel sad, and humiliated, and incompetent, and overwhelmed.

'Mr Rogers,' she tells the head of department, a stoop-shouldered trauma surgeon with a shock of white hair and a nicotine-yellow twirly moustache – both the moustache and its wearer are legends in our city – 'I have a complaint.' My heart sinks. Mr Rogers looks up from his paperwork.

'Tell me, Dotty,' he says, gravely.

'It's outrageous that this inexperienced doctor was sent, alone, to tell a wife her husband was dead with no senior assistance and no nurse to act as witness or support!' declares Dorothy, and my jaw hangs slack with surprise. 'You've been talking for ever about training our young doctors to be good communicators, but how will they ever learn that if the seniors either act alone or send the youngsters alone? It's not fair, and this young doctor has been punched in the face by a shocked and angry relative.'

He surveys me, narrow-eyed, over his half-moon spectacles, shaking his head and tutting.

'Bashed, were ye?' he says in his gentle Scots accent. 'Are the police involved?' He asks this mildly, in the way you might ask someone to pass the salt.

'We don't need the police, do we?' I hear myself say. My voice is neither mild nor gentle. I don't recognise its high pitch or breathless catching. 'It was my fault! I shocked her. I didn't mean to, but she was so appalled by the news she lost control of herself.

Her husband has just died. Please don't involve the police!' To my dismay, I am sobbing.

Rising from his desk and pushing his spectacles up the bridge of his nose with a massive finger, Mr Rogers takes two paces to stand in front of me and squints through his glasses at my cheek. 'That won't need a stitch,' he observes, and I am bathed in his tobacco-flavoured breath, 'but a Steri-Strip would help.' It's only now that I am aware that my cheek is visibly damaged. 'Sniff!' he commands, putting that beefy finger against my right nostril so that I must breathe through the left, on the side where my face aches. He probes my cheekbone, feels around the edge of my eye socket, the huge hand surprisingly gentle. 'You'll do,' he says, satisfied.

'Right, Dotty. Sort her cheek out. We'll have to talk to the team about chaperones for bad news. Again . . .' and Mr Rogers turns on his heel, resumes his seat and lights his pipe, hospital smoking rules notwithstanding.

Dorothy tugs the sleeve of my white coat and leads me to the staff room. I am told to sit quietly and before I can protest, she has gone. I am grateful and shocked and, I discover, very sore. And very tired. And so sad. Cold, shivery. A bit nauseated. I sit down and wrap a nursing cloak around myself.

Dorothy reappears with Steri-Strips and a dressings pack.

'Now, my pet,' she soothes, taking the chair next to me. With practised hands she opens the pack and spreads the sterile towel on the table beside us. She pours the disinfectant, swabs my cheek (*ouch*) and then uses another damp cotton swab to wipe round my chin. *Oh, dear. I've been walking around the department with a bleeding cheek wound.*

She places the Steri-Strips with care, eyes locked on the task, her tongue protruding with the effort of concentration. I am grateful for her quiet kindness. But there's more.

'How are you feeling?' she asks, and I want to say 'Fine' but my tears tell the truth and she strokes my shoulder reassuringly. I'm starting to be able to see my cheek beneath my left eye as the injury swells. I shiver inside the cloak. 'Do you need a sick bowl?' she asks, perspicaciously, and I realise what an intuitive and consummate professional she is. I blink away my tears and shake my head. The nausea is abating.

'That's been quite an experience,' she tells me. 'They were wrong to ask you to go alone to break that terrible news. We have protocols. You should always have someone with you: someone to offer care to the poor person who is about to have their world upended, and also to be your back-up. We work in teams because that's what keeps us safe and well, able to keep doing this work. They didn't look after you – and look what happened!'

'But I should have done it better,' I sigh. 'I should have done it like you did. Slowly. A step at a time. I should have sat down. I should have been . . . oh, I don't know . . . *more human*, somehow . . .'

'Well, I've been doing this for over ten years,' she replies. 'I've had a lot of practice. I've been watching you when you come here on duty: I know you are kind to your patients, so I can't imagine you were brutal to her. No, this wasn't your fault, and Mr Rogers needs to remind everyone again about working in teams, using chaperones, teaching these skills to you newbies.' She says 'newbies' with the tenderness of a proud mother. I am speechless at her compassion.

'You getting bashed will be a good story to use in teaching,' she continues. 'It's incidents like this that change people's behaviour when all the telling in the world makes no difference to them. It's stories, not rules, that change people.'

Stories, like lifetimes, are experienced as they move forwards but can only be fully understood when looking back on them. This story is no different. The young doctor who broke bad news 'by the book' was shown how enabling the other person to receive that news into their own understanding of the story-so-far was a way of giving truth with kindness. Dorothy was one of many teachers in the art of storytelling, of how telling begins with listening. The young doctor I was then will learn to listen, to enable others to narrate their stories, to find ways to incorporate difficult truths and unwelcome news; she will learn how to support people as what they hope for changes from success and life goals fulfilled to peace of mind, understanding, being understood. Her patients will teach her that success is not a destination, although it is sometimes an experience on the road; that what really matters in the end is gratitude, forgiveness offered and received, acceptance and love.

Dorothy will carry on being the backbone of her department, speaking truth to power and consoling trainees who feel overwhelmed by the tasks of the ED. Over three decades later, I will meet her during an event at which the hospital's palliative care service, not yet even imagined on this troubled day, is presenting a public-awareness session about end-of-life planning. She is now a governor of the trust that runs the hospital; I am the palliative care service lead. 'You won't remember me,' she begins, and my heart wells at her humility, before I open my arms to hug her. 'I always knew you were a good 'un,' she whispers in my ear, and looking back over Dorothy's shoulder I see the path that has led here: the story makes sense. I understand exactly how Dorothy's skill and kindness on that difficult day so many years ago shaped my practice, my career decisions and my approach to communication skills training.

Dorothy may not have rewritten the book, but her influence has made this book happen.

Opening the Box

To offer somebody help or support, we must start from where the person is, and understand their situation from their perspective. That sounds so simple, and yet it can be difficult to do. Our impulse to be helpful often overrides the need to begin by taking stock, a bit like setting out on a self-assembly project without first reading the instructions and counting the components.

There is an art to participating in conversations about matters that touch on strong emotions. There are skills we can use and habits to develop so that we offer support without overwhelming the other person, we show our willingness to listen without being intrusive, and we hold a space in which they feel able to discuss their distress if they wish to do so. We offer, and they choose. It is very likely that you already have these skills: the art of the tender conversation is to use and trust them in circumstances that may feel emotionally heightened.

The next few stories offer a style guide: a set of skills to recognise in, or add to, your repertoire that are useful in any conversation and especially during emotionally charged discussions. None of these skills is difficult to learn. All of them will become easier to remember and to use, and to use well, with practice. Eventually, instead of reaching for these skills as 'add-ons', they can become habits: part of your conversational style. That's the good news.

Talking about sad, frightening or frustrating things never feels easy. That's the bad news. No matter how much we practise, when the conversation really matters, and especially when it's with a person we love, our own emotions have a way of joining in and making it feel more challenging.

That's why it will help to practise the skills. Every conversation is an opportunity to use them, whether it is discussing a friend's indecision over a purchase or a colleague's interest in a hobby. Use everyday situations to try out the suggestions in this book, and see what happens. As you experience success, those skills will flow more easily into your conversations.

Once we open the box, the stories inside will provide some simple principles of supportive conversational style. We'll look at how to begin a tender conversation, and what puts people off trying. Then we'll look at some skills for making sure we are listening well and really getting the other person's perspective as the conversation progresses: paying attention, checking our understanding, allowing time for reflection. We'll look at ways to reach a safe conclusion to an emotional or deep conversation; and we will consider when we should call for help, either for the other person or for our own support.

Getting Started

It can be difficult to start a conversation about anything that raises strong emotions. It doesn't matter whether it's asking someone out on a date or talking about our funeral arrangements with our dear ones: sometimes our own emotions and sometimes our concern about theirs hold us back. Finding a way to begin that allows both people in the conversation to feel confident of being respected and heard sets a tone of collaboration for the rest of the discussion.

'Doctor Ma'am, have you got my scan results back yet?' Mr Majumder has asked me this several times a day for three days, every time I pass his bed as I tend my patients on this surgery ward where I am completing my first year of being a Real Doctor. Six months in a surgical ward has convinced me that at heart I am a physician and not a surgeon, and yet I love the technical skill I am sometimes privileged to watch as a surgical assistant in the operating theatre.

Mr Majumder has become alarmingly yellow. His brown skin has taken on a vaguely grapefruit-coloured glow and the whites of his eyes look like lemon slices. The scan is part of a battery of investigations: as the results of blood tests, X-rays and biopsies come back, I am forming a picture of why Mr Majumder is jaundiced. And I know it won't be good news. The scan result will be the last detail in the picture, and then the surgeon in charge of his care will be able to tell him what is already becoming clear: Mr Majumder has cancer in his pancreas, and he will be lucky to live another six months.

Usually I smile ruefully and say, truthfully, 'Not yet, Mr

Majumder! But when I do, you will be the first to know!' However, today I know the envelope is in the office, and the time for that conversation is approaching.

Mr Majumder is visited twice each day by his devoted wife and one of his brothers. His wife wears rustling silk saris and walks like a queen; her calm grace dignifies the plastic chair beside his bed. His brother wears a business suit and never sits down. He cracks jokes, shuffles from foot to foot like a nervous foal, talks loudly, claps his brother on the arm and hurries away, wiping tears from his eyes once he turns the corner. Mr Majumder takes extra painkillers before visiting time. 'I don't want them to worry about me,' he tells the nurses. 'I must not cause them any burden.'

I approach the bed on heavy legs. He smiles at me hopefully. My mouth is dry; my smile feels false. A voice in my head informs me that my demeanour is screaming 'bad news!' to the whole ward. I try to ignore it.

'Mr Majumder, I think we should have all the test results back today,' I begin. I am too junior to be the bearer of his bad news; I don't have enough knowledge of the disease, and any possible treatments. Or so I tell myself.

Mr Majumder holds my gaze. I feel myself blushing. My stomach flips. *What if he asks me outright?*

'If it's good news, Doctor Ma'am, I would like to hear it soon,' he says. 'If it's bad news, then I would prefer my brother to be here.'

I don't know what to say. The brother never pauses for breath: he talks and talks so that there is no room for conversation. Anecdotes, jokes, have-you-heard-the-one-about . . . his brother is terrified. How could he support Mr Majumder?

'Is your wife visiting later?' I ask.

He says yes. 'She's an excellent wife. She is a good mother. She visits me every day.' He pauses, a frown playing across his face before he continues, 'I take great consolation from her goodness.'

I can imagine how her quiet gentleness would console him. I am about to suggest that perhaps his wife, rather than his brother, might be here to talk with the surgeon, when he says, 'And that is why she must not be told any bad news. She must have hope. She must be able to take care of our children without sadness.'

He knows. He already knows. Relief and dread compete in my mind: *what should I say?*

'Mr Majumder, I'll get all the results together and make an appointment for Mr Castle to see you and your family this evening when he finishes operating. He usually talks to his patients and their families at six p.m. Is that convenient for you and your . . . brother?' *I nearly said wife. Oh, I want his wife to know.*

Mr Majumder agrees. He is kind enough to ask me no more questions. The stage is set for later. I have done my best. But I have ducked an opportunity to explore what he might have guessed; I know it, and he knows it, and I know he knows I know he knows. Surgery seems simple compared with communicating well. I have so much to learn.

It can take courage to begin a potentially emotional conversation. Concerns that deter us from getting started include thoughts like:

What if I get emotional?
I won't start because I don't feel calm enough.
What if I make them feel upset?
They might want to ask something I can't answer.
How will we be at the end of this conversation? What if we're both distressed?
What if they don't want to talk about this with me?

All of these are realistic, important ideas. They show us that getting started isn't the only hurdle: there are other things to consider, like how to check that the other person is willing to join in, how to navigate the conversation once it starts, and how to get it to a safe place, whether or not the discussion is complete, before leaving. We will look at all these ideas in future chapters. Like any enterprise, a conversation must have a beginning, a middle and an end. Here, we're looking at the beginning.

To get started, we need to bear in mind whether the circumstances are right. 'Right' has to mean 'good enough', because we'll never find the perfect moment. If the time is right, and the setting allows us a chance to talk, that is probably about as good as it gets. The style guide has two pieces of wisdom here: the first is that the other person has a right to choose, too. If the time is not right for them, that is their decision to make. The second is that we don't have to get the whole issue sorted in one go; we can 'press pause' on a conversation after some discussion, and pick it up again on another occasion. We can invite someone to dance and respect their decision to join in or not; once on the dancefloor, we are not obliged to dance ourselves to exhaustion.

How do we know whether this is the right time for them to talk? How do I know if I am a person they would choose to talk to? Instead of trying to guess what is on their mind or struggling to frame a pithy phrase that will sum up the whole conversation, it can be helpful and calming simply to offer to talk, or to ask the other person to have a conversation with you.

I know – ridiculously simple, isn't it?

'It looks like there's something on your mind. Would you like to talk about it?' or 'I've got something on my mind. May I talk it through with you some time?'

'There's something I want to discuss with you. When would be a good time? I'm free now if you are.'

Using cues can be very helpful: 'Did you see that programme about . . .?' is an easy, neutral introduction to a conversation. 'I'd really like a chance to chat to you about something I read about/ saw on TV recently. Would that be OK?'

'I've been worrying about something and I'd like to talk to you about it. Do you mind mulling something over with me?' Most people will not turn away from a request for help. This is discussed in more detail on page 194.

Once you have made your invitation, *Please may we talk?* (or its variant, *Would you like to talk?*), you are ready to find out where they would like to begin. Another simple question solves that dilemma: *Where would you like to start?* It sounds too simple and obvious. But that is how to find out where someone wants to start.

Beginning a conversation about difficult truths can feel daunting because we fear making somebody feel distressed. Of course, a conversation does not cause the distress: the difficult situation the person is in causes their distress. Talking about the situation – whether it is concerns about a family member, losing your job or being bereaved, mental health or financial problems or having a serious illness – doesn't make it worse. In fact, many people describe a feeling of loneliness when their family and friends, scared of causing upset by talking about 'it', simply avoid them altogether. Being distressed and not being able to talk about it can feel worse for many people.

It might be that the conversation has started because someone else has asked you for advice. In that case, instead of *Where would you like to start?* you may find it more helpful to begin with *Tell me what you already know* or *Get me up to speed with what I need to know*. By using questions or prompts to invite the person to tell us what they want to talk about, we avoid blundering into parts of the situation that they don't want to discuss with us today.

Starting with an invitation to talk opens a door into a conversation, and it also allows the other person to accept or to turn down that invitation, and to make some mental preparation for a serious discussion. This is a form of consent, and it is important because a conversation works best when the power balance is as even as it can be.

A thorough discussion of a challenging situation is more likely to work if it feels like a collaboration rather than one person forcing something on another. You may intend to invite, yet a work colleague who is not your equal in the hierarchy, or a person who relies on you for employment or other security, may not feel able to decline: how might you make it clear that the choice is theirs?

The place where the conversation takes place bears consideration, too. Can you arrange the seating so that you are on a similar level? Can you meet in a place that feels secure for the other person? What can you do that will make your conversation feel more relaxed? In my medical career, I made cups of tea for patients and families to accompany our more tender discussions; it's a small act, yet it changes a 'consultation' into a conversation.

A safe place will usually offer some privacy. It might mean freedom from interruption, or somewhere that is familiar and reassuring. It may mean waiting for the person's supporters to join them, either to listen or to be participants in the conversation, giving the person a sense of security; or it may mean beginning sooner, so they can seize a chance to talk without the pressure of extra people in the room.

The right time may mean when the person feels secure. It may mean freedom from symptoms: when someone is seriously ill, for example, they may want a chance to take their painkillers or to have a snooze before an important conversation, so they are able to concentrate better. They can advise us when is a good time to talk. This is an invitation: we are offering someone a choice.

Thirty years ago, Stefan was my neighbour. He was a great gardener, and he used to advise me on the pruning of my roses. Sometimes our conversations were about other matters, and often they were about his wife, Irene, a wonderful cook and a talented flower arranger. Stefan managed their garden so that there would always be something that Irene could put into a vase and make beautiful. One spring, over a series of pruning-advice visits, he chatted to me about his wife's health.

Stefan has noticed that his wife is breathless when she walks up the stairs. She wakes up at night 'feeling funny' from time to time, and potters down the landing to their spare room to sleep the rest of the night propped up on five pillows. She tells him not to fuss, we're all getting old, that's all. 'We're in our eighties, Stefan!' she sighs. 'As long as I can manage the housework, there's no need to worry.'

But Stefan *is* worried. Not talking about it isn't making it go away. He tells me about friends who had lung disease and heart disease who were breathless to begin with, and it got worse until they died. Stefan can't imagine life without his Irene. If she's sick, he wants her to see her doctor. He wants me to come round and tell her. But this is something they need to deal with together. Irene is a very private person. Instead, I snip my roses and Stefan tells me his worries.

Stefan says that he mentions it every day. 'Irene, you were up again with your breathing last night. I'm making you an appointment with the doctor.'

'Stop fussing me, Stefan! It's nothing! The doctors have better things to do!'

It's an impasse. He pushes; she fights back. And her breathlessness continues. None of us likes to be told what to do, do we? I ask Stefan if there is anyone Irene might trust whose advice he can ask.

Stefan phones Irene's sister, Paula, to ask her to help. Paula is a few years younger than Irene, and the sisters meet in town for coffee and cake each week. Stefan describes Irene's symptoms, and how she won't see the doctor.

'You know how she is, Stefan,' says Paula. 'She's always been stubborn. If you say up, she'll say down. Maybe you need to back off a bit.'

'But if I back off, she still won't go,' he says. 'I don't know how to deal with her, and I've been trying for fifty years . . . Will you talk to her?' And Paula agrees.

Paula takes a different tack. She phones her sister, and says, 'Irene, I'm not going to beat about the bush, and I don't want you to, either. Stefan tells me he's worried about your breathing, and now I'm worried, too. I'd like to know a bit more. Do you think we can chat about it? Perhaps not today – just when you're ready.' The invitation is issued and left. It's now Irene's move. Irene wants to be cross: her family members are talking to each other about her. But she knows it is concern, not malice, that motivates them. And, she has to admit to Paula, she is a bit concerned herself.

'Well, I'm happy to chat whenever you're ready, Irene, but our café mightn't be the best place,' says Paula. 'Lots of wagging ears there. Where would you like to talk about it? Would you rather talk to me or to Stefan? Or both of us together? I know he gets worried and that makes him pushy. Would you like me to come and be your back-up?' By offering Irene some choices, Paula is giving responsibility to Irene rather than forcing her hand.

'Why not come over, Paula? I'll make us a pot of tea, and we can chat with Stefan. And then we two can go out for cake and a bit of peace!'

Stefan is delighted. Now she is being invited rather than pushed, Irene has chosen the time, the place and the people she will talk to.

The power of that invitation was to give Irene a sense of control. That simple change enabled her to choose when to talk, and she also decided what to do to cheer herself up at the end of the conversation. That was the beginning and the end sorted. I'm sure they managed the middle.

Listening to Understand

When was the last time you really felt listened to? When you felt that someone appreciated not only the words you were saying, but why the matter under discussion was important to you? How did that person show that they were paying attention to you? What we're considering here is not simply being listened to, but being heard.

It's clinic day. I am a very junior doctor in a medical clinic; the consultant in charge is a professor, a world authority on thyroid disease.

The young woman in my examination room has been sent by her GP with a typical overactive thyroid history: weight loss, sweating, trembling hands, palpitations, a sense of being unable to feel at ease. She's called Leonie and is the same age as me; she works in a shoe shop – in fact, my favourite shoe shop – in town. We have discussed her thyroid problem and the tests I will need to arrange; we have discussed peep-toe shoes and heel heights. It's time for the professor to review her, to check that I haven't missed anything, and to approve my plan of investigations and care. I'm feeling rather proud of my rapport with this patient. And we all know what pride comes before, don't we?

'It's a really simple overactive thyroid situation,' I tell Prof outside the door. I recount the battery of blood tests and scans I have in mind. I report that our patient isn't pregnant so radioactive iodine will be a safe treatment. Prof nods and opens the door, ushering me back inside to introduce my patient.

Prof is tall and elegant. She perches on the side of the

examination couch to bring her eyes level with her patient's as Leonie sits propped up on the couch, covered by a sheet. She takes Leonie's hand, smiling. I know she'll be using that physical contact to look for pulse rate, sweating palms, trembling hands as she chats. 'When is your wedding planned for?' Prof asks.

Wedding?

Leonie flushes bright pink, takes a deep breath and her large, round eyes begin brimming with tears that run down her cheeks.

Prof waits. She pulls a tissue from the box beside the couch and puts it into Leonie's other hand. The hand with the engagement ring that I hadn't noticed. Leonie dabs her eyes, gulps, swallows.

'All right?' smiles Prof, sympathetically. Leonie nods.

'That was emotional, wasn't it?' says Prof. 'Want to tell me about it?'

There is a pause before Leonie says, 'I can't get married looking like this . . .' and begins to cry again. Prof lets her hand go, and waits. The silence is long. I haven't noticed before how loudly the wall clock ticks; how much traffic noise thrums through the opaque windows; and in this silence, how loud my own heartbeat sounds.

'The dress . . .' Leonie begins, before stopping and swallowing again. 'The dress . . . It's too big, and it's gaping, and the bulge in my throat looks huge . . .' and she starts weeping once more.

People with overactive thyroids lose weight. Leonie is very slender. I know (because I have taken a very careful history) that she has lost ten pounds in three months. *But it's easy to have a wedding dress taken in. Far harder to deal with if she had put weight on.* She does have a small thyroid swelling, called a goitre, that will go away once she gets treatment. It's hardly visible; I had to examine her carefully to find it. *It won't show in photographs.* I can see many consoling things to say.

But Prof says none of them.

She says, 'It sounds as though you feel very different, and it's upsetting you a lot.' Leonie nods, dripping tears as she does so. 'I don't look like me any more,' she says. 'I wouldn't blame Luke if he left me.'

Prof nods again, waiting to see if Leonie is going to say anything else. When Leonie doesn't break the silence, Prof speaks. 'You feel very different, and you worry that it may affect how your fiancé feels about you?' she summarises, and Leonie nods again. 'Does it affect how you feel about yourself, too?' probes Prof, gently, and Leonie nods, rocking on the couch, hugging the sheet to her diminutive body. I begin to understand. It's not whether the dress fits Leonie's body; it's whether Leonie's body fits Leonie.

Prof has asked four questions. There has been more silence than conversation. And yet she has established, within a few minutes, the crisis at the heart of this consultation. I knew everything about this patient: her height, weight, pulse and shoe size. It turns out I knew what was the matter with my patient, but not what mattered to her.

In the rush of daily life, we consume information without taking a lot of it in. We have to, or we would be overwhelmed: radio, TV, social media, family, friends, colleagues, clients; phone calls, text messages, emails, conversations – we are bombarded by 'communications', yet it's rare that we feel we are truly communicating.

During an important conversation, when we want to communicate effectively, how we listen can be more important than what we say. Careful listening helps us to understand the perspective of the person we are talking to. Our understanding helps us to pace the conversation: not too much at once; taking their view into account; hearing their thoughts; noticing their emotions. We are keeping in step, dancing with care.

First of all, let's forget about speaking. We're going to listen without trying to formulate what to say next: listening, not to answer, but to understand. This may mean there are silences: while the person gathers their thoughts; while we reflect on what they are saying; if one or other of us becomes emotional. *Listening to understand* means we can't plan what we are going to say next until we have fully absorbed what the person we are listening to has just said.

Accept without judging. Every model of psychological practice has this advice in common: to listen without judgement. The person speaking needs to be able to describe their experience, partly so that we can begin to see the situation as it looks and feels to them, and perhaps more importantly so that in describing it fully, they too can gain a new perspective on something that they may have been immersed in too deeply to allow clarity. Fearing that the listener may be judging their words, their story or their coping will discourage transparency. They need to tell their story 'warts and all', and that is quite a daunting prospect. Talking to a stranger may be easier than telling the story to someone whose good opinion matters to the person; it may be particularly difficult to speak candidly to someone who is a beloved family member or friend (for example, for fear of upsetting them), or to someone who is perceived to be in a position of influence like a teacher or senior work colleague (perhaps concern about disapproval or impact on career progression). The only judgement that is helpful as a listener is to judge ourselves privileged to be given this confidence, and to be aware that we should do our best to be worthy of it.

Value the silences. The silences during a conversation are when both participants do their thinking. If a discussion is simply to give information, it doesn't need much silence. You may be telling me what time we are meeting this evening, and where. If I am familiar with the place and the journey to get there, our conversation can be brief:

'See you tonight? Seven-thirty outside the cinema?'

'Yes, fine, see you later!'

But if there's more than one cinema, or I'm not certain how long it will take me to get there, I may need a pause to give me thinking time before I say, 'I'm not sure I can be there by seven-thirty. What time does the film start?'

Now you need some thinking time, too: to remember the start time, or to calculate whether the advertisements before the film will allow us some leeway, or to remind yourself if there's a later showing of the same film.

The presence of silences during the conversation has the effect of slowing everything down. Slowing down allows us to focus better on what is being said, and for many people this slowing also reduces any anxiety they felt coming into a conversation that might be important, emotional or long-awaited. Remain aware, though, that an 'expectant silence' can seem threatening to someone who does not feel ready to explore their uncomfortable thoughts: there is more about using silence safely in 'Using Silence' on page 75. Punctuate the silence without puncturing it, by using short expressions of encouragement: 'It's OK, I'm here.' 'Take your time.' 'There's a lot to think about.' Be aware that gazing directly at someone can make them feel flustered or rushed to answer, while gazing away or downward offers them thinking space.

Silence helps conversations to work. Give it space. Don't interrupt it.

Check your understanding. Listening to understand also means checking to make sure that we *do* understand. This is another truth so obvious that it's easy to overlook. When someone tells us about a problem that is concerning them, it's helpful for them if we occasionally check that we are getting the message. A question like 'So, if I've understood you properly, your main concern is . . . Have I got that right?' or a statement like 'It sounds as though the thing upsetting you most is . . .' and a pause for them to confirm, or to put us right, helps to make sure we are getting the right idea.

These occasional interruptions to check understanding don't usually put the speaker off. In fact, they help the speaker to feel properly listened to. They also further slow the conversation. Reducing the speed at which someone pours out the mixture of ideas and emotions and words and memories and possibilities swirling around in their head helps them to express it more clearly. Often simply saying it out loud helps the person to review the whole situation and see a new way to deal with it.

'Thanks,' they say. 'You've really put that into perspective for me.' In fact, they did all the work: the listener simply provided a safe space and listened well.

Summaries and check-points are so important that I teach my students to think of listening as a waltz, a dance that progresses in triple time: question, question, check; question, question, summary. Without frequent recaps and summaries to check understanding, it is easy to drift into believing that we have understood the story when in fact we have formed inaccurate assumptions about what we have heard. Checking our understanding is essential in listening to understand.

Listening to understand is not just about words: it means noting how the person is feeling as well as what they are saying. There may be tears or clenched fists; a wobbling lip or excited shouting; there may be emotional words in what the person says, or it may be the way they say it and clues from their body language that communicate the emotion in the conversation. Noting the emotion helps us to understand the person better; checking our understanding of their emotion is as important as checking our understanding of the story.

We can check our understanding of the speaker's emotions using questions like 'Is telling me this making you feel sad?' or

'Do you feel angry while you are remembering this?' Or we can name the emotion we observe, and check our observation for accuracy: 'You sound excited about this. Are you?' or 'To me, this all sounds quite scary. Does it make you feel anxious?' Offering our interpretation of the emotions we are observing may give the speaker pause for thought: they may have been so caught up in their emotions that they have not processed them. They may need silence to consider our observation; they can do this most easily if we offer our ideas for their consideration as questions, avoiding the suggestion that we can fully understand the complexity of the situation as it feels to them.

Asking the other person to summarise from time to time is another useful way to share responsibility in a conversation, and it is particularly important if they are receiving new information as the discussion progresses. In conversations in which I have given patients or their supporters new medical information, or discussed treatment options for them to think about, I invite them to summarise things by asking 'How will you explain our discussion to your parents?' or 'How will you describe those treatment options to your family?' It helps them to check their understanding and to practise saying the new information aloud, and it helps me to notice any details that they may have over-looked or misunderstood. Communication is the responsibility of both parties: if something has been misunderstood, we need to go back together and discuss it again because my previous explanation was not well enough expressed. The question that checks understanding is not 'Do you understand?' but rather 'What have you understood?'

Accept that the solution is not simple. There may seem to be obvious solutions to the dilemma being described. If any of the solutions you can think of was an easy fit for the speaker's diffi-culty, they would almost certainly have solved it by now: offering quick solutions is not only unhelpful, it also shuts down the telling of the difficulty.

Accept that emotions are high. Likewise, hearing how upset the speaker feels as they describe their situation may make you want to reassure them, or to change the subject to reduce their distress. Of course, that situation is still in the speaker's thoughts; not talking about it doesn't make it go away, and reassurance is false when the difficulties are real. Although it may feel uncomfortable for us, listening to understand requires us listeners to acknowledge the difficulties, allow the emotions and not to stifle their expression.

Remember: you don't need to know what to say. Listen fully, and don't be distracted by wondering what to say next, how to sort this out, or any of the other thoughts that jump into your mind. Ignore your inclination to work out something consoling to say. Just listen. Trust yourself; just like feet move in rhythm to unfamiliar music, when it is time to speak words will come to you, and they will come from your heart instead of your head. The task is not to solve, it is simply to listen.

'Papa's driving me crazy!' Eloise's mother shouts down the phone. Eloise, carrying a backpack of groceries, pushing her toddler's stroller with one hand while managing her phone with the other, finds a patch of shade at the harbour front and parks the stroller where the baby can see the ferry boats loading and unloading passengers.

'Hi, Mum!' she says. Her mother has called and launched into a diatribe about Eloise's father without even greeting her. 'Is Papa with you now?'

'He's gone into his greenhouse. Needs to spray his tomatoes, he says. But it's the middle of the night! And it's February – freezing here! What's he playing at? Why is he trying to upset me like this?'

A familiar band of fear grips Eloise's heart. They are so far away; here in New Zealand she can picture her parents' cosy Scottish home, Mum using the old-fashioned phone attached to the kitchen wall. When Eloise visited them at Christmas, she tried to talk to her parents about her father's failing memory and increasing distractedness, but they were very defensive, and she returned to New Zealand anxious for them both.

'Mum, what's he wearing?' she asks. Mum tells her Papa has pulled his gardening jumper on over his pyjamas. 'He's wearing that ridiculous old bobble hat, too! He knows I hate it!' Eloise feels her mother's distressed bewilderment down the line. She seemed to believe that her husband's erratic moods and behaviours were some form of elaborate teasing on his part, designed to provoke her. Eloise understands that, in some way, that belief is easier for Mum than facing the possibility that Papa is trapped in a confused world of his own.

'Mum, do you remember that I tried to talk to you about Papa's moods while I was over there at Christmas?' Eloise asks, carefully. The baby is crooning at a seagull perched on the harbour railings. Mum is silent. Eloise waits.

'Mum? Are you still there?' she asks after a while.

'I'm here,' says Mum. 'I don't like it when you talk about Papa like that.'

'I know, Mum . . . I know. I do love you both. And I worry about you both, too.' She waggles the stroller, and the baby laughs. 'Mum, do you feel worried at all about Papa?'

'Well, of course I do! He's outside in the cold in the middle of the night!' shouts Mum.

'Yes, it is a worry that he's out in the cold, Mum,' says Eloise. 'I'm worried about that, too. But I'm worrying about other things . . . Are you?'

During the next silence, Eloise shrugs off her backpack to find food for her toddler. This might be a long conversation, and much overdue. She knows that in this silence Mum will be fighting back tears, struggling to find words, thinking about the changes in Papa's behaviour. She will be deciding whether it would be disloyal to mention them, contemplating the awful reality of saying them out loud. Eloise waits.

Finally, she hears Mum say, 'I think he's getting confused, El. I think he's not all right . . . I don't know . . . I just don't know what to do.'

Oh, thank God! At last! She's said it! thinks Eloise to herself. Out loud, she simply says, 'So . . . you think something's not right . . . And you don't know what to do about it . . .' She waits. There is no response. 'Did I hear you right, Mum?' asks Eloise.

There is a pause before Mum replies. 'I think he hasn't been right for a while, but I kept thinking I was imagining it. But . . . but . . . Oh, El! Yesterday I think he didn't recognise me for a while. He thought I was a cleaner at his office.' Mum's voice breaks, and Eloise's heart stretches to reach around the curve of the earth, to soothe her mother's tears. She has no idea what to say in response to this revelation, or to the bereft note in her mum's voice. She lets her heart speak, saying, 'Oh, Mum. That must have felt very sad for you.'

Half a world away from her parents, waggling the stroller again to keep baby Bonnie entertained, Eloise feels her own heart breaking. 'Thank you for telling me, Mum. It all sounds so sad. So . . . you seem to have been noticing changes for a while, but just didn't feel sure . . .?'

There is a babble of voices on the line: Mum's voice and Papa's. He must have come in from the greenhouse. Good. It's far too cold to be outside in the early hours of a Scottish February morning.

'Mum? Papa? Are you there?' she asks. Mum's voice comes back on. 'He's back inside. I'm going to make us both a cocoa and we'll go back to bed. I'll call you in the morning, love, and thank you for listening.'

'Bye, Mum. Give Papa a kiss from me. And from baby Bonnie. She's watching the seagulls. We're about to get the ferry home.'

'Papa says that baby should be in bed,' says Mum. 'He can't remember it's a different time in Auckland. But at least he realises it's bedtime here! Speak later. Bye, love.' Mum hangs up.

Eloise wipes baby Bonnie's face, pulls on her backpack and heads for their ferry. Somehow, by not being face to face, or because of the crisis, or because she has used questions instead of telling her mum what changes she noticed in Papa, or because she managed to listen instead of giving advice – Eloise wasn't sure exactly what was different in this conversation – at last her mum has confided that something is wrong with Papa. This is a first step. A huge step. Eloise reflects that at Christmas she tried to give Mum 'a good talking-to', when in fact what would have helped her was a good listening-to. She wheels the stroller up the ferry's boarding ramp and looks for a seat by a window. Bonnie can watch the other boats on the calm, sunny bay while Eloise contemplates the storms ahead for her beloved parents.

Eloise listened, allowing silences and checking her understanding of what her mum was telling her. She recognised that this was a complicated situation with practical challenges and enormous emotional implications, and that her mum felt anxious, afraid for her husband, worried about the future. Eloise named her mum's sadness and checked that she had properly grasped her concern – her belief that she saw changes in her husband's thinking. By the end of their short conversation, Eloise and her mum reached a new understanding with each other, a place of common ground that Eloise will be able to come back to, when her mum feels ready to explore what to do next.

On Tenderness

I've been using the word 'tender' to describe sensitive conversations for several years now. Initially, it was a spontaneous counter-response to the vocabulary of fear: 'courageous conversations', 'challenging conversations', 'difficult conversations' all evoke a self-defence response that is the very opposite of the 'I'm here for you' mindset that these conversations require. Tenderness seemed to me to conjure the disposition most helpful for discussions that are painful for one or both parties. It acknowledges the presence of pain not as something to be overcome, but as an experience to be held with sensitivity and respect. Instead of holding myself back, I give myself. It's not about difficulty, courage or challenge. It's simply about being intentionally, fully present.

Tenderness: a sensitivity to pain. We are all familiar with physical tenderness, whether it is a toothache and fear of that wince-inducing shard of agony that follows chewing, or belly ache and fear of being touched or jostled from a position of precarious comfort, or the throbbing after-pain of a newly twisted ankle that warns us exactly how excruciating the next step on that injured limb might be. Tenderness sits at the edge of the pain experience, warning us not to take any risks. Emotional tenderness is an exact parallel: an awareness of distress lying close by, and a desire to minimise the risk of plunging into it.

Usually tenderness is an individual's sensitivity to their own pain. As a doctor, I was trained to examine a tender abdomen with great care for the patient's discomfort: to explain why I needed to touch, and to ask permission; to promise I would stop if the pain was too bad; to watch the patient's face throughout for signs of distress; in children (and often in adults, too), to let them hold my examining hand so they could guide it and feel some sense of control. The patient has a tender tummy; the doctor must proceed with caution. The doctor, in fact, must be tender for her patient's pain throughout the task.

In a similar way, the conversations that we are discussing are more likely to flourish when one person is sensitive to the other's pain: a tenderness-exchange where we tread softly to reduce the threat of another person's distress. Just like examining that tender abdomen, when we participate in a conversation that may cause the other person to feel pain then we must be sensitive to their tenderness, and yet not shirk the task.

The search for a positive, alternative description to 'difficult', 'courageous' or 'challenging' for these important conversations was initially an instinctive and simple idea. Subsequently, though, my use of language has been more deliberate. To give any discussion a problematic label drags that suggestion, with all its negative overtones, into the interaction. How could these important exchanges be described in ways that fit the true tone of the task? These are *benevolent* conversations in that they intend good even though they may evoke very painful emotions. There is need for a word that describes *giving attention*; *valuing* the conversation; approaching it with *gentleness*. The *delicacy* of the task requires *sensitivity* on the part of the person taking it on.

There is also a need for *caring*: if a policeman must break bad news, or a doctor has a serious diagnosis to impart, there is no way around the distress that the news is likely to cause. Their task is to give the information in as *supportive* a way as possible. Sometimes we can aim only for causing the least hurt: avoiding the task, failing to step up to that life-changing conversation, would be a further harm.

For friends or family who invite or are invited to a conversation that supports somebody in their distress, there is a need for *generosity* with their time and attention. For all these conversations, we need to be aware that our words, our questions, our very attitude can offer consolation, but also that we will be touching close to matters that hurt. The person has a wound; our response must be to recognise that injury and its sensitivity to pain. We are recognising their tenderness.

So, for reasons that begin with the person to be supported rather than with the person giving the support, tenderness offers a description that includes their vulnerability and also encompasses the attitude we need to bring to bear. Tenderness. These conversations, whatever the circumstances, require tenderness from the news-bearer or the companion in the dialogue, in a direct response to the tenderness of the other person's pain. These are tender conversations.

In case there is any doubt, it is worth using a dictionary not simply for the definitions and synonyms of tenderness, but to look at its opposites. There, in a list, are the words I have heard wounded people use to describe horrible conversations they have had with people as diverse as medical advisers, family members, lawyers, and telephone respondents for banks, insurance companies, government agencies and utility companies. Conversations they describe as *brutal, callous, cruel, hard-hearted, unfeeling* and *unkind*, an A to Z of insensitivity. Conversations lacking any sense of empathy; lacking acknowledgement of their suffering; failing to take their tenderness into account. Non-tender conversations that cause unnecessary pain.

How would communication skills training be interpreted if, instead of learning techniques for 'Breaking Bad News' or 'Difficult Conversations', people were invited to step into 'Tender Conversations' training? How would we feel about the 'Awkward Conversations' we must address with colleagues, family or friends if we regarded them as moments of shared tenderness instead? How would bearers of unwelcome news perceive their task if they understood that, upon breaking such news in a tender and supportive manner, the distress the recipient will inevitably feel will enable them to frame their response to the situation? We do not cause their pain, the situation does.

When we engage in a tender conversation with somebody, we create a safe place for them to suffer:* we don't cause their suffering, but we can accompany and support them in it. In taking time to be with them as they absorb the unwelcome news, we show them that their situation and its emotional repercussions are worthy of our time and attention. Our tenderness to their needs offers succour in circumstances that have the potential to feel brutal and lonely. Our ability to remain alongside as they experience their emotional storm does not lessen their distress, but it prevents the additional pain of feeling abandoned in a place of suffering.

We tender our quiet attention in their service. We validate their tenderness.

These are tender conversations. They require our courage, skill and determination. They involve our own willingness to be vulnerable. Tenderness is a virtue, and its application requires our strength.

---

* The expression 'a safe place to suffer' was coined by psychiatrist Dr Averil Stedeford in her book *Facing Death*.

Curiosity

The curiosity of young children seems insatiable. The questions never stop. They pause to examine small details of the world that may pass adult attention by: the ladybird on a leaf, the person wearing an interesting hat, the range of barks among various dogs, the difference between their left hand and their right hand. Their curiosity drives their discovery of the way the world works. As they accumulate information they catalogue and compare it; they file it; they retrieve and reorganise it as new experiences match or challenge their previous understanding. Each new discovery is fascinating. They don't see answers as 'right' or 'wrong', as 'good' or 'bad', even as 'probable' or 'improbable'. They simply collect information and use it to decipher their experience.

In this skill of curiosity and questioning, children are our role models for our conversational style. Curiosity helps us to frame questions that explore and clarify complicated information. Let's join an explorer of ideas in action.

'Yes, but why?' Polly is sitting on a rock beside the ocean. The tiny crab in her red bucket is called Hattie, she has informed me, and Hattie needs a friend. But the water in the bucket is warming in the sunshine, and we are due to meet Polly's parents for ice creams on the seafront soon, so it's time to put Hattie back into her rock pool.

'I want to collect a friend for Hattie and take them home as pets,' growls Polly, three years old and determined. 'Mummy would let me.'

I'm a novice at this child-wrangling business. I'm taking Polly rock-pooling while her parents attend her mum's appointment with their obstetrician, checking on the progress of my friend's pregnancy with what will be Polly's new baby brother in a few months' time.

This is an impasse. I don't want to cause a scene, so I sit on the rock beside Polly and we peer into the pool together.

'Why is the sea so far away?' asks Polly, looking up from our rocks and over her shoulder across the vast expanse of sand to the ocean, lying at low tide and making our rock-pooling expedition possible. Now there's a question. Tides. Gravity. The moon. The earth. Where do I start?

'The sea moves backwards and forwards very slowly every day,' I tell her. 'Later on today, the sea will come right up to these rocks, and cover them up.' Polly's head describes the arc from the rippling waves lapping the distant sand to our seat on the rocks. It's a long way.

'When?' she asks.

'About six hours from now,' I say. 'Which is around your bedtime tonight. When the sea covers this little pool over, all those tiny shrimps and fishes can swim in the big sea again. And if Hattie is here, she can play with her friends who live in other rock pools.'

Polly isn't going to be diverted into the conversation about Hattie's fate. She has just been informed that the sea moves. The sea moves backwards and forwards. This is a Big Deal.

'How does the sea know how far to come up the beach?' she asks.

'I don't know,' I admit. 'I think it just gets as far as it can reach before it's time for it to move backwards again.'

'Does somebody turn the taps off before it gets too high?' she asks. I am stumped. 'Daddy turned the taps off when the bath was too full,' she explains, patiently. 'He said we might cause a flood.' She pauses, and a frown furrows her brow. 'What *is* a flood?'

'A flood is when there's water in the wrong place, like all over the bathroom floor,' I say. 'Sometimes, if rivers get too full, the water runs over the riverbank and into the fields or onto the roads by the river. And sometimes the sea comes in so far that it floods the road by the beach.' Now Polly looks impressed. 'That road there?' She points to the seafront.

'Yes, where the ice-cream shops are,' I say.

'Well, that must be messy,' she says, sagely. 'Someone should turn the taps off sooner in the sea!'

'The thing is, the sea doesn't come out of taps.' I am a bit concerned we might be here all day discussing the water cycle. 'The sea is just there all the time.'

'Well, how does it get bigger and smaller? Does somebody take the plug out?'

'It just slides very, very slowly up the beach, and then down again. When it comes up our beach, it slides down another beach far away. And then when it slides down our beach, it goes up the other one.'

'So Hattie could swim to another beach through the water in the sea?' asks Polly, with round-eyed wonder.

'She could! She might have visitors from other beaches here, too,' I agree, 'but she'd miss them if she wasn't here, wouldn't she?' There is a long pause. A gull swoops low over us and circles off towards the seafront. There are Polly's parents, waving from the road.

'How about . . .' I suggest, 'how about we take Hattie to show Mummy and Daddy while we have our ice cream? And then let's bring her back here, and leave her in her pool to wait for her friends to visit tonight when the sea comes back over the rocks?'

Nailed it. We've learned a lot: Polly about the sea and me about curiosity. We've earned that ice cream.

Curious questions simply seek information. They are open to whatever arises, nothing is ruled in or out. In these exploratory conversations we use curiosity to discover the other person's experiences, knowledge, beliefs and uncertainties: their viewpoint. We may be listening to their concerns about a situation at work or school, a health problem, an opportunity to be engaged with or a disagreement with a friend. We may be talking about a decision to be reached, listening to find out what information they have and what remains to be found out, or what their preferences are. We may be wondering whether someone has previous experience to draw upon as they confront a new challenge, or what their expectations and assumptions are about the situation in hand.

The way we listen affects the speaker's confidence. If we listen as 'experts', the speaker may fear exposing their uncertainty, or they may move from useful problem-solving to seeking our advice. If we listen as 'critics', to judge or point out errors, they may fear exposing their mistakes. If we listen with a vested interest, they may feel unable to explore negative emotions or hurts.

To be a good listener, then, we need to take on some particular qualities. These are the conversational equivalent of moving to the rhythm of the music in dance, a basis for everything that follows. Just as even pre-verbal children will spontaneously move in time to music, our child-teachers bring the innate qualities of curiosity during conversation.

Open-mindedness: with interest and curiosity, simply to accept the thoughts, beliefs, memories and assumptions of the other person as the way they currently see the world. It may be that there are gaps, mistakes, misperceptions or prejudices in their interpretation of a situation: the time to address those will come later. To begin with, our task is to understand how things appear to this person. We are listening with open-minded curiosity about their view, in order to understand it as much as any person can ever understand another. Our understanding is the baseline for any further dialogue. Children accomplish this perfectly: things are as they are.

Humility: by being open to the ideas and opinions of the other person, we allow the possibility that their view is valid. We may have personal differences in values, whether political, moral or otherwise; during this task of open-minded listening, we will suspend our urge to oppose their values or argue the case for our own. Instead, remaining curious enables us to listen and to ask further questions as we build our understanding of their view.

Listening is a soul-to-soul task. When we meet as equals, we create a space to listen deeply. The person with a dilemma or concern is an expert in how they are feeling and what they are going through: we must recognise that expertise.

Genuine humility always levels up. Levelling up is especially important when we are listening to someone with whom we are in serious disagreement. To hear them, and to allow them to feel heard, we must listen to their views with the same respectful interest we would expect were the roles reversed.

To listen with genuine humility is rare and precious; it's also hard. When we listen with humility, we are prepared to search for the truth together, as peers. We acknowledge that whatever our paths through the world have been thus far, we are both human beings: different in experience yet alike in dignity; of equal worth. A child assumes that their conversation is a dialogue between equals until the world begins to temper their self-esteem; in their innocence there is no hierarchy of importance, there are only people.

Our humility must extend to tolerating not knowing. Experts are vaunted for what they know, for finding solutions and solving problems. In this act of curious listening, even the expert starts from not knowing. Being prepared to not know reveals willingness to share the task of discovery. Being able to resist offering solutions and advice prematurely holds the space for the person to explore their situation and gradually to reveal it to their attentive listener. Even as they make it clear to the listener, they are often also making it clear to themselves. The thoughts are no longer swirling in a mixture of hopes and doubts: they are named and expressed out loud. By avoiding the pseudo-helpful solution of offering reassurance as though 'I know best', we leave room for their real and important distress and after it, for new possibilities.

Curiosity communicates, 'I want to understand this better. Tell me. I'll listen.'

'OK, Jake. Take a seat.'

Jake is pacing the school's tech room. Mr Anover sits at his desk and waits.

'Something's really got to you, hasn't it?' observes the teacher. Jake spins round to face him.

'You're all the same!' he shouts. 'It's never about me, is it? It's always about Kyle, isn't it? Kyle this . . . Kyle that . . . Kyle would have . . . Kyle used to . . .

'Well, get this, everyone: I. Am. Not. My. Brother!' Jake stands still. A silence falls across the tech room. Mr Anover nods, holding Jake's furious gaze. Then suddenly, the rage is over. Jake drops into the nearest seat and stares miserably at Mr Anover.

A few minutes ago, as he walked from the tech room towards the staff room for his lunch, Mr Anover had heard Jake shouting in the stairwell. He recognised the voice: he has a soft spot for this underachieving teen and he knows that there is untapped potential behind the too-cool-for-school façade. Standing at the foot of the stairs, Mr Anover gazed up towards the second-floor landing. From within the stairwell he could hear a second, softer voice: the careers adviser who is in school that week, seeing each year-eleven student for a career guidance interview as they choose their subjects for A-level study next year. The softer voice is trying to calm Jake, and Jake is having none of it.

'You don't even KNOW me!' Jake is shouting. 'How can you tell me anything about my life? This is shit! I'm not coming back in. It's all *shit*! It's . . .' In the pause, Mr Anover says calmly but with immense clarity that echoes up the stairwell, '*I* know you, Jake. I think perhaps you could give me a hand in the tech room so Mr Copperfield can get back to his interviews. Can you spare me ten minutes?'

Jake's face appears over the banister. Tech is Jake's favourite lesson. Mr Anover is Jake's favourite teacher. He blinks down at his teacher, heaves the world-weary sigh of the indignant teenager, and shouts, 'It's about to be lunch, sir!'

'Better get a move on, then,' replies Mr Anover equably. He hears the sound of feet descending the stairs in jumps, and wonders at the agility of these youngsters.

Then there is Jake before him, descending the last flight three steps at a time. He stops on the bottom stair and looks Mr Anover in the eye. 'Just ten minutes?' he asks.

'Just ten minutes,' confirms Mr Anover, and they leave the stairwell together.

Jake is now perched on the front of a wooden school chair, his fists clenched, his elbows resting on his knees. He moves his chewing gum into his cheek, looks up at the tech teacher and sighs.

'Want to tell me what happened?' asks Mr Anover. 'And while you do, I need a hand to get that year-eight model into the storage bay. Can you carry the other end for me? It's heavy, mind.' He gestures to a six-foot board on a workbench, with a scale model of the town hall built on it, amid landscaped gardens. It is destined for a display in the real town hall next year; small groups of year-eight students have been working on it all year and now it is painted, and surprisingly impressive. 'Shame to see it damaged before it gets there,' says Mr Anover as he and Jake position themselves at either end of the board.

'You lead,' says Mr Anover. Jake knows the drill: Mr Anover has taught his students to work in teams to move large objects of their careful creation. One leader, clear the route, plan the manoeuvre, share the weight, count to lift and count to place down.

'Is it going on that low shelf?' asks Jake, nodding towards the storage bay.

'That's my plan,' says the teacher.

'Will it fit?'

Mr Anover smiles. 'Excellent question, team leader,' he says. 'I did measure it, but you can check if you like.'

Jake grins back. 'I'll take your word for it.' He gazes across the room from the model to the storage bay, then says, 'I think if we keep it parallel to the corridor wall, and you walk backwards, we can turn in front of the storage bay and slide it in sideways. Sound OK?'

Mr Anover smiles back. 'Sounds good. Tell me when.'

'Lift on three,' says Jake, as Mr Anover has taught all his students. 'One . . . two . . . three', and they lift the large display board, manoeuvre it along the classroom, turn on Jake's instruction and move sideways into the storage bay. Mr Anover sees the concentration on Jake's face and observes that the rage is draining away.

'Stop . . .' Jake instructs. They pause. 'On three,' he says, 'bend your knees, not your back . . .' and Mr Anover keeps his delight to himself as his student leads their safety-aware teamwork to slide the model onto the low shelf.

'Thanks, Jake,' says Mr Anover. 'Good job you were around. I needed someone reliable with that, it's a very precious piece of work.'

Jake nods to accept the compliment, and the lunch-break bell rings. There is instant clamour in the corridor outside the tech classroom as students stream through the school towards their lockers or the canteen. Mr Anover stands still. 'I know it's lunchtime, Jake, but I'd still like to talk about what happened to make you shout at the careers adviser like that. Want to give me the gist of it?'

Mr Anover sits down and gazes at Jake across a workbench. Jake sits opposite and drops his head.

'In your own time,' says Mr Anover. 'I'm just going to listen . . .'

'It was the same stuff I keep getting, Mr A,' says Jake. 'Grades are low, behaviour record isn't great, what kind of job am I aiming for? What are my hobbies, do I have any talents they don't recognise in school? That smarmy claptrap. Then he said he remembered my brother, and there were some smart people in my family so did I think I could raise my game. *Raise my game.* And I am just sick of being Kyle's brother. And from that . . . that . . . stick insect who wouldn't know cool if it bit him!'

Jake's estimatation of the careers adviser is that he looks about as old as Jake's brother, but less cool. Tie. Suit. Trying too hard. His brother would cut a dash in school: everyone always wanted to be like Jake's brother. Good at sports. Good at school. Good at university. Now good at his job in a graphic design company. Yeah. Cool.

And the adviser remembers Kyle. The athlete, the high-grades star. His own brother was in Kyle's year. So even though some of Jake's grades are . . . shall we use the word disappointing, Jake? We both know that there are smart genes in your family, and . . . well, shall we ask ourselves whether you could raise your game?

'I just lost it, sir. I blew up. Raise my game. *Raise my game* . . . I'm not Kyle. My dad is the same. Kyle's this, Kyle's that, what are you doing, Jake? It's never about what I can do, or what I think. Even in my own careers interview, it's still about my brother!'

'No wonder you feel fed up,' says Mr A. 'I'd feel fed up, too.'

There is a silence.

'Well,' says Mr A into the silence, '*have* you got any plans for after school, Jake? Got a career in mind? Or are you just . . .' Jake braces himself for 'snoozing your way through life' (his dad's opinion) and is surprised again when Mr A says, '. . . just an open book waiting to discover what your own adventure story is going to be?'

'Erm . . .' Jake gulps, trying not to swallow his gum. 'I think I'm that one. A book with nothin' in.'

'You've got something in, Jake,' says Mr A. 'You've got lots in. You just haven't got the next few chapters planned, but there's loads of stuff already in there. Loads.'

Jake blinks. This isn't what he was expecting.

'For example,' says Mr A, 'you've got all the things you're already good at in it. What things are they?'

Good at? In school? This is not a normal conversation, Jake thinks. No one talks to me about what I'm good at. Only what I'm bad at. Which is pretty much everything. He swallows again, and shrugs. This is a trick. But Mr A is always a straight-talker. He's always fair. Everyone knows it.

'OK, how about if I give you this pad and pen,' says Mr A, doing that, 'and you start a list? What are you good at? Not just in school – anywhere. Hobbies. Music. Friendship. What you do at the weekends. What do you like doing?'

'Well, skating,' says Jake, truthfully.

Mr A smiles. 'Write it down,' he says. 'Tell me about your board.' Jake describes his skateboard; how he has modified it; painted it; made his own logo for it. Mr A knows that Jake's doodles are often skate-related and that he once crafted a minia-ture skate park in this very tech room.

'Is that the logo on your T-shirt, too?' asks Mr A and Jake nods in surprise.

'So, because you like skating, what other skills has that given you? I wonder whether you have good balance. Courage to have a go at new moves even if you fall off a few times. Determination. You stick at something and practise it. Stuff like that, yeah?'

'Yeah . . .' agrees Jake, beginning to sense that he isn't being tested or teased here: Mr Anover might be on his side. 'Well – I practise and learn new moves. Some of the jumps are scary and you do fall off a lot until you get good. But I am good! Well, pretty good . . .'

'Put them on your list, Jake,' says Mr A. 'Determination. Balance. Courage. Practice. Sticking power. I saw your balance as you jumped down those stairs earlier – remarkable!' Jake adds them to his list.

'What other things do you know about yourself that might surprise some of your teachers?'

'I've been designing and selling T-shirts,' says Jake. 'Is that what you mean?'

'Exactly what I mean! Tell me about that,' says Mr A.

Jake admits that sometimes his brother helps him a bit. 'It's his job, like, design and that.'

'Great!' enthuses Mr A. 'How much of the design is his idea and how much is yours, would you say?'

'Well, I draw them. He shows me how to make them fancy, maybe put a frame round them, change colours and stuff – make them stand out, see?'

Mr A nods. 'So could design ideas go on your list, too?' Mr A points at the pad and Jake adds the next item. 'And business sense,' prompts Mr A. Jake keeps writing.

'Quite a list already,' says Mr A. 'Now what about school things? Sports? Art? Maths? Tech skills?' Jake pulls a face, but Mr A laughs. 'I know you've got tech skills, Jake, and your skate-park model needed maths as well as creativity. What were your best results in your mock exams?'

Jake can feel his face flushing. 'I didn't get good grades, Mr A

. . .' he begins, and Mr A waits, listening quietly. 'But . . . my least bad grades were maths, IT and art. And tech, of course – the skate park . . .'

'And where did you get the marks for your model?' asks Mr A, who knows the answer but wants Jake to remember, too.

'The idea . . . the design . . . the discussion of measurements and curves . . . not so good on the selection of materials . . . and the finished product was OK . . .' Jake has one eye closed as he concentrates on the final project report for his design project.

'So . . .' summarises Mr A, 'ideas, creativity, geometry, concentration, eye for detail, even artistic flair . . . Are they all on your list yet?' Jake is increasingly surprised. It's like Mr A is bigging him up. He wants to find things Jake is good at.

Mr A looks squarely at Jake. 'We're starting to see that your open book has lots in it already, Jake. Lots of potential to think about the sort of career you would find interesting and rewarding. What about the things you know you don't like? Are you good with discipline, for example?'

Jake laughs aloud. 'I bet you know how often I'm in trouble!' he says.

'There will be reasons for that, though,' says Mr A. 'Being in trouble is no fun. But what can you learn from it?'

'How do you mean?' asks Jake, curious. This sure is a funny conversation.

'Well, some people get into trouble because they just can't get up in the mornings. They shouldn't choose shift work. Others have trouble keeping rules. They probably wouldn't like the army. Some are fighters. Maybe they should learn to fight well and earn money from it. So – what does your discipline record tell you about yourself?'

Thoroughly astonished, Jake knits his brows as he thinks about why he is so often in hot water. 'I cause trouble in the classroom. Make people laugh. Tell jokes. Impersonate teachers and famous people. Get told to sit in a corner. Or to go out of the room.'

'And *are* you funny, Jake? I mean, could you stand up and do jokes in front of an audience?'

'Dunno . . .' admits Jake. 'But I get a laugh in lessons.'

'Well, if you like an audience, there's a whole lot of careers to choose from there, too.' Mr A leaves the suggestion hanging, before saying, 'You could add "I like an audience" to your list. Although maybe choose a less disruptive way to practise your comedy skills?'

Mr A points at the list; Jake begins to write. The teacher smiles as Jake's pen moves down the page; forgetting to be anxious about the rules, Jake resumes chewing his gum as he notes his creativity, his comedy timing, his impersonation skills. His love of an appreciative audience: something he never gets at home, in the shadow of his brilliant brother.

He looks up and hands Mr A the list.

'Lots to go on here, Jake,' says Mr A. 'Here's the plan. Photograph the list – yes, I know you'll have your phone in your pocket, whatever the rules are. Take the list away and see what else occurs to you. Keep writing this list. Make it as long as you like.

'Then start to think about what kinds of qualifications you'd be interested in getting that use some of those talents.

'We can meet up again in a month to chat about this some more if you like. Unless you'd rather have another session with the careers adviser?' They both laugh as Mr A puts his pad and pen on his desk.

'And Jake,' says Mr A, locking the tech-room door as they leave, 'I didn't hear you swear at the adviser, did I? Because that would be unwise, and involve the loss of a lunchtime . . .'

'No, sir, you did NOT,' agrees Jake. Somehow Jake looks taller.

Mr Anover's conversation with Jake could have gone very differently. The teacher was well aware of Jake's poor school discipline record, his academic underachievement and his casual interpretation of school rules, like the gum he was chewing when they met on the stairs. By suspending all judgement and offering him a space for shared thinking, Mr A surprised Jake, who was expecting a disciplinary conversation.

The teacher used curiosity to let Jake generate a list of his interests; Mr A used additional questions to get details and to open up Jake's own understanding that he has talents that don't get mentioned at school (and possibly at home), as well as summaries every now and then to confirm what they discussed: 'your open book has lots in it already'. Mr A did not press his own expertise: he elevated Jake's self-esteem by levelling up, and he tolerated the possibility that there won't be a clear career route ahead for this student. He even gave the key task, the list-writing, to Jake. Mr A wasn't trying to be 'in charge'. By accepting not knowing, by acting with humility, this experienced teacher encouraged Jake to see career planning as something to think about and engage with, instead of another task imposed by school.

Using curious questions and summaries, levelling-up with humility, and applying the attributes of a good listener, Mr A transformed Jake's self-perception in a single conversation.

Using Helpful Questions

When we create a space for someone to tell us their story, we may find that the person, though willing or even pleased to talk, has difficulty giving their account. They may be emotionally overwhelmed by the circumstances, and we hesitate to continue in case it is too hard for them to bear. By combining our curiosity with the skill of asking helpful questions, we can offer them stepping stones through their story.

Using questions as stepping stones can help if we want to support somebody but we're not sure where to start. It can help if they begin to tell us their story and then feel uncertain how to express an enormous situation in words. Using questions also helps if we know some of the story already, but don't yet know how the other person is processing the details and meaning. Helpful questions never suggest a particular answer; these are curious, open and open-minded questions that allow us to explore a situation together. In answering our curious questions, people choose how much to say, reveal only what feels safe to them and they often gain new insights that they might previously have overlooked.

The key to staying in safe territory is to be curious and supportive. When we ask someone questions, they can decide how deeply they want to answer. Helpful questions invite the other person to think, reflect and share their ideas, instead of replying with a simple 'yes' or 'no', or one piece of information. Questions that invite these short answers are called closed questions ('Have you fed the cat?' 'Are you vegetarian?' 'How old are you?'). Questions that invite detailed answers are more helpful in gathering a story.

These are open questions; they often begin with 'What . . .', 'How . . .', 'When . . .' and 'Where . . .' Other open questions are constructed as invitations to 'Tell me about . . .' or requests for more information such as 'I'd like to know more about . . .' ('Tell me about your family', 'What are your holiday plans?', 'How did you get interested in cooking?')

Open questions are *helpful to the asker*, because they allow us to build up a picture of the situation as it is experienced by the other person, rather than by making assumptions. Compare, for example, 'Are you scared of flying?' (assumption) with 'How do you enjoy air travel?' (open question).

Open questions are *helpful for the person being asked*, because they show the asker's interest, and they allow the person being asked to reflect and consider how to answer. Using the skill of *listening to understand* (page 25) alongside that of *asking helpful questions* is a powerful way of enabling somebody to feel safe, accompanied and understood as they talk about their experiences, hopes and fears.

Helpful questions and prompts to explore the current situation:

Tell me more about. . .
How do you feel about that?
What else did you think/say/do/feel?
What do you think about that now?
Could we be missing anything here?
Is there something else?

The final question is surprisingly powerful: it invites the speaker to add more or go deeper. Its cousin, *'Is there anything else?'* is more likely to close exploration down, evoking 'no' in response. The specificity of 'something else' evokes reflection and invites further exploration.

By asking what the person already knows, we help them to tell the story so far. This means that as the conversation progresses, we move together towards a shared understanding of the context. Making sure that we understand the story properly is important. A good way to do this is every now and again to sense-check: offer short summaries back to the person, using the 'question, question, check' and 'question, question, summary' waltz.

Our questions also help the other person to examine aspects of the story, and to notice things they may have overlooked or where they may have made assumptions that are untrue or unproven.

A recurring theme in helping by listening is the importance of enabling the other person to be in control of describing and exploring possible solutions for their difficulty: this means we must avoid giving unsolicited advice. Once the story has been told, sticking to questions can be helpful in looking for ways to deal with the situation. Using questions avoids slipping into advice-giving, and helpful questions will encourage the person to look at how they might approach the problem.

Helpful questions to explore possible ways forward:

Have you had any ideas about what to do next?
Is there something about this that could easily be changed?
Do you have any other information about this situation?
Could there be a different interpretation?
Have you ever dealt with a problem like this in the past? What did you do? Can you apply any of that experience here?
If a friend had a problem like this, what would you advise them?

Being immersed in a difficulty can reduce someone's sense of their own ability to act, and trap them in 'behaviour habits' that may help them to feel safe but make it difficult for them to solve their problem: staying away from a person they disagree with instead of broaching their differences; avoiding taking a health worry to their doctor for fear of bad news; studying relentlessly and becoming exhausted; assuming the worst to avoid being disappointed later; taking all (or none) of the responsibility for a situation. Questions that help someone to remember their own resilience or to come up with possible actions to address their difficulty can enable them to begin problem-solving. It is astonishing how often people who feel completely stuck can nevertheless think of advice to give a friend in the same position – using questions helps to change perspective. By using helpful questions, we enable someone to explore whether there could be another way of looking at this dilemma.

Louise is a volunteer in a cancer information drop-in. She has been attending a training course to learn about using cognitive therapy skills in supporting drop-in visitors, and I am one of her group's trainers. One of my favourite parts of the course is when participants bring back mini case stories to report on how they have used their new skills in real life. Today the group is feeding back about using curiosity and questions; this is Louise's story.

'This isn't actually a work case,' she begins. She looks around the circle of fellow trainees, including cancer nurses, dieticians, a physiotherapist, two chaplains and other volunteers from drop-ins around the UK. 'In fact, it's about my teenage son and his best friend.' There are smiles around the group: we all love a good story.

Louise's son Foster and his friend Leo have been pals since nursery. Now fifteen and at senior school, they still spend their free evenings and weekends together; they study, watch sports on TV and play video games. Their mums have become friends, too, through the many conversations that they have shared from nursery days to more recent times while picking up or dropping off their boys at each other's houses.

Recently, Leo's mum, Tracy, has been diagnosed with breast cancer. She had surgery, and now she is having chemotherapy.

'I've worked really hard to just be Tracy's friend, and not turn into a drop-in adviser when she talks about her treatment,' says Louise. 'We just chat, or I drop shopping off for her, and sometimes Leo sleeps at our house if it's chemo week and she's feeling very sick.'

Louise explains that the boys had planned a weekend together at her house a couple of weeks ago; they were going to play online games, watch some films and had promised to get their homework done, too. 'So it's Friday afternoon, I've stocked up my fridge with boy-snacks and cola, and I'm ready for them,' she tells us. 'I'm peeling potatoes and getting the dinner ready, and I can hear them coming through the backyard. Usually there's a racket – but they seemed a bit quiet. They came through the back door into the kitchen and Foster flops into a kitchen chair; but Leo just hovers by the door. I still didn't really notice there was anything wrong, I just shouted out to them to make me a cuppa and find themselves a snack.'

When neither of the boys moves, Louise looks up from her potato peeling.

'Everything OK?' she asks. Foster catches her eye and jerks his head towards his pal; Leo looks at the floor and Louise realises he is struggling to hold back tears.

'Fos, get the kettle on,' she instructs as she dries her hands and walks towards Leo. 'Leo, want to talk?'

Leo shakes his head and a tear falls onto the kitchen floor. He coughs and sniffs.

'No need to say anything at all,' says Louise, touching his shoulder, 'but you know where I am if you change your mind. Any time, OK?' Leo nods and another tear splashes to the floor. 'Come and sit at the table by Foster. You want tea? Cola? Water?'

Foster produces tea for his mum and cola cans for himself and

Leo. They pull the rings, pretending to squirt each other (they have done this for as long as Louise can remember) and then Leo says, 'Mum's in hospital, Lou. She's sick . . .' and his words tail off. Louise is standing behind the boys; she takes a seat at the end of the table.

'Tell me all about it, Leo,' invites Louise and Leo, who just said he didn't want to talk, describes his mum's cough and sore throat, high temperature, calling a GP overnight, seeing an ambulance arrive and Tracy being taken away by paramedics, his dad telling him from the back of the ambulance to be sure not to miss school tomorrow.

'So now,' Louise tells the group, 'I want to just reach out and hug him and promise him everything will be OK. But I also know that it mightn't be. And I'm really not sure how to play it, and that's when I think I'm going to try the questions approach from our training, and see how things seem to Leo.

'I was shaking!' she tells them all, and they nod in encouragement. 'I mean, I love Tracy and I love Leo. Fos has never had to deal with a situation like this before. Tracy is like family to him, and if she dies I don't know how . . .' Louise stops speaking and gathers herself. She shakes her hands as though to dispel her difficult thoughts and then resumes her story.

Louise asks Leo how his mum is today, and Leo says he doesn't know because the ward will only speak to his dad, who is at work. 'He doesn't answer my texts when he's at work,' growls Leo.

'Obviously,' Louise tells the group, 'I want to phone Leo's dad and tell him to get over here and tell us all what to expect. Because usually, that's what I do, you know? Sort things out. Get busy. Make a plan. But I stuck with the questions, and I was brave – I asked what was Leo's worst thought, just like we all practised in here.' They nod. I catch the eye of my co-trainer: we are proud of the way our trainees put their training to use. And Louise is a natural storyteller: the group is spellbound.

'What's worrying you most, Leo?' asks Louise. Foster watches his friend's face contort as he struggles with his emotions, before Leo whispers, 'I don't want her to die, Lou . . .' and tears stop him speaking. Foster watches in silence.

'It's scary, isn't it, Leo?' Louise says, naming Leo's emotion. Leo nods silently. Louise touches his hand across the table. Foster fiddles with his ring-pull, scratching shapes onto his cola can.

'Do you think she really is dying?' asks Louise. Leo looks baffled. He rubs his chin with one hand and scratches his head with the other.

'I dunno. I just thought if she's gotta go to hospital she must be dying, but they sent me to school!' he says. 'She's trying to stop me seeing her die.'

'Well,' says Louise to the group, 'I knew it wasn't very likely Leo's dad would go to work if his wife was dying, so I expected there might be other things going on. But I stopped myself saying that, and I remembered to acknowledge Leo's thoughts before I asked questions about other possibilities.' Members of the group are leaning forward to hear her; several are giving thumbs-up or signing silent applause.

Louise looks at Leo; Leo looks at his cola can. 'Hmm, that's a scary thought,' she says. 'But I wonder if it could be anything else . . . Did she show you that leaflet they gave her when she started her chemo?' Leo's eyebrows gather in conference, then he looks straight at Louise for the first time as he says, 'The one about going bald? And germs? No visitors with colds and that?'

'That's the one,' says Louise. 'What did it say about if she had a cough or a sore throat?'

'Erm . . .' Leo is really thinking deeply now, trying to remember the information the family discussed before Tracy's chemo began three months ago.

Louise tells the group, 'Honestly, you could see him thinking – trying to remember what else he knew. All that helpful information just flies out of people's heads in a crisis, doesn't it?'

Finally, Leo says, 'I think it said she can't fight infections, so she needs antibiotics fast in a drip if she gets a sore throat or a cough . . .'

'Yep, that's what I remember, too,' agrees Louise, who has read this leaflet many times in her drop-in role. 'And what will the antibiotics do?'

'Erm . . . well, they'll . . . well, they're to make her better, aren't they?' says Leo, sitting up straighter suddenly. 'They are to stop her from dying of an infection, aren't they? *That*'s why she's in hospital, isn't it?'

Louise sips her tea and nods. Her helpful questions have probed Leo's worst fears, and then helped him to remember things he had overlooked in his terror.

'After we've had supper, shall we go in for evening visiting at the hospital?' offers Louise.

'Brilliant, yeah, let's do that, Lou. Can we have chips?' says Leo.

'*Chips!*' Louise reflects to the group. 'It was an instant mood shift! I was so relieved – and I was a bit proud of how my questions got him to reassure himself – it was like he was a different lad. A different, hungry lad!'

There is an enthusiastic round of applause from the group for her story and her courage, and from the delighted trainers at such a beautiful example of the power of helpful questions.

Louise gave no advice. She asked questions, named Leo's fear and gave him space to feel upset. She also asked him whether there was any other information available to consider, wondering (with curiosity) whether there could be any other explanation for Leo's mum being in hospital and helping him to remember the leaflet he had read but forgotten about in his panic and sorrow.

Helpful questions and tender listening; a gentle way to get alongside someone in distress.

Getting Alongside: 'Being With' Distress

Encountering someone who feels overwhelmed by their distress can feel discouragingly difficult. They may have agreed to talk about their troubles, or even have asked us to chat with them, but it's hard to know how to respond if the conversation becomes very emotional. There is a worry about causing harm; fear of overwhelming someone; nervousness about blundering into areas they don't want to discuss; even fear of the power of the emotions at play – both theirs and ours.

'Don't cry' is a common response to seeing distress. It is kindly meant. It doesn't imply 'You are bad for crying', but rather 'I wish you didn't feel so upset that it makes you cry.' It suggests 'I want to make it better for you', and signifies concern. The problem is that this wish for a distressed person to appear less upset translates into a judgement that their emotions are inappropriate. Our exhortations to 'Cheer up!' or our attempts to change the subject to something more positive simply tell a distressed person that their suffering is not welcome here.

The fear of making things worse for someone is rooted in a belief that 'I should know what to do.' But what if we approach this conversation from a different perspective? What if we come not as a problem-solver, but as a person prepared to share their uncertainty and support their distress?

To make space for suffering, and allow somebody to process their distress, is an important component of support and care. Being a companion in suffering requires us to hold a space for them where suffering is not judged, discouraged or minimised.

'Oh, no! Oh, please don't cry . . .'

I just happen to be passing when Agnes emerges from the dean's office in our university faculty; she had been unexpectedly summoned there from our seminar twenty minutes earlier. Twenty life-changing minutes. Agnes's face is a mask of sorrow, her eyes brimming and her mouth contorted by the effort of containing the suffering that threatens to overwhelm her. We are first-year medical students and we hardly know each other, but I sense that I must not walk away. Something dreadful is happening, and I want to put it right.

Agnes slumps onto an ancient wooden chest that is the only furniture in the wood-panelled portico of the academic building. She leans forward and sobs, heaving shuddering breaths between her howls of pain. I look around anxiously: who might be near by? *Who can help? What can we do? What is going on?*

Crouching down, I take Agnes's hand in mine. She allows this, and her sobbing intensifies, her whole body shuddering with each breath.

'Agnes, what's happened?' I ask, supposing that a summons by the dean is likely to mean Agnes is in some sort of trouble. Has she been suspended? Dismissed from the course? It's clearly something major. Agnes shakes her head and tears scatter, one warm drop landing on the back of my hand and running down to seal the place where my skin meets the soft black skin of Agnes's hand. A baptism.

Looking up, Agnes meets my gaze; she shakes her head while her lips move in an effort to speak, before her mouth grimaces again and a new shower of tears spills from her eyes.

I don't know what to do. I sit on the floor and give Agnes's hand a gentle squeeze as my heart hammers inside my chest. What is she going to reveal? How on earth can I help her? I imagine the shame I would feel if I were to be dismissed from the course. How would I tell my parents? How would I cope with the disgrace?

And Agnes – gentle, smiling Agnes: she comes all the way from Ghana and her family is far, far away. We had shared a cup of terrible vending-machine coffee in freshers' week when neither of us had quite enough coins to purchase a drink each, and we swapped personal details, but Agnes was living in a different hall of residence and I had hardly seen her. We'd always smiled as we passed each other among the ocean of students coming into or out of lectures: I felt a sense that we had a friendship waiting to happen.

But now this. What *is* this?

'Agnes, you can tell me. Please don't cry. Nothing is that bad. Whatever it is, we can sort it out . . .'

Agnes, whose own life has just been irretrievably altered, now changes my life-view with three words.

'My mum died,' she says, quietly. 'My mum. Oh, Mama!' Agnes crosses her arms in front of her chest, stroking her shoulder-tips with her hands and rocking back and forth as though embracing her lost mother. And I am overcome with shame for my selfish thoughts. I understand in an instant that all my projections of shame and humiliation and the loss of her course would be welcome instead of this dreadful truth. On a different continent, too far to reach, Agnes's mum lies dead, and the dean has had to break this awful news to his student.

I can't make this better. I can only sit on the floor, silent and appalled at the loss Agnes faces; picturing my own mother's smile and imagining how that loss could be borne; horrified by the emotions I know Agnes must be feeling, and aware that I have nothing to offer; nothing but my inadequate presence and my witness to her love and sorrow.

In the wood-panelled portico of their medical school, two doctors-to-be have discovered that the world asks us not to cry. I understand that I can never undo the words I said, the assumptions I made. I sit in shamed silence, waiting for Agnes to find the strength to stand up. I am determined to sit here with Agnes for as long as I am needed. I will take her home and help her find the coins necessary to phone her family from the students' payphone. I promise myself that I will never again make assumptions, never again promise that we can fix what is broken.

Of course, I went on making assumptions. We all do. We see the world through our own lens, and we draw conclusions based on limited evidence, conjecture and supposition. What I did learn, though, was how my own discomfort at Agnes's distress caused me to try to change what she felt: to assure her that nothing is that bad, nothing is irresolvable, that there will be a solution for this. I just wanted to 'fix' it. I know I am not alone in wanting to fix things: most people experience a natural, kind wish to make things better. But sometimes things can't be made better. Some things can only be carried.

When someone is suffering, their thoughts and emotions are theirs alone. It is the extent to which we are prepared to see their perspective, acknowledge their experience, and allow ourselves to feel discomfort on their behalf that dictates whether our response is perceived as pity, sympathy or empathy. Often we do not fully discriminate between these responses ('tea and sympathy' can be a maxim for any of them), but the differences are important when we are engaged in support for a person in distress.

Pity recognises the other person's perspective and acknowledges that their situation is unfortunate, but it does not progress to evoking personal emotions in the observer. Pity watches suffering without entering into it: pity is about me, not about the person in distress. Someone might have recognised that Agnes was leaving the dean's office in a state of distress and walked away with a sense of pity: 'Poor thing. Another person getting a dressing down about their exam results.'

Sympathy is about the other person's feelings; it is less self-conscious than pity and includes clear concern about the other's distress. Sympathy identifies with someone's suffering enough to want to fix it. When we reach out in sympathy, we do so from a place that feels safe to us, a place where we feel in control. Generally, sympathy wants to 'make it better', although this is at least in part so that we can feel better. The very suggestion that their distress could easily be 'fixed' means a sympathetic response can demean the person's suffering. A passer-by's decision to stop may originate in sympathy, for example 'Oh, she looks very sad. I'd hate to be alone feeling like that. I'll see if she's OK and help to make her better.' Attempts to 'make it better' can take the form of offering solutions ('Why don't you . . .?'), reassurance ('I'm sure everything will turn out OK.' 'The doctors will be able to fix this.'), distraction onto other topics of conversation, even admiration ('Oh, you look so well!' 'Wow, you're so brave.' 'I don't know how you stay so strong.'). Worst of all are crass attempts to 'cheer up' their sorrow, often taking the form of 'At least-isms' ('At least he's out of his suffering now.' 'At least you have other children.' 'At least your wife still has a job.'). At first sight, trying to reduce someone's distress sounds like a good thing to do, but attempts to diminish their expressions of suffering do not solve their difficulties. Instead, these well-intended efforts to reduce their emotional upset simply tell them that this is not a safe place to express their emotions: the person, and not their distress, becomes diminished.

The deeper emotional responses of empathy and compassion arise when we are prepared not only to identify with the other person's emotions, but to connect with them on a level at which we, too, feel deep emotion. Empathy is entirely focused on the suffering person; self-awareness is used to bring our personal experience and imagination into their service. An empathic response offers companionship in their place of suffering, and being prepared to witness, validate and accompany their distress. Empathy identifies with suffering and recognises that either there is no way to fix it, or that the solutions must belong to the suffering person. Instead of focusing on 'doing something', empathy offers to be with someone in their suffering. It is 'feeling with' someone.

By being aware of the sufferer's perspective, recognising their emotion and connecting with a similar emotion inside ourselves, we allow ourselves to be vulnerable. We move with them to the rhythm of their sorrowful music, taking their lead, recognising and reciprocating their vulnerability. The empathic supporter has stepped inside the sufferer's experience as best they can, and instead of trying to change the experience they simply seek to accompany it: they have moved from observer to companion. Having no personal experience of the death of a parent, I found myself reflecting on the depth of loss I would feel in Agnes's situation, and that insight transformed my understanding of the complexity of her distress. I had engaged as an act of sympathy, but I stayed because I had found empathy for my classmate's distress.

Compassion is the action-arm of empathy. Grounded in empathy, compassion goes further, seeking to support someone in finding their own way through their suffering by joining their dance. A compassionate response to a bereavement might be to acknowledge how difficult the everyday tasks of running a home might feel and so to offer practical support with meals, laundry, dog-walking or child/elder care; or to recognise the unpredictability of emotions in grief and offer a regular check-in, which the bereaved person can accept or decline as they feel inclined; or to ask how to help honour and celebrate the dead person. Compassion offers support without insisting. Compassion suggests, 'You will find a way through this, and I will give the support that you decide is right for you.' It is 'being with', not 'doing to'.

Sympathy is expressing concern through a doorway; empathy enters the place of suffering to offer companionship there;

compassion is the solidarity that seeks the other person's good, for the other person's sake. I was a bit slow, but I got there in the end.

Someone who has experienced an emotionally intense event will go over their story until they have made sense of it. This processing is an important part of coping: it helps us to move an experience from the here and now into our memory of past events. For some people, this processing is internal reflection but for many it involves a retelling out loud. We are familiar with new mums' telling and retelling of their birth stories from first contraction, in eye-watering detail, until they are safely holding their baby for the first time. The same need to narrate applies to difficult events, but people may not feel welcome to retell their tale of the midnight knock on the door by a policeman with bad news, or their slow-motion experience of being in a traffic accident, or the birth story that ends in sorrow. Yet the need remains to process our stories until they make sense to us, so once a person with a distressing story finds someone who is willing to listen, expect to hear their story repeatedly, sounding the same (often with new details) and eliciting the same distress, until gradually it softens into the memory of 'a bad thing that happened to me in the past' instead of being an active and current distress. Failure to transfer a distressing event to our memory in this way is a feature of post-traumatic stress disorder. Being able to tell the story in a safe space is a protection once the person feels ready to tell their tale, although imposed early debriefing, however helpfully intended, can be harmful: we can offer to listen, but we should never force someone to re-experience events.

People who view themselves as 'kind' can fall into the trap of over-helpfulness. They jump in to reassure, to promise help and support, to problem-solve. It is a particular struggle for many people who work in caring roles because they are motivated by the notion of being helpers, taking action to solve others' problems.

Learning to listen quietly, to accompany people in their distress and even to use helpful questions to explore that distress more deeply can feel uncomfortably challenging to them, as though allowing expression of all those painful emotions is a failure of kindness, a lack of helpful action. In fact, sorrow shared is a different way of helping, one that is deeply appreciated by people in distress and often remembered long afterwards.

Alan is lost for words, gazing at his wife. Laura sits silently, pale. They are together on two functional plastic chairs in a tiny room in the maternity department, and their world is falling apart. Their precious IVF pregnancy, their baked-bean-sized baby, has died. Laura is bleeding, and a scan shows her womb is empty.

Two weeks ago, in this same room, they saw their baby's tiny heart beating on Laura's first scan. They left the hospital ecstatic with excitement. Yes, they knew it was early days. Yes, they knew it was too soon to assume anything. But they were pregnant. They were going to be parents. In fact, they were already parents; their baby's heart was beating. They called their baby Jamie, a name suitable for a boy or a girl. They wanted a surprise on delivery day, to meet their baby and learn its sex. They would decorate the nursery in mint green and primrose yellow: colours of spring, hope and anticipation.

A knock at the door; a softly turned handle; the door edges open and a head appears. Long, dark hair, tied up. Nurse uniform. Smile.

'I'm Pete,' he says, softly. 'I heard about your baby. I am so sorry . . .'

Pete steps into the doorway, and asks, 'Please may I join you?' Alan reflects that it's his department, and then notices that Pete's question implies that the space is theirs. Pete waits, not assuming permission. Laura nods at Alan, and Alan says, 'Yes, Pete. Come in.'

Laura leans sideways in her chair to rest her arms on the

examination couch, then drops her head onto her arms. Her shoulders shake as she sobs. Alan touches Laura's elbow, his own tears running unchecked down his face. Pete kneels on the floor beside them, and very gently touches them both on a shoulder, forming a ring of silent sorrow.

Pete says nothing at all.

'I'm sorry . . .' sobs Laura, looking up at Alan. 'If I'd only . . .' and she dissolves back into tears. Alan lifts Laura's hand and kisses it, and Pete sits back to give them space, dropping his arms.

'It's just so hard, isn't it?' he says, into the empty space between them. They nod, and sigh, and look at Pete.

'If you'd only what, Laura?' asks Pete. He knows women often blame themselves for a miscarriage. The grief is hard enough, without adding guilt.

'I . . . I . . . Oh, I don't know!' she says. 'It just seems like I must have done something wrong to lose the baby. I don't know what. But I was supposed to be the safe place, and I wasn't safe enough . . .' and she stops to blow her nose, wipe her eyes and gaze sadly at Alan.

Pete nods, then remarks, 'I hear people say that all the time, Laura. Even though I know they have all had the leaflets, the data. They have all been told that even with a positive pregnancy test, one pregnancy in ten is lost in the first twelve weeks. I know you knew that, didn't you?' and he looks from one to the other as they nod.

'And knowing that just doesn't make this any easier, does it?' he asks. They shake their heads. He sits back on his heels.

Pete waits, kneeling in silence before them, waiting to see whether they have any more questions, waiting to gauge whether they feel ready to move out of the clinic room.

'I've come to invite you into a different room,' Pete says eventually. 'It's more comfortable than this room, and there's a kettle and cups. You can sit in there for as long as you like, while you just process all this sadness. There's no hurry. And I can make you a coffee there, or get you a cold drink.

'Do you feel safe to walk along the corridor with me? We won't pass the waiting area, only offices. You won't bump into anyone except staff who work with me. How does that sound?'

In the new room there is a sofa, two upright armchairs, a soft rug on the floor. In the corner is a shelf with china cups above a gleaming sink; a small fridge; jars labelled 'tea', 'coffee' and 'sugar'. A low coffee table with a vase of silk flowers and a box of tissues. Pete shows them the facilities, then says, 'There's a sofa for closeness, or if you need your own space those armchairs are comfier than they look. You can lock the door from inside, and I'll pop back every now and then to see how you're doing.

'I'm going to leave this notebook and pencil. If you have any questions, jot them down. I'll try to answer them, and if I can't there are people around I can ask.

'Is there anyone else you'd like here? Your family? Our chaplain? Invite anyone you like. This room is your space for as long as you want it today.

'I'll be back in half an hour.'

Pete is good at his job. As a specialist nurse in early pregnancy loss, he regularly meets women and couples facing the sorrow of an abruptly ended pregnancy. He knows he cannot make this better. He knows that every loss is as individual as the hopes of the heartbroken parents he meets. He knows that after leaving the hospital, many will face friends and family who, in a desire to manage the hurt, offer redundant messages that minimise the loss: *at least you know you can get pregnant; well, have a holiday and try again; at least it wasn't a real baby yet; at least . . .* Or they 'helpfully' avoid mentioning the pregnancy, the baby and the loss altogether. Some will even cross the road to avoid a conversation that might involve sorrow, kind in intention but wounding to the core of those left lonely in their grief.

By offering a room dedicated to making space for sorrow, Pete and his department are making a bold statement. This is a loss. Your baby has died. This hurts. We see you. We are listening. Pete spends time there with each grieving mother and her companions, sitting with them in silence, witnessing sorrow and not trying to make it better, not belittling their pain.

Pete calls back regularly to check on Alan and Laura. He makes himself a coffee and sits on a chair to listen as they talk about how to tell their family and friends their sad news. He asks them what responses they anticipate, and he gently warns them that not everybody will understand the depth of their sorrow. But mainly, Pete listens. As they talk to each other, Alan and Laura will feel their way through their grief to a point at which they are ready to go home. Pete escorts them to the stairwell that avoids walking through the waiting room, and watches until they turn the corner, out of the department and into the unknowing world.

People like Pete know and practise this important truth: we can't always make it better. But we can always hold space for it.

Using Silence

Let's change seats, and think about being the person listened to. Talking aloud about a situation, a memory or a fear is a way of making sense of it. As we tell our story to someone else, we hear that familiar story in a perception-changing way. Taking it out of our minds and framing it into words changes the way it feels, sometimes even the way that we understand it. This is emotional work. Sharing difficult news or personal struggles reveals the painful emotions involved to both narrator and listener, making a discussion uncomfortable for both parties in the conversation.

The listener may want to comfort or console us, believing that the less we speak of our pain, the less we will suffer. In fact, the opposite is true: the suffering lies within us, waiting to be attended to. By offering us their attention, a listener provides the space where we can face those issues we alone can wrestle with, within our inner silence; a place to review the components of our distress, understand them better and find ways to move forward. By listening and allowing the heartache, a compassionate listener helps us to create a container strong enough to hold it. Often their best contribution is an accepting silence.

Craig has just picked his teenage daughter up from a night out with school friends. Tomorrow is Saturday; she can sleep late and then catch up with schoolwork, art activities and her music. It was easy to find her: in the sports club car park there was a jostling, laughing cloud of youngsters flitting like moths in the pools of light beneath the lamp-posts, glad to have finished the week with a game of football and some social time in the sports club café-bar. They can't drink alcohol, of course, but they like the music there and they gather to chat, dance and gossip, skittish and giddy on the freedom of a weekend ahead. Sacha waved him down, air-kissed the two girls beside her and slid into the passenger seat, where she sits scrolling through photos on her phone, silent.

'Good night, Sacha?' asks Craig, pulling out of the car park. Sacha doesn't reply. Her head is bowed to her phone screen that glows blue in the dark car interior. As they move between streetlamps, orange flashes illuminate her face and her spiked, purple hair. Glancing sideways, Craig sees a tear glistening on Sacha's cheek.

'Wanna talk?' he asks. The car curves into the darkness as the lamp-lit city street becomes a dark highway across the countryside. Craig drives, eyes ahead, silent. Waiting.

Sacha sniffs and blows her nose.

'They laughed at my shoes,' she says, glumly. Craig feels a surge of relief. Shoes! Only a fashion tiff. He'd been as riled as a bear whose cub had been threatened. A surge of fatherly helpfulness sweeps through him as he says, 'Oh, sweetheart. It's only shoes. What's the big deal? Come on, you're just tired. Let's get you home to bed. If you like we can go shoe shopping next weekend. OK?'

Sacha nods, turns off her phone, pulls up her scarf and closes her eyes. If he can't understand about the shoes, how can she tell him about the other stuff?

Craig is glad he made his baby feel better.

Processing bad news, contemplating future difficulties, remembering past troubles: these are all parts of being human. Our magpie minds assemble our predicaments and garnish them with fear, shame and guilt. They can build the pile of sorrow baubles so high it is hard to see anything else. These are unpleasant to face and lonely to contemplate, feeling too heavy to carry and too bitter to share.

Yet sharing our difficulties is one of the keys to surviving them without becoming completely broken. To tell the story of a complex inner struggle takes physical and emotional energy, and involves the risk of judgement, censure and rejection. Emotional reasoning is inherently biased, suggesting that feeling bad means we *are* bad, and we may be found out if we tell our tale. Finding a non-judgemental listener is a validating experience, and it allows the story to be told aloud – to be heard anew by the narrator as they explain it to the listener. This simple re-hearing can be as powerful as any external advice.

The way the listener behaves is crucial to opening up or closing down the safety of the conversation. The listener may be the person who has had to break bad news, or they may be the person who happens upon us in our distress. The listener may be familiar and trusted, or may be a stranger. In some ways, their identity is not important. Listening isn't about the listener, it's about the listening.

We unwrap our sorrows like an onion. The outer layers are least complex. We are able to reveal some of these layers without taking too much risk. As we do so, we gauge the response of our listener. Are they shocked? Disgusted? Angry? Perhaps they are showing an excitedly prurient interest. Perhaps they are simply dismissive. These responses warn us to keep the deeper layers well wrapped. A calm, curious, non-judgemental response may indicate it is safe to go deeper. Those layers are more emotionally laden; harder to tell, hurtful to encounter. As we reveal our hurt, we again assess the listener's response: calmly accepting, gently encouraging listeners offer safe ground to continue. Echoing our distress shows we are understood. But responding by reassurance or attempting to minimise the hurt interrupts the unpeeling and shuts it down.

No wonder it's difficult to be a good listener. It requires being empathic: aware of the person's distress, and able to see their perspective, yet holding back the impulse to comfort or console prematurely lest this closes the safe place. To make space for our suffering, and allow us to process our distress, is an important component of support and care. Being a companion in suffering requires a listener to hold a space for us where our suffering is not judged, discouraged or minimised.

In a conversation, we speak and we listen; we ask questions, we wait for answers; we make statements, and we wonder aloud. But deep conversations also include silences. There are points when nobody is speaking, and the silence is doing the work. Silence is where we ponder, where we bring together different ideas and assemble new possibilities, where we reach new understanding, where we make a decision or change our minds. In other words, silence is where the real work happens.

One aspect of communication that can tie us in knots is eye contact. There is a widespread belief that 'genuine' communication requires direct eye contact. When we really examine that proposition, though, we realise that prolonged, direct eye contact when we feel emotionally vulnerable can be intrusive and disconcerting. In fact, many intimate conversations take place while we are walking shoulder to shoulder, or engaged in a shared hobby where our eyes are on the task, or in cars where one participant is driving and so there is little or no exchange of eye contact. Although in everyday conversation we instinctively use gaze to give each other signals like 'your turn to talk' or 'that surprises me', often it is when one participant gazes away that they offer the other person that pause for their own thoughts, or they indicate that they are not yet ready to take their turn to speak. To allow silence as 'thinking time' may require paying attention to gaze: looking away to show that we are respecting this moment of silence; noticing that the other person looks down as they consider their thoughts and ideas while we hold silence; or looking back at the person to indicate that, when they feel ready, we are waiting for them to speak and we will not interrupt the silence before them. When we cannot see each other, whether we are alongside gazing outwards together or talking on the phone, we find other ways to signal our listening, our thoughtfulness and our turn-taking, and we still use silence as a valuable component of our most thoughtful conversations.

Understanding the value of silence is key to tender conversations. The hope is not to avoid distress. Rather, it's to allow the conversation to include the difficulties, sorrows and frustrations of the situation and to accept the emotions that arise as reasonable and expected. By being companions in those uncomfortable emotions, listeners show compassion and give permission for us to feel whatever we feel without being judged.

At the same time, by holding that space, they allow us to process our thoughts and emotions; we are considering, reviewing, reshaping and understanding our ideas and concerns in the thoughtful depths that look, on the surface, like a simple silence. It is the pause in the dance, where we gather our breath.

Let's take Craig around the block before he picks up Sacha. He's a bit early, anyway, because he feels very protective of his daughter. She is a precious miracle. It's two years now since her bone-marrow transplant. Her leukaemia has been cured by the gift of a stranger. Sacha is back in school, catching up with lost progress. All her friends are in 'the football crowd'. Most of them play, but Sacha has been left with permanent nerve damage by her chemotherapy, and isn't always steady on her feet. She can't play football but she loves sport and cheers on the touchline on Friday evenings before heading to the café (the kids call it 'the bar' in an attempt to sound grown up) to socialise and celebrate the weekend.

Sacha walks more slowly than her friends. She sometimes trips on the football touchline because the ground is uneven. She can't wear the heels or platform shoes that are in vogue; she simply falls over or twists her ankle. Although her feet don't tell her brain exactly where they are, they certainly tell her exactly how much they hurt.

Sacha dressed carefully today because she had a special idea in mind for this evening. The patent leather air-sole boots, an iridescent kingfisher blue, were the confidence-boosting flourish of her outfit. At the after-football gatherings, Sacha has been getting to know Toni, the captain of the girls' football team. She has found a strange, sweet pleasure in Toni's company, and Sacha believes they are falling in love with each other. Tonight Sacha planned to ask Toni on a date.

But Toni didn't join the gang at the bar. She dashed straight from the changing rooms to the car park, where an older boy was waiting in his car. 'Bye, everyone!' she waved from the passenger seat window as her beau drove them to the exit. 'See you on Monday!' Sacha watched the car sweep out of the car park with her dreams on board, a ripping sensation pulling at her chest.

'C'mon, Sacha! You should be at the front of the queue in your shiny shoes!' shouted a friend as they trudged across to the café. But the shoes are pointless. The hope is pointless. The love is pointless. Sacha's heart sank to her boots. These stupid, hopeful boots. She would like to throw them, pointless yet stabbing her, into the nearest bin.

Let's bring Craig back to the car park to pick Sacha up, broken heart and all.

'Good night, Sacha?' asks Craig, as they drive away. Sacha doesn't reply. Her eyes are fixed on her phone screen that glows inside the car. The light from the streetlamps flashes across her face and her spiked, purple hair. Glancing towards her, Craig sees a tear glistening on Sacha's cheek.

'Wanna talk?' he asks. The car moves from the lamp-lit city street to a dark highway as they enter the countryside. Craig drives, eyes ahead, silent. Waiting.

Sacha sniffs and blows her nose.

'They laughed at my shoes,' she says, glumly. Craig is surprised. Sacha isn't usually fussed about teasing.

'Oh, Sash, I'm sorry,' he says, holding his thoughts to himself. 'I thought you looked sad . . .'

Craig feels as riled as a bear whose cub has been threatened. His precious daughter is sad, and some other kid has done this. He maintains a silence, glancing at Sacha from time to time as she scrolls and sighs. After several minutes, he prompts Sacha with 'I'll listen if you want to tell me about it, you know.'

Sacha puts down the phone. 'I wore these boots specially, Dad. I chose them because I like someone who likes these boots. I wanted to show we were on the same wavelength . . .'

Craig waits. This is Sacha talking about liking someone. She's never had a boyfriend, but she's reaching the age when all that starts to happen. His mind races to a million terrifying destinations: heartbreak, sex, pregnancy, more heartbreak, losing her to a boy who doesn't deserve her. He checks himself, remembers dating from his youth, remembers the fun and the awkwardness and the self-esteem crises.

'So you like someone . . .' he invites, and falls silent again.

'Yes, and I thought . . . I thought they liked me, too,' she says, her voice choking miserably.

Ah, that old unrequited love thing, he thinks, relieved. Heartbreak is all part of growing up. But it hurts, so badly. He waits.

'So . . . what happened?' asks Craig into the dark silence beside him.

'They . . . they went off with somebody else,' sighs Sacha. 'I didn't expect it, you know? I thought they liked me . . .'

'Oh, that's hard, hon',' says Craig. 'I hate that heartbreak feeling.'

'But you've got Mum, and I've got *nobody!*' she says. This wounds Craig: *you've got us!* he wants to shout. But well done, Craig, for keeping those thoughts inside his head. He nods in the darkness. He waits.

'Nobody will ever love me,' sobs Sacha. Craig wants to tell her there are plenty more fish in the sea, she'll meet someone, there's plenty of time. But those consolations aren't for now, while her heartbreak is raw.

'I guess I read too much into it . . .' Sacha is mulling it over. 'I mean, we talked about boots. And football. And we both like the same music. And we just seemed to click, you know?

'But I hoped for more, and I was excited to think maybe . . . they did, too. So I feel silly as well. But at least I hadn't said anything yet. I haven't been humiliated. But . . .' and another tear glistens silver in the light of a passing car.

Sacha is using the silence to review her hopes and assumptions. Did Toni encourage her, or did Sacha misread their friendship? Is her hope of happiness over for ever, or has she discovered something about relationships? Does her dad realise that Sacha is talking about a girl? Is he ready for her to come out? Is *she* ready to come out?

There is a lot more to be unpeeled, when Sacha is ready to tell it. But this dark car, this patient dad, this open-minded silence, has given her a safe place to begin.

This is definitely not about shoes. Well done for holding the silence, Craig.

The Opposite of Listening

Craig could have derailed his intention to listen by diving in to help: such a natural impulse whether the person we are listening to is our daughter, our friend, a colleague or a client. Trying to make it better is almost the opposite of listening: it is intended to reduce the distress and yet the only distress it reduces is the listener's.

Here are some 'opposite of listening' behaviours to recognise. Like all of us, to start with you may find you have already taken some of these actions; some may even be your regular habits. That's fine: noticing is the first step towards change, and we call it insight. Next time you notice the impulse to act, smile inside at your insight and just keep listening. Don't get distracted by 'what I would do if I were you'. Remain present, listening. It gets easier with practice, and the successes reinforce future use of listening.

Interrupting: let the person tell their story. Avoid finishing their sentences, or assuming their story will follow the route you expect. Giving reassurance is a form of interrupting.

Telling your story: this is their story. Avoid telling them that 'it's like a time when I . . .' Empathise by saying 'I'm listening' instead of telling your similar, but probably not similar, story.

Offering advice: if there was an easy solution, the person would have sorted the dilemma out already. Listen. If it sounds simple to solve, it's harder than you have understood – yet. Keep listening.

Over-identifying: 'I know just how you feel.' No, you do not.

Minimising distress: if they are upset, sit with their emotions. Don't try to save them, don't try to distract or divert the conversation: just let them know you will stay with them through this distress.

Trying to fix it: that isn't yours to do. They will fix it, if it can be fixed, when the time is right. Just keep listening. Ask more questions. Try to understand more.

Making assumptions: those tears may be sadness, but they may not be. They could be tears of ferocious pride, an overflowing of tenderness, a river of regret. The boots were not the problem for Sacha, but what the boots meant was highly significant. When we sit in silence to be present with someone in their distress, we must avoid assuming we have understood the whole story. A recent death may be an unimaginable blow, but it may be a relief after a long period of waiting, or the complicated loss of a person who was difficult to relate to. The loss of a job may be a release from years of bullying as well as a frightening step into financial insecurity. Failing an exam may mean other life plans are put on hold: the disappointment may not be about the exam result at all. Ask, don't assume. Check your understanding.

Finishing Safely

The conversation has begun. You have told your news, or you have heard somebody else's. You have listened, and I hope you have been listened to as well. It's time to bring the discussion to a close: if you have communicated well together, the tenderness of the conversation is still in the air. If it's been a bumpy conversation, there may still be sadness, hurt or anger. It may be both: a recognition of hurt and also a deeper understanding of mutual concern.

How do we bring the discussion to an appropriate close? With an abrupt change of subject? By making a rush for the door? Should you crack an awkward joke? We've seen all these, haven't we? We know we would like to finish this exchange as kindly as possible: ending in a safe and supportive manner leaves the way open for the conversation to be picked up again, as and when it's needed.

Finding the right time to finish is a balancing act. It depends on a variety of things, some that we can control and some that simply are. Sick people run out of energy quickly: a conversation of a few minutes may be all they can manage, and we must be sensitive to their ebbing energy levels. One of us may be limited by other time pressures: catching a bus, getting back to work, picking up children. The time we are alone may be curtailed by other people arriving, expectedly or not. With deep, attentive listening time passes surprisingly quickly. We may suddenly discover that we have to leave the conversation but wonder whether it is insensitive to mention it. Yet by managing the way we close the discussion, we can ensure that everyone involved is able to move back from any strong emotions raised without feeling rushed, damaged or raw.

I've always found time management in these tender conversations a challenge, and over the years I have discovered some ways to deal with that. The first is to make the time available explicit at the beginning, in a way that shares responsibility for it.

'I've got half an hour free now, if you'd like to tell me about what's on your mind.'

'If you feel you'd like to talk about this now, what time do you need us to finish?'

'This sounds like an important thing to discuss. Is this a good time to talk, or are we likely to be interrupted by anyone arriving who you don't want to hear this yet?'

'I'm glad you're willing to talk to me about this. Please help me keep an eye on the time so I don't miss school pick-up.'

Or, if you are not in a position to give time and attention right now, recognise the opportunity and make a clear offer to listen soon, like 'I can hear that this is important to you, and I'm sorry I can't listen right now. Can we talk about it later/ tomorrow? When? For how long?' This is not unkind: you may have another appointment, you may be too tired or hungry to pay good attention, and self-care is important for good listening.

Sharing responsibility for timekeeping has been a complete game-changer for me. Before, it felt rude to check my watch and I was torn between an honest, overt sweep of my eyes to my wrist (that could make me look disrespectful or distracted or bored) and an awkward fumbling of one hand to nonchalantly push back the sleeve of my other arm and so allow me covertly to consult my watch – probably very much more obviously than I hoped. Once timekeeping is explicit and shared, I can check my watch to say, 'We're fine – still plenty of time' or 'I can see it's getting close to time for your bus/my next appointment/

time to take you home', and so begin a short, careful closure conversation.

Closing is not the same as finishing the discussion. There may be more to think and talk about; we may only have reached the point of understanding how much remains to be discussed. Closing is a temporary measure and if we close well, we reach a shared agreement that we can leave the conversation for now, put it somewhere safe and pick it up again together at another time. This dance is done, but we can dance again in the future.

There have been several examples so far in this book of conversations begun and then closed, ready to pick up once more. Eloise and her mum (pages 32-5), Jake and his teacher (pages 46-53), and Craig and his daughter Sacha (pages 75-82) all have more to discuss. By breaking their discussions into shorter conversations, they have begun a process of exploring both the issue at hand and also how it can be talked about. They have left their dialogue ready to be picked up again, either with an agreement (Jake was invited to think further and then to come back to talk more) or when the moment seems right (Eloise has opened a long-awaited discussion with her mum and knows she can mention it again next time they talk; Craig has shown he can listen, and Sacha is considering whether to continue her revelations to him).

This is another example of something that feels slightly awkward being most easily managed by simply stating it.

'I think that's enough for today. We can carry this on another time.' 'I'm sorry I have to go now, so we'll need to leave this conversation for today.' 'You look tired now. Shall we stop talking and pick this up another time?'

Before we part, or turn to other matters, it will help to check that both of you are feeling ready to finish the conversation. This is another instance of working together, sharing responsibility for the discussion. Again, it's not complicated.

'Do you feel OK to leave it there for today?' 'I know you have to go now: do you feel all right?' 'It's time for me to go soon. Do you feel ready for that?'

Expressing appreciation is a useful way to finish. 'Thank you for listening to me.' 'I'm glad you talked to me about that: thank you.' 'I know that wasn't easy – thank you for taking the time to mull that over with me.' 'I know there's still more to talk about, but I'm glad we have begun to discuss it.'

We can also arrange how we will follow up our conversation. 'I'll give you a call tomorrow.' 'Would you call me when you've had a chance to think over our conversation?' 'When shall we check back with each other about this?'

If you are on the right terms, the end of a tender conversation may be an appropriate time for a hug, a kiss, a moment of expressed tenderness. Follow your heart.

The summary of this whole philosophy is:

Listen. Be quiet, make space, pay attention. This is a shared endeavour.

When to Find Help

Some difficulties may require more than time, space and tender listening, and it is important to recognise when professional or specialist help may be needed. That may be help for the distressed person or help to support a helper, including you.

If somebody tells us about a possibly serious health concern or an experience that sounds dangerous or damaging to them, we may need to explore options for getting more advice or help for them than we can offer alone. What if they disclose a behaviour of concern like compulsive gambling, drinking or drug use? What if they tell us they have 'found a lump' or another symptom that could be a serious health problem? These are difficulties that require the help and support of specialists, and while we can listen to support the person, it is right to suggest that our support is not enough to keep them safe.

They may disclose or make reference to a situation that suggests rape, domestic abuse, abuse during their earlier life or flashbacks to traumatic experiences like accidents, combat or other occasions marked by a sense of their having little or no control over the difficult events. It's important not to assume that only events like these would be traumatic: I have met people left traumatised by being lost in an unfamiliar city or by becoming disoriented on a well-planned trek.

The experience of loss of control is traumatising, so helping the person to have a sense of control about what to do next is important. If they want to talk about it, we can support them best by listening calmly. Remember that forced debriefing can be harmful, but we can turn our curiosity towards thinking about how they might deal with their distress. What have they tried in the past? Is anyone else already supporting them with this trauma? Would they like your support to find more help? It is important to say that you would like to call on extra help: they may assume that you will be their helper, but you should take care of your own wellbeing, too.

'I want to help you to deal with this. Shall we look for someone who can give us expert advice?' 'I don't know enough to help with this. I'll support you, but I'd like us to find someone to give us advice.' 'Would you like me to come with you if you decide to talk to your GP/the police/a counsellor?'

There is help and advice about PTSD on the Mind website.*

What about suicidal thoughts? It may surprise you to know

---

* https://www.mind.org.uk/information-support/types-of-mental-health-problems/post-traumatic-stress-disorder-ptsd-and-complex-ptsd/about-ptsd/

that about one person in five has entertained ideas of suicide at some time in their life. Mainly these are fleeting, but for some people they can become overwhelming. Research shows that suicidal acts are often preceded by a period when the person feels distanced from the world, their troubles and distress, and so they may appear calm yet be entirely engrossed in the idea of taking suicidal action. Making conversation when they are in this state can 'burst the bubble', bringing them back to safety. This is the essence of Samaritans' *Small Talk Saves Lives* campaign (see page 273).

Suicide is one of the conversational taboos. But just as talking about sex will not make someone pregnant and talking about death will not shorten someone's life, talking about suicide will not make someone act to end their life; rather, it opens the subject up for discussion.

People who have suicidal thoughts rarely talk about it directly, but they may make statements like 'It's all pointless', 'I'm worthless', 'Who would miss me?' or 'It's not worth going on'. Noticing these cues and responding with curiosity can open up their thoughts and ideas about suicide, which could range from a vague wish not to continue living to a clearly thought-out plan for ending their life. Most people with suicidal thoughts do not want to die; they want to live, but with a better quality of life or with specific difficulties solved. Asking about these ideas is usually a relief to the person with suicidal thoughts.

Using questions like 'How do you feel about the future?' 'Have you ever thought about harming yourself?' 'Have you had thoughts about suicide?' is safe: if they have had no suicidal ideas, your suggestions will not plant them. If they have been thinking about suicide, though, they may be afraid of their own thoughts and isolated by fear of admitting them, or they may feel guilty or ashamed of their thoughts. Your non-judgemental enquiry can offer an assurance that it is safe to talk, and you can suggest helping them to find support. Samaritans' website offers further advice about helping someone who is having thoughts about suicide, from how to respond in a crisis to how to assist them to set up a support network.*

* https://www.samaritans.org/how-we-can-help/if-youre-worried-about-someone-else/

Towards Change

The first chapters of this book have given an overview of beginning conversations that we may feel hesitant about, and ways to reach an understanding of the other person's viewpoint, their dilemma or situation. We considered the basic 'dance moves' of careful listening using curiosity and questions, allowing silences and remaining present with someone in distress. Following a principle of offering a welcoming space for the person to tell their story and to consider their options, we help them to reach a broader or deeper understanding of their situation. Often this is enough. They feel accompanied in a time of difficulty; they feel understood and acknowledged; they may use their sharpened understanding to solve their problem or to find a more comfortable way to deal with it.

Sometimes, though, a clearer understanding may not help to change things. The situation may be more fully recognised and better understood, but it still feels stuck. Let us move on to look at how, if there is any potential for change, we might support someone to find a way to begin. The good news is that it is usually possible to make helpful changes: even if circumstances cannot be improved, the way someone deals with them can make a difference to their wellbeing and comfort.

Is there bad news? Well, that depends on your perspective. If you want to fix things for someone else, the bad news is that we are not going to attempt that. 'Fixing' is our solution, not theirs. The principle we will follow is that each person is best placed to solve their own difficulties; the style we have adopted is one of curiosity and interest, being present as a companion and not as an expert or 'fixer'. That is the style we will maintain as we enable people to move through their distress and stuckness towards making changes for themselves.

As a dance increases in complexity, the dancers maintain the same balance and poise: even though they may be moving faster or changing direction more often, they use the same steps. The dance remains a collaboration; the rhythm still marks the pace; the space is still shared. In the same way, we are now going to look at the conversation skills we have already met, using them now to enable someone to take a deeper look at their situation and to consider possible ways forward. Ideas developed for use in cognitive behavioural therapy (CBT) will be applied to help us to describe people's experience in more detail, and we will consider how listening and accompanying someone in their distress can provide them with a platform to take stock, reframe and begin to move forward.

To make progress we must trust the music to guide us. In complex conversations that is about trusting ourselves, trusting the principles and trusting other people to be the best solvers of their own difficulties.

Listening, Noticing, Wondering

After I was trained as a cognitive therapist, I realised that the 'CBT model of emotional distress' is, in fact, a model for 'how humans are'. The CBT skill set offers a framework for listening and noticing, because when we listen attentively we observe behaviours and emotional responses as well as attending to the language used, the tone of voice, the fluency or hesitancy of expression. This careful listening leads us to wonder about the person's inner experience; about the way they interpret the events they are describing and about how their interpretation affects their wellbeing. CBT encourages this curiosity to be shared by the listener: by wondering aloud together we shape a conversation that explores the possibilities as well as the facts.

The CBT model describes four cornerstones of our inner experience: our thoughts, emotions and physical sensations, and the behaviours all three link to. Any moment in life can be mapped by paying attention to these four domains and to the relationships between them, and yet we spend most of our lives paying them scant attention, perceiving only what is superficially obvious to us and ignoring, discounting or missing the rest of our experience.

Working as a cognitive therapist, my task is to help a client to notice all four areas: how their thoughts respond to the situations they find themselves in and how those thoughts then drive their emotional and behavioural responses. It is fascinating to see how different we all are in so many ways, including our self-awareness. Some of us are keenly aware of our bodily sensations yet surprisingly tuned out of the way we think and talk to ourselves. Others of us feel our emotions very strongly yet we don't connect them to the thoughts that drive them or to the bodily responses that are aroused by them. Some of us live in our thought bubble, conscious of our thinking yet unaware of its relationship to our mood or behaviour.

Whether I am teaching a person to understand their own inner world or teaching carers to understand those they care for, this is the diagram that I use to explain the four cornerstones concept:

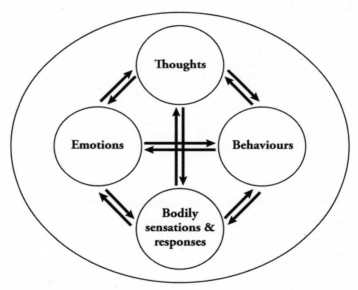

In addition to the four cornerstones of thoughts, behaviours, emotions and bodily sensations, I always ask them to try to identify the specific circumstances that were present, or the trigger, in the situation they are describing to me.

It is often easier to observe the relationship between thoughts, emotions, behaviours and body state in other people than it is in ourselves. Think about a child (or possibly adult) who is hungry and becomes angry as a consequence ('hangry'): grumpy, unbiddable and unhappy, and becoming delightful company again five minutes after their wise parent/long-suffering colleague has fed them a biscuit.

In the case of the hangry person (we all know one, so I hope this makes you more sympathetic, and possibly better prepared), here is how that diagram would look:

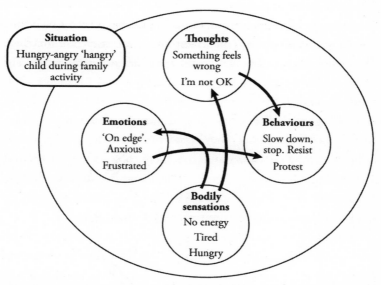

What we observe – the protests or grumpiness, the slowing down of responses or movements – are **behaviours** that are a result of **bodily sensations** of tiredness and hunger. Yet some people are not 'tuned in' to their bodies, and so they do not take action to feed themselves as their energy stores are depleted. What they may be aware of, rather than the physical sensations of hunger or tiredness, is the **emotional** disquiet of feeling edgy and anxious, driven by their **thoughts** (which they may not notice) that there is 'something wrong', or their **emotion** of frustration with their own tiredness or with people around them making 'unreasonable' demands.

The biscuit is not magical: it simply restores normal blood-sugar levels, which allows the return of a physical sense of safety, stopping the anxious sense of 'I am not OK' and allowing the child (or spouse, or colleague) to feel well enough to become cooperative and happy again.

This model of interlinking processes is commonly used in cognitive therapy to help clients to become better observers of themselves and more aware of their whole experience. The diagram is referred to in therapy as a formulation, and it is used like a map to describe specific occasions when the client has encountered difficulties. They then learn techniques to test out the potential benefits of changing their behaviours, or to examine and challenge their thinking, and in this manner they find new ways to engage with and manage their difficulties. A good therapist does not solve their client's problems; rather, they teach the client how to solve the difficulties they are facing and give them tools to use for the rest of their life. This is not a book to teach cognitive therapy, but we can borrow some theory and skills from that school to apply to the art of tender conversations.

The cognitive behavioural model, looking at thoughts, behaviours, emotions and bodily sensations, can help us to be self-aware, so that we are aware of our own body and mind; and it can give us listening awareness, helping us to notice where another person is focused, what parts of their experience they may not be discussing and what aspects they may not even be conscious of.

Self-awareness

To be truly present to another person, we need to recognise how our own thoughts and emotions can change our attention and behaviour. This interplay of thoughts, emotions and responses can influence the way we participate in, hear and interpret a conversation. In the same way, the other person's interpretation of our conversation will be affected by their emotional state. Being aware of our own inner processes will allow us to keep an emotional balance as we conduct a conversation. We can develop the skill of noticing our emotions, taking account of our thoughts and their potential biases of attention, and maintain a sense of centredness as we participate in the discussion.

How do we manage that? Self-awareness is a habit of attention to our inner experience. Noticing what happens to our thoughts and emotions, acknowledging our bodily responses and being mindful of our own conduct as we prepare for and then join in a conversation of significance gives us clues and information to help with the task. By listening to ourselves in this way we can use our observations and reflections, our emotional reactions and our hunches, to shape the way that we respond as the exchange progresses. Scanning all four cornerstones helps us to sit 'four-square' and keep our own balance as we talk to someone who is seeking balance and clarity of their own.

Thoughts

Thoughts are the vehicles of activity in our minds. We may think in words or pictures, in colours or numbers, in shapes, sounds or sensations. Sometimes we think in a linear way, joining thoughts together to compose a timeline of events; sometimes we may assemble a mental collage or flow chart to summarise our understanding of lots of different pieces of information; some thoughts are commentary on events, others are memories or imaginings of past or possible future events. Thoughts drive behaviours and emotions: the thought *I'm late* may change our behaviour (hurry; take a shortcut; call a cab) or make us feel anxiety, frustration or guilt, depending on the circumstances. A thought that is a mental picture of a potential future event might trigger hope, sadness, anger, despair.

When we are present at a tender conversation, we will be

holding some thoughts deliberately in mind: the information we want to give or receive, what we already know of the other person, and the situation to be discussed. During the conversation new thoughts will emerge. Some will be related to the discussion, as we gauge the other person or people's responses, listen to their questions and comments.

Some of our thoughts will be less 'managed' and more spontaneous: the inner commentator that experiences the world through our sensations and that judges, critiques, prompts emotions, nudges us into actions and forms a distracting chatter that can get in the way of our intention to listen well. These are thoughts like *I might upset him, Did I lock my car? I'm making a mess of this* . . . An awareness of this 'inner background noise' can help us to avoid responding to it and allow us to focus instead on the task at hand.

It is important to realise that not every thought we have is true. I am going to say that again. Just because we think it, or even believe it, does not make a thought true. We are very prone to jumping to conclusions, treating assumptions as though they are facts, and all kinds of other inaccuracies in our thinking. Thoughts are not necessarily facts. This is as true of our own minds as it is of the person we are listening to. We must be guided, but not fooled, by our thoughts.

Emotions

Emotions are important indicators of our inner condition. They influence our attention and our behaviour. When we feel anxious we pay more attention to possible threats; when we feel sad we more easily access our unhappy memories; when we feel contented we find relaxation easier. Paying attention to our emotional state can help us to navigate tender conversations with insight. How do I feel before this conversation? My inner emotional state is likely to be apparent to those around me, possibly more than I am aware. Will my emotions affect the way that I communicate with the other person, and if so, how? Does this have implications for the timing or set-up of the conversation? What support might I need before, during or afterwards? How do I feel during this discussion? Noticing the flow of our emotions while a conversation is going on can help us to be aware of our own needs as well as those of the other person: to adjust our responses accordingly when the mood changes; to maintain our own safety with clear yet gentle boundaries; to beware the way our anxiety can undermine us or our anger confound our ability to speak clearly.

Sometimes the story we hear triggers strong emotions in us. This is natural, but it can be uncomfortable and it may even threaten to take over the conversation. While we are paying attention to somebody else's emotions, we may need to damp down our own, and so it's important to take some time afterwards, perhaps alone or by talking to somebody else (maintaining the person's confidence, of course) to acknowledge our distress and to process it. Professionals and volunteers in listening roles have access to 'supervision' – a confidential and supportive space for talking about the emotional impact of listening to others, and for dealing safely with the strong emotions that can arise as a result. This helps to keep them emotionally healthy. If you are the regular 'go-to' person in your family or friendship group, it's worth thinking about how you can set up a way to maintain your own emotional wellbeing by finding someone who will offer you the same non-judgemental and supportive space that you offer to others.

Self-awareness helps us not to be ruled or knocked off course by our emotions.

Bodily Sensations

We are embodied beings, and when we attempt to devote our mental attention to listening and supporting someone through a tender conversation, our body may help or hinder us. When we feel tired or hungry that impacts on our mood and our ability to concentrate, as do those important sensations from our bladder and bowel, sometimes to the extent that it is worth mentioning and dealing with it.

'I want to hear your story, but I am so tired today. Do you mind if I make us both a coffee while we talk?' 'This is important and I want to listen carefully. Please give me a moment to visit the toilet before we go on.' 'Can we grab something to eat while we talk? I'm hungry, but I want to listen to you, too.'

Bodily sensations can also tell us about our responses to someone's story: headache may suggest we are feeling tense; tears, a lump in the throat as we experience sorrow at the story; a dry mouth, knocking heart or breathing changes if we feel anxiety, fear or even anger. This flow of physical sensations can also alert us to emotional responses that the other person may be experiencing, too, and that we can check as part of our curious questioning.

Self-awareness enables us to avoid being distracted or diverted by our bodily sensations.

Behaviours

Our behaviours may be our greatest asset and our most profound weakness. If we can stay centred and remain curious, holding the space for the conversation to be non-judgemental and for the other person to explore their situation in response to our questions, our calm behaviour and unhurried use of questions, reflection and checking our understanding offer a secure framework for the discussion to take place at their pace and respecting their autonomy. These are excellent 'helping behaviours'.

But oh! – how we want to advise. How we want to propose solutions, offer comfort, interrupt the answers to tell our own stories of that time when . . . Managing our impulses to 'help' or 'solve' relies on us overriding these behaviours, which are almost automatic. Observing ourselves and noticing our urges to act allows us to refocus on the task of listening; to resist the drive to take over; to attend to maintaining the space, remaining curious, seeing the other person as the agent of their own solution. This urge to solve is reported even by experienced therapists, who find themselves mentally 'sitting on their hands' to stop themselves offering solutions.

Being aware of our urge to act allows us to modify our behaviour.

Listening Awareness

While observing ourselves to ensure that we are offering space and not allowing our own thoughts and beliefs to take over, we are also paying close attention to the person we are listening to. The mind of each person engaged in a tender conversation is experiencing that same interplay between thought, emotions, sensations and behaviours. We can use the same model to aim for balance in our dialogue.

In English, we use the verb 'to feel' in several ways, and this may lead to some confusion when we look at that cognitive model. 'I feel' may express thoughts (I feel lonely/misunderstood/abandoned; I don't feel ready/brave enough/listened to), emotions (I feel sad/furious/hopeful) or physical sensations (I feel sick/cold/hungry). As we observe the person we are in discussion with, we may see they are flushed, flustered, hesitant, jumpy. We may notice they are tearful or trembling. When we ask 'How do you feel?' we may elicit emotions, thoughts or bodily sensations; we can be clear by asking 'What is going through your mind?' 'What emotions do you notice?' and 'What sensations do you notice in your body?'

The model is useful in helping us to notice not only what they are describing, but also what they are missing out. We wonder what might fill those gaps, and our curious wondering can be framed as questions that help them to reflect and notice more about that part of their situation and their response to it. Together, we reach a fuller understanding.

One person may tell us a lot about how badly they are sleeping, how they have lost their appetite and how they feel on edge all the time. As we notice that they are describing only their bodily sensations, we can wait for a chance to ask gentle, curious questions about their thoughts when they lie awake, their emotions when they notice they feel on edge, how they respond when they don't feel hungry at mealtimes.

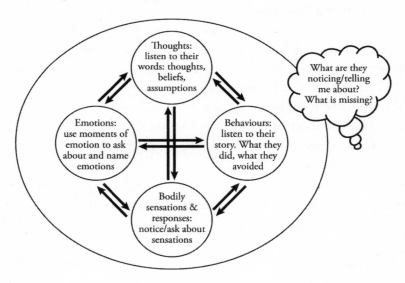

Similarly, we may be supporting somebody who is very aware of the troublesome thoughts going through their mind: predictions of difficulties and obstacles that make them feel stuck. By asking about what actions (or inaction) their thoughts lead to, we can help them to notice how they get tied up in knots, or how they escape from their difficult situation without solving it. For example, thoughts predicting that they are 'bound to fail that driving test' lead to emotions, or 'feelings', of anxiety that drive unpleasant physical-reaction 'feelings' like a dry mouth, churning stomach and nausea; and the nausea causes them to cancel the test – which might then relieve all the symptoms. That is a vicious circle, yet they may not have put it together in that way. Using curious questions about what someone notices first, and what happens next, and what that leads on to, and so on, can help them to see how they are getting stuck in that loop.

We can use the model to help us to ask questions that establish more details, and even to help the other person notice the links between their emotions, thoughts, behaviours and bodily sensations. Helpful questions will enable the person to discern some aspects they may not previously have attended to, or to perceive links between different parts of their challenging situation that may aid them in finding new ways to engage and respond.

Don't be fooled by the thoughts.

Don't be ruled by the emotions.

Don't be diverted by bodily sensations.

Don't let behaviours sabotage the connection.

Staying Present

During a conversation that requires long silences, we can begin to feel awkward. Should I speak or stay silent? Is this too hard for them to bear? Should I rescue them and change the subject? If it is a phone conversation, we might even wonder whether the line is still connected, if the other person is still there.

Yet we also know that the silence is where the work takes place: holding that silent space is one of the skills we can use to give the other person room to consider all their difficulties, the components of a dilemma or potential solutions to a problem. How, then, do we show we are holding that space?

It's almost midnight on the student helpline. Charlie and Pippa are tonight's volunteers. It is spring, and exam season is approaching. This is the helpline's busiest time of year. Generally there's brisk business in the early weeks of the first term as new students encounter homesickness, loneliness or the loss of family support for long-term mental health problems; established students find new pressures challenge their friendships in shared accommodation, or face difficulties paying their rent, or anxieties about their success as they begin their final year of studies or writing up dissertations. There is a flurry of activity around Christmas, the loneliest time of year for anyone whose lifestyle doesn't match that of the cosy families depicted in the seasonal films, adverts and TV shows. But the busiest time is spring: exams approaching, summer plans being made, submission deadlines for degree-making or -breaking assignments, jobs being sought with multiple rejections before the relief of success. Beach bodies to be buffed, or to feel ashamed of. Parties to attend, or to be left out of. So much to aspire to. So much to feel crushed by.

The phone rings and it is Charlie's turn to pick up. There are always two volunteers, with a member of the university's pastoral care team on call if they need support. Charlie presses 'Speaker' and says, 'Student Helpline. Thanks for calling us. What's your name?'

There's no answer, only the sound of traffic in the background. This caller is out of doors. It's a warm evening, but it's late. Although possibly not that late in a student day that has its own circadian rhythm: this might be breakfast time for some of the more nocturnal crowd.

'Hello,' repeats Charlie. 'I can hear some traffic but I can't hear your voice. Can you tell me your name?'

'Farah. I'm Farah,' says a woman's voice. The silence returns, punctuated by the swishing of traffic and a distant fire-engine siren.

'Hi, Farah. How are you doing tonight?' asks Charlie. He is asking about this specific moment because his caller may have concerns so widespread that a bland 'How are you?' can make the task of explaining feel overwhelming. Keeping the conversation in the present moment helps the speaker to focus on right now. Charlie is inviting his caller into the conversational dance.

'Can I ask you something?' says the voice, joining the dance.

'Sure, ask away. I mightn't know the answer, but we can think about it if you like,' replies Charlie. Pippa gives him a thumbs-up.

'How can I . . .' Farah hesitates.

Charlie waits. The silence continues. Traffic noise. Distant, drunken shouting. Bells tolling midnight. Charlie waits a little longer, then says, 'How can you . . . what, Farah? Can you say any more?' and he waits again.

'How . . . how can I . . .' she trails off again, and Pippa points to the other phone. She wonders whether this might be a question about self-harm and, if so, their policy is to work in pairs, one on the call and the other as supporter, who can call their supervisor if necessary. When Charlie nods in agreement, Pippa takes her phone off the hook to prevent her line becoming occupied by another call.

Down the line, they hear Farah take a sobbing breath before she says, 'I can't marry him! I can't do it! How can I tell my parents? How do I tell them?'

Pippa and Charlie catch each other's eye, and Pippa nods as Charlie says, 'Oh, that sounds like a big concern, Farah. Is that what you rang to talk about?'

Silence again. They can hear her breathing and what sound like footsteps. The traffic noise is fading. Pippa notices that the hammering of her own heart is reducing. The sound of traffic always spooks her: she has had students phone in desperation from beside busy roads, contemplating suicide. She feared this might be such a call. But Farah seems to be walking away from the road.

Into the silence, Charlie says, 'There's no rush, Farah. Just tell me when you feel ready.' Farah's breathing sounds laboured. 'It sounds like you're walking pretty fast,' says Charlie. 'Do you feel safe, Farah?'

'It's Eastgate Hill,' she pants. 'I'm safe, I'm on my way home. I've been out walking to get my head round all this stuff, but it just keeps going round and round.' She stops talking, breathless, and Charlie waits once more. Sensing that it's safe to do so, Pippa replaces her phone on its receiver, ready to take calls again. She keeps listening, with Charlie, to his call.

'OK, Farah, that's quite a hill,' says Charlie. 'While you get your breath back, let me check I've understood what you've told me so far, OK?' He pauses. Farah doesn't respond; she's still sounding breathless, so Charlie continues: 'You've been out walking tonight because you've got a lot on your mind, and you wanted to think it all through, yes?' He waits while Farah considers his summary.

'Yes,' says Farah, but no more.

'And the thing that's bothering you the most is about telling your parents that you don't want to get married. Have I got that right?' He waits again. The footsteps stop, and Farah says, 'I'm home. I'm standing in the hallway. I'll have to whisper so I don't wake them up . . .'

'OK,' says Charlie. 'I'm glad you're home safely. Who is at home?'

'My friends,' says Farah. 'My flatmates. We share this house. But they don't know about this . . . They are all excited that my parents have found me a husband, and they don't understand that's not what I want. They are all waiting for their families to introduce them to faithful, kind men. But I don't want that. And I don't know what to do!'

Pippa's eyes are wide in her pale face. This has been a long shift and she is very tired. But this call is fascinating. It sounds as though Farah lives with companions from the same community, and she seems to be struggling with traditions that she doesn't completely share. Charlie stays focused.

'Farah, are you telling me that your parents have arranged a marriage for you?' he asks, checking.

'Yes, that's right. To a lovely guy. He's the perfect match. But . . .' and Farah lapses back into silence. Charlie waits.

'Hmmm,' he says, after a while. 'It sounds like you have a lot on your mind.' And he waits again.

'My family is very traditional,' says Farah. 'My parents have a very happy arranged marriage and so does my sister. It's not that I think it's a bad match, or a bad system . . .' and she stops speaking.

'I'm such a bad daughter!' she blurts, and the sound of sobbing radiates from the speakerphone. Charlie listens, and when the sobbing continues he says, 'Thanks for telling me, Farah. I can hear how hard this is for you, that you see yourself as a bad daughter. I'm in no hurry. Take your time . . .' Pippa gives him another thumbs-up. There are so many questions Charlie could ask to clarify this situation, but now is not the right moment. For now, Farah needs a confidential space to feel her strong emotions knowing that a companion is with her. Charlie is saying simple things, things Farah won't be distracted by, so she can process her thoughts and emotions without interference, while Charlie's short and simple phrases tell her that he is still with her.

'I'm still here,' he says. Farah's breathing is quiet now, no more sobbing. 'Lots to think about,' says Charlie. The silence continues. 'It's a lot,' he says. More silence.

Then Farah speaks. 'I have never said any of this out loud before,' she says. 'I feel very disloyal to them. They've always called me the Difficult Daughter.' She stops. There is a pause.

'The Difficult Daughter?' asks Charlie, using her words again to show that he is paying attention. A short laugh sounds down the phone, the kind that acknowledges bitter truth and heartbreak.

'Yeah, difficult . . . "So headstrong! So wilful!"' Farah is now impersonating someone else's voice. '"You behave like a boy!"' she accuses herself, repeating phrases she has clearly heard for many years.

'Oh, *that* kind of difficult,' says Charlie. 'It sounds as though you are thinking lots of things through tonight . . .' He's keeping the conversation in the present rather than asking about the difficult past.

'Yeah . . . lots. I am a disappointment to them. Not a good girl. They thought coming to university would improve me. But it's shown me lives I could live. A different way of life . . . I'm an engineer. I am a *good* engineer. I'm on track for a first-class degree and I already have a job offer . . . But how can a good, obedient wife be an engineer?' and Farah's voice trails away as she lapses back into thought.

While she thinks, Charlie stays beside her in spirit, saying only, 'Mmm . . . yeah . . . That's a lot to think about.'

'Thanks for listening,' says Farah. 'It feels so different saying all this out loud. It makes me realise what a difficult daughter I really am.'

'Does it make anything else feel different, now you're talking about it, Farah?' asks Charlie, and he waits while she frames her answer.

'Mmm . . .' they hear her musing. 'Well . . . actually, saying I want to be an engineer out loud sounds quite reasonable. It sounded wicked in my head, but it doesn't seem at all shocking now I have said it out loud.'

Pippa's phone rings. Charlie switches his call off speaker so that Pippa can answer and he can continue his conversation with Farah. Now that she is engaged by the call, Farah has become more talkative and in response to Charlie's specific questions she tells him that her greatest hope is to be a bridge engineer; that her worst dread is to disappoint her parents; that the marriage thing was the last straw, a tipping point for her growing realisation that she wants to live a more independent life and that she will have the financial means to do so. Charlie asks where she could get supportive and culturally sensitive advice about how to tackle this conversation with her parents, and Farah tells him she had intended to ring the university's Islamic Society, but they closed after hours and that is how she came to call the university helpline. Tomorrow she will ask the Islamic Society for guidance. She's certain they will have experience of a dilemma like hers before.

'Thank you,' says Farah. 'I don't even know your name, but I feel like you have been a great friend to me tonight.'

'You're welcome, Farah. I'm glad you called. We're here every day and night if you feel like talking. It won't always be the same people, but there's always someone here to listen.' The line goes dead.

Charlie sighs and stretches: it's the very early morning and he hears Pippa saying, 'I can hear you're very worried about your cat.

I'm sorry the fire brigade couldn't help you. Do you want to tell me a bit more about what's going on?' He smiles ruefully and makes a cup sign to Pippa, who nods. More coffee will get them through this shift, listening volunteers for their community.

Charlie has enabled Farah to think through her dilemma. By using a thoughtful *silence*, saying simple, *encouraging phrases* to indicate he was still listening and *repeating* some of Farah's own words and phrases to show he was paying attention, Charlie encouraged Farah to 'think aloud'. He used *questions and curiosity* to give Farah support to expand her story, and summaries to *check his understanding. He gave no advice*; he did not share his views or pass any judgement on Farah's dilemma. He held a space for her thinking, and Farah used it to decide what her next steps would be, and to give herself the advice she believed could work for her. Charlie used the components of a skill set known as *active listening*; Farah felt safe and heard.

Giving Away the Power

When faced with a difficulty, we feel less overwhelmed if we can find our own way to solve it or to decide how and on what terms we will live with it. Facing the struggle and coming up with our own solutions is empowering and we usually know the best next step to take. We can feel humiliated or disempowered if someone else comes along and takes over, even if they solve the problem for us. Recognising this truth asks us to rethink how we support others with their own challenges so that our 'help' doesn't take away their power.

Often in a time of trouble, we assist most by being alongside someone without 'helping', and so supporting them to be architects of their own solutions. It can be hard to do, as every parent knows. Accompanying instead of taking over involves accepting risk, tolerating our own anxiety and resisting our impulse to 'fix' things. We are giving the power to the other person.

It is an act of wisdom, of courage, and even of love.

It's physics homework. I am in tears. I have read and reread this question until I can recite it; I have looked at every piece of information and tried to fathom which formula will solve it. Each time I read the question, it seems to ask me something different. I feel panicked, humiliated and stupid. I will never pass this exam; I will never get into medical school; I should have taken different subjects, stayed with art and writing essays, stuck to safe ground.

My dad is patient.

'Explain to me how gases expand,' he invites. He is a scientist. He gets this stuff. I want him to tell me the answer. I want him to make me feel better. When I was tiny, we used to dance together: I would stand on his shoes and hold his hands and laugh as he danced me around the room. I want that now: Dad in charge, me a happy passenger. But he is teaching me to think instead. He insists on asking me questions. I breathe the deeply tortured sigh of a teenager dealing with an uncooperative parent and explain how gases expand. That's the easy bit.

'Now tell me what happens when the volume of a cylinder of gas is made smaller,' he asks. Now I am furious. I know this stuff! I need to answer this question about temperature, why is he asking me about volume? And how will I do this in an exam, on my own? Panic and anger grab my breath and the tears well again. Sniffing, I describe the way gas molecules behave as the volume is reduced: pressure increases as they cluster together, colliding and generating heat.

The lightbulb moment isn't instantaneous. I am too grumpy at being asked ridiculous questions by someone who knows the answer but won't tell me, so it takes a moment to realise that I am talking about temperature even though we started off with volume changing the pressure in the gas cylinder. I have just answered the homework question – *not because my miserable, unhelpful dad helped me but because I worked it out for myself.*

See what he did there? I didn't. I just took the credit, did the homework, passed the exam. *Sorry, Dad.*

When we help people by helping them to help themselves, they won't always be grateful. If we support them well, they may even believe they managed entirely on their own. As they danced with us they found their own power. That's a real triumph: you gave them what they needed so gracefully they didn't even notice. I try to take the same approach with my own children. It reminds me how much I owe my parents, who quietly supported my struggle to work things out and then let me tell them I'd solved it all by myself.

The impulse to help is innate: we are a cooperative species that has survived through millennia by working in groups. Working together saves time, reduces the individual effort of group members, conserves energy, and we can often achieve more together by harnessing the varied talents and combined strength of a group than we can by individual efforts. Co-working is a good thing.

Co-working involves the *mutual consent* of the co-workers. Each is involved in the endeavour; each will benefit from the results. Co-working is subtly different from helping. When we offer help and it is accepted, we have become a co-worker by agreement. When we simply do something that solves another person's difficulty without being invited or asking permission, we have not established that mutual consent criterion. Instead, we are 'helping' and working to our own agenda: to cheer the person up, to diminish their suffering, to keep life tidy, to minimise our own distress. Without their consent, our act of help is an assault on someone's autonomy. It makes us feel good to be helpful, but it makes them feel 'done to' instead of 'worked with'.

The expression 'do-gooding' refers to exactly this situation, and most of us have fallen into that trap at one time or another. Helping without seeking permission is a shortcut to resolving a problem, and we mistake delivering the solution for a supportive act. The supportive act would be to *offer* to help, and to allow the person to consider the offer and accept or decline it. In the same way that the route into many necessary but uncomfortable conversations is to invite instead of insist (see page 20), so the action that turns helping into supporting is to offer help without insisting.

There are occasions when giving immediate help is exactly the right thing to do: rescuing a child lost beside a busy road; calling the fire brigade when we see a house on fire; attending to a person who has collapsed at the shops. Waiting to seek permission wastes time that cannot be regained; better that the fire brigade gets several calls than that everyone who sees the fire thinks they shouldn't interfere without permission while the house burns down. On many or possibly most other occasions, helping without asking is perceived as interfering. It disempowers the person 'helped' and although it may have been intended as a good deed, it may be the wrong help, address a peripheral problem, cause offence or undermine that person's self-esteem.

By offering to help and then carefully listening to the way the person would like to be helped, we can offer them the support they are prepared to accept. We give them control over our input; we give away our own power to build theirs. Once again we are back to listening, to curiosity, to discerning what we can provide that will be an acceptable contribution to this person's problem-solving. How can I be with you in this difficulty, in a way that supports you best?

Being with, walking alongside: not doing to.

Ellen was an overnight care assistant in a hospice, and in her time off also a volunteer bereavement counsellor for a non-profit organisation. Ellen had been a lifelong helper; helping others gave her life meaning. She was attending one of our cognitive behavioural therapy 'first aid' courses. She'd had some difficulty getting on the course, which required attendees to have degree-level health or social care qualifications as a condition for funding: her counselling experience and her enthusiasm to join the training were so great that we found a way to include her without the usual qualifications, and from day one it was clear that she was a skilled communicator.

Halfway through their training, students are asked to present a case study to describe how they are putting their new skills into practice. This is Ellen's case study.

Ellen's hospice was looking after an elderly man with cancer. She called him 'Jim'. Jim had no family and he had lived alone; he was unable to look after himself because of pain in his legs and back when he tried to walk. He valued his independence, so he had been reluctant to be admitted to the hospice. He arrived unkempt and smelling of stale urine – hardly surprising given his difficulty in getting to the bathroom. He stayed in bed in his single room all day, except when the physio persuaded him to go to the exercise room where there was a huge TV showing live football. Distracted by the football, Jim tolerated the discomfort of having his thin legs stretched.

Jim's hair was matted, and as the days went by his stubble became a straggly beard littered with food debris. Yet he refused to let anybody help him to wash or shave. He had too much pain to get to the toilet, but he declined a urinary catheter and struggled to use urine bottles, with spills in the bed and on the floor. He accepted clean hospice pyjamas with a disinterested snort. 'He was hard to help and hard to like and hard to get to know,' said Ellen. 'We all hated the idea of not liking a patient. But he just kept everybody at arm's length.'

Ellen's case study was about using questions to understand someone's perspective and to discern how they would like to be supported. She reported that Jim had become steadily less well, needing more painkillers and becoming less interested in eating and drinking. He even stopped going to see the football on the exercise room TV. One night he kept ringing the bell to call the nurses. Each time they attended, he told them he felt dirty and he wanted to get washed. Each time they offered to help him wash, he turned them down. They felt helpless and exasperated. 'And a bit cross, if I'm honest,' admitted Ellen.

Ellen decided to try out her new CBT-style questions skills. She went into Jim's room. By now it was nearly midnight; all the night-time medicines had been given out and most patients were asleep. This gave Ellen more time to sit and talk with Jim.

'Jim, you seem very restless tonight,' she said. 'Is there something bothering you?'

'There was a very long silence,' reported Ellen. 'I thought he was trying to ignore me, but I just sat tight. Then he said, "I won't be worthy like this." And he looked sad enough to break your heart.

'"Tell me about being worthy, Jim," I asked. And he stroked his beard and said, "Filthy. Unworthy." I didn't know what he meant. I asked him how worthy would feel, and he told me he would need to be clean to be worthy.

'"Jim, do you want a shave? A wash?" I asked, and he said, "Yes, but I want to do it myself." I offered to get him a bowl of hot water, but he got hold of my hand and shook it – he looked quite cross – and shouted, "No! In the bathroom! Like a man!" But we both knew he couldn't walk and could hardly sit up without pain . . .'

Ellen's fellow CBT trainees nodded and murmured. They recognised this situation of the hard-to-help person, and the gap between what someone longs to do and what their body is now physically capable of.

Ellen continued her story. 'I went and told the qualified nurses that I was going to wheel Jim into the bathroom and set him up for a wet shave. They didn't want me to do it in case he fell on the tiled bathroom floor – he could easily break a bone – but I told them that it was very important to Jim in a way he couldn't really explain. They gave him an extra dose of painkiller to get him through all the moving around and they helped me to ease him into a wheelchair. Then I wheeled him into the bathroom, helped him to use the toilet, and wheeled him to the sink. Every movement was sore, it took about thirty minutes just to do that. I ran him a sink full of hot water, and I found him a comb, and a clean razor and some shaving soap.

'"Give it to me," he said. "Leave me to do it." I was pretty anxious about leaving this agitated man on his own with a sharp razor, but it was clear he wasn't going to let me shave him. I told him I'd wait outside the door. And I also told him . . .' Ellen flushed and her voice wobbled; the classroom was silent, hanging on her every word. 'I also told him that I was proud of how manly he was being. And then I asked him to be really careful, because I would get into trouble if he cut himself.

'I was scared that he might use the razor to harm himself. And if he did, I would probably lose my job. But I could see that being alone in this bathroom was so important to him.

'I waited for half an hour. Honestly, it was the longest half-hour of my life. I was desperate to peek around the door: he'd agreed to leave it ajar in return for being left alone. I could hear him breathing, and the swish of the shaving brush in the water and the scrape of the razor on his skin.

'Eventually he shouted my name, and there he was: hair combed back, and clean-shaven cheeks. He let me finish shaving his neck around his Adam's apple and I took him back to bed.

'"I need clean pyjamas," he told me. So I went to our cupboard and got a few pairs, and he chose the ones he liked best. I changed all his sheets, and the nurses came to help him back into bed and we all told him how handsome he looked.' Ellen smiled, and shrugged, and told us that they left him propped up on pillows, smiling, while she went to make him a hot chocolate.

'And when I got back to his bedroom, of course . . . well, he was dead, wasn't he? That's why he'd needed to get shaved and washed and to wear clean pyjamas. To be worthy . . . of whatever it was he could feel coming. He knew he was dying, and he wasn't ready until he was clean.'

This remains one of the most powerful stories of sincere listening, of serving, of *being with* instead of *doing to*, that I have ever heard.

The Power of Not Fixing

The skills and approach discussed so far have assumed that people are the best designers of their own solutions. Helping someone by listening and asking questions that clarify and expand their story to offer them new insights, or by asking someone to own their story as we give them new information to add to it, keeps them in charge of their personal narrative.

Conversely, simply solving someone's problem at their request without giving them agency does not provide them with the tools to solve similar problems in the future. Rather than enabling, over-helping builds dependence: they dance on our shoes as we make the steps, but they don't learn the steps for themselves. Keeping the space between us, each standing on our own feet (or moving our own wheels), allows us to dance together, to consider their dilemma or challenge, and to move towards possible solutions that they can own and manage for themselves.

Of course, not every difficulty can be solved by listening and thinking aloud. Some situations need practical action to correct a problem: a breakdown van, a plumber, a doctor, an interview-skills course. Other situations cannot be 'corrected'. There are some difficulties, like bereavement, disappointment, frustration, sorrow, that can only be carried. The task of a companion in distress is not to make it better, but to make it less lonely to bear.

The power of not fixing, but remaining alongside, is that it holds a space for someone to work through their difficulty and to own the possible solutions. It gives them power, it encourages their commitment to seeking solutions, and it demonstrates solidarity and support as they work their way through their trouble. We offer more consolation by holding a lost hand in a dark place than by shouting instructions from the safety of the light.

The Voice Within

Listening is not always about hearing others. One of the most important and perhaps most overlooked voices is the voice within. How often do we stop and listen to ourselves?

Our inner voice has many modes and moods. It can be our guide and our critic, offer praise or censure, cheer us on or hold us back. Unlike the advice and opinions we hear from other people, we often accept the voice within without question, believing its content and commentary are true, fair and balanced. But are they?

Learning to hear our inner voice is as vital for our wellbeing as listening to anyone else. But we need to listen, to hear ourselves and then to pause to consider before we take our own advice. Our inner voice can offer us a lifeline, or it can lead us astray. Just because we think something doesn't make it true. We must learn to listen to and question our inner voice if it is to be a supportive guide rather than an undermining detractor or a reckless imp.

This story shows one way of helping someone to notice their thoughts and then to question them instead of simply believing them. We can help another person to do this, and we can use the same approach for ourselves, too.

Christie is explaining rap music to me. His eyes are shining and he's waving his arms as he talks, the chunky metal rings on his expressive fingers glittering. He is seventeen years old, choosing university courses, fighting with his mum about curfews. The world lies before him. But only for a while. Christie is unlikely to live to see his thirtieth birthday. This is a hospice outpatient clinic. He is pale, thin and sallow, enveloped in a baggy checked shirt and the fashionably loose trousers that mean he has to keep hitching up his waistband as he strides around the room, in case he exposes more than the regulation amount of his boxer shorts.

This is my cognitive therapy clinic and Christie has been referred by the local cystic fibrosis team. He has been losing weight, experiencing diarrhoea and becoming increasingly withdrawn at home. He confessed to his dietician that he had stopped taking his enzyme capsules that replace the long-lost digestive functions of his pancreas, because everything seems 'pointless'. Yet when seen by a psychiatrist, Christie did not meet the criteria for depression. Rather, he seemed to be overwhelmed by the same concerns that loom large for all teens at this time of life: the transition to adulthood, the pressure of exams and future planning, relationships – both friendly and adverse at school – and feeling misunderstood by parents.

In fact, by 'pointless' Christie is not describing a death-wish. For him death is a constant companion and several friends he has made during hospital visits have already died of CF. He is simply acknowledging a truth: without a lung transplant in the next few years, his life expectancy is cruelly short and the long-term career planning of his school friends feels irrelevant to him. Why struggle to pass exams if you might not live to finish a degree? Why look for a job when there's no prospect of using your income to build a future?

But rap. Well, that's different. He is explaining to me about his latest hero, Dizzee Rascal, who is still a teenager himself. 'He's making music, he's talking about real stuff, he's been stabbed and hospitalised and he bounced back – he's amazing!' says Christie. 'And my mum hates him!' he grins.

'You look very pleased about how much your mum disapproves,' I smile back at him. I am probably around his mum's age. I'm not sure I would relish rap music resonating through my home, either. But I'm not here to judge, I'm here to enquire. 'Tell me more about that,' I invite him.

Christie continues to pace around the room as he talks. 'She's so *careful* about everything,' he sighs. 'Careful could be her middle name.' He gives a rap-style imitation of his mum. '*Be careful, Christie. Don't jump about so much, Christie. Where are you going? When will you be back? Who'll be there? Have you taken your meds? Is your homework done?*' He's good. I have to smile.

'Do you perform?' I ask. He says he goes to open mic nights at a local club that will admit over-sixteens with a responsible adult.

'Who's your responsible adult?' I ask, assuming it's unlikely to be his Careful Mum. He pauses, and considers, eyes sliding sideways momentarily as he decides what to say to me. 'My cousin,' he answers. And with that, he abruptly takes a seat in the armchair provided for patients. He waits for my next question. I wait for him to say more. The change in demeanour is startling. I sense there's a story here.

He begins to fidget in the silence. I wait. He makes beat-boxing noises. I wait. He says, 'Well, he's like my cousin. He's really my mum's cousin, but he's closer to my age than hers. He's got decks, too.' I must look blank, because Christie regards me pitifully and sighs. I suddenly feel like his mother. 'Mixing decks,' he explains. 'He works in a club two nights a week and he raps, too. So we're music mates. He lets me mix. We riff off each other.'

'So he gets why you like rap, and he gets you into the club,' I summarise. Christie nods. 'But . . .?' I offer, naming the awkwardness that floats in the air.

He bites. 'But . . . well, he seems to think he's my parent. He gives me pep talks and tells me to be nicer to my mum. Sometimes he's my "look at us, like bros" guy, and then suddenly he's like a teacher, all rules and "why don't you" at me.'

'So you get mixed messages?' I check my understanding.

'Sometimes he's your pal, and sometimes he's more like a parent?' Christie nods. 'And he tells you to be nicer to your mum . . .' I leave his repeated words hanging, and wait.

'She must hate me,' he says. His head sags, chin on his chest, and he looks downcast, his thin fingers playing with the loose rings on his hands. 'I'm a real bastard to her. I know I've ruined her life . . .' He falls silent, sighs and looks up at me, eyes wide and round in his too-pale face.

'That's a pretty strong thing to say,' I reply. 'You think she hates you. You think you've ruined her life. That sounds hard to deal with.' I wonder whether his young and earnest cousin has thrown those accusations at him, or whether he has acquired these beliefs from somewhere else. But I wait. This will need time. There's no rush. This clinic is where we think about thinking, and how those thoughts impact on us.

'Can you explain to me how you've ruined your mum's life?' I ask.

'Obvious, isn't it?' he replies. 'I was born with this shitty disease. I was a runty baby. I cried all the time with belly ache. I didn't grow properly. My dad left my mum because she gave me all her attention. She's left with this skinny kid who's sick all the time, no prospect of more kids, no life for her. If I hadn't been born, none of that would have happened.'

'Is that what someone has said to you?' I ask. 'Or is it something you told yourself?'

'She's too kind to say it. But it's true, isn't it? It's all my fault.'

'You deliberately gave yourself CF to make her life hard?'

He scowls at me. I imagine this is a look his mum is familiar with. 'Well, nooo . . .' he says in a sarcastic voice. 'Obviously it's genetic, so I didn't choose it.'

'Tell me about the genetics,' I invite, and he explains perfectly about the recessive gene that he has inherited two copies of, which means he isn't a carrier (just one recessive gene) but a person with CF. I ask how he got two copies. He rolls his eyes in exasperation at my stupidity: *one from each parent*, of course.

I pause before repeating, 'One gene from each parent. So . . . you didn't give yourself CF. Did they give you CF?' His chin jerks upwards and he meets my eye. This isn't the direction he'd expected the conversation to go, clearly. He drops the teenage scowl and his eyes narrow as he thinks.

'Well, no . . . but . . . kind of . . . I mean . . .' he falters, gazing forwards blankly as he tries to process his thoughts. 'They didn't know they were carriers. So it's not their fault, even though they gave me the genes.' I nod. I wait. He carries on thinking. 'And my mum says if she'd known, she'd have had me anyway. Not a termination. She told me that.' So this is a conversation that has been aired at home. That's good.

'OK, so do you mean that your mum and dad aren't to be blamed for your CF, even though they gave you the genes?' I check again. He nods, firmly, gazing straight at me. I nod with him. 'And even though you think your mum's life would have been better if you had never been born, she has told you she would have wanted you anyway?' He nods again, and I see a tear in the corner of his eye.

'Help me out here, Christie,' I ask. 'I'm stuck. Who says you ruined your mum's life? Your mum? Your cousin? Someone else? Or . . . is this the opinion of the voice in your head?'

He wipes the tear briskly with the back of his hand and shakes his head. 'No one ever said it out loud. But I just worked it out myself. I'm the problem.'

'Can we look at that in a bit more detail?' I ask. He folds his lips and nods, sadly.

'I want to write down some of the things you've told me,' I explain as I reach for my writing pad and pen. I place the paper where we can both see it, and I draw a line down the middle of the page. I write 'Beliefs' on the top left, and 'Evidence' on the top right.

'This column here, these are some of the things you've told me you believe over the last few minutes,' I say. You've said, "Dizzee Rascal is amazing", and I write it as I speak. 'You've also said, "My mum hates Dizzee Rascal". And I have to say, you sounded quite amused about that!' He grins as he looks at the page. 'Now, this column here is where we check out our evidence for the statements in the first column. You told me lots of reasons why DR is amazing: tell me some now, to write here.' He tells me about DR's chart success, his gang fight and recovery from stabbing, his new music post-recovery. I write it in the 'Evidence' column.

'Right: now the evidence that your mum hates DR,' I smile and he laughs as he says, 'She tells me to "turn that racket down" and "Why can't you like nice music?" and "That guy is a thug!"' I write it all down.

'What we're doing is making sure the statements fit the evidence, see?' I show him the page. 'And so far, it looks like it does. Right, what else have you told me? Well, you said "My mum must hate me".' I write it as he watches. 'And "I've ruined my mum's life". And "I'm a real bastard to her". And "It's not my parents' fault that I have CF". Is that OK? Have I caught you right there?'

Christie scowls at the paper. He's an intelligent young man and I can see he's already thinking about what we might discuss next. The evidence. We start with 'My mum must hate me'.

'We need evidence,' I tell him. 'Has she said she hates you? Does she do cruel things? It's OK to tell me if she does.'

He shakes his head. 'She tells me off a lot,' he says.

'About who you are? Or about things you do?'

Again that sharp upthrust of the chin as a new concept hits him. 'No, she never says bad things about me. She sticks up for me when my aunties complain that she doesn't make me get a job and stuff. She gets annoyed if I make too much noise. Or if I don't take my meds properly. Or if I miss my chest physio. I've never thought about that before . . . it's what I do, or don't do, that makes her mad. But not who I *am* . . .'

He is quietly thoughtful, as I say, 'And you told me she annoys you because she's so careful. Worrying about where you are and when you'll be back. Whether you're looking after yourself. Did I understand that right?'

He nods, looking surprisingly earnest.

'You're not making a great case for this statement that your mum hates you,' I observe. 'In fact, so far, there's no evidence for the prosecution. And a fair bit for the defence . . . I'm going to change this page a bit', and I draw a new line down the centre of the 'Evidence' column, marking the two new columns 'For' and 'Against'.

'Can you give me a single instance of cruel and unreasonable, hateful behaviour to write in the "For" column to support "My mum must hate me" as a belief?' I ask.

He starts to smile. Then a wide grin breaks across his face as he says, 'No, haven't caught her yet!'

I smile back, give him the pen and say, 'OK, now the evidence against. I'd like you to write the evidence that she doesn't hate you, just there.' I point, and he writes, 'She worries about me. Tries to keep me safe. Puts up with my noise. Tells aunties she's proud of me. Wants me to get a lung transplant.'

'Wow. Look at that list,' I say, watching him capture the evidence against his belief *Mum must hate me.* 'How do you know all that evidence?' I ask.

'Because I've heard it and seen it. She doesn't hate me, does she? But I do make her sad.' He looks despondent.

'Just to check again: do *you* make her sad? Or is it things you do, or say, or don't do that make her sad?' Before I have finished asking the question, he is nodding and his hands start to quiver with excitement.

'Yeah, yeah!' He is positively enthusiastic. 'It's not me, it's what I do. I drive her mad! But sometimes I don't mean to . . . and sometimes . . . yeah . . . sometimes I do. Sometimes I'm mean to her.'

'OK. Are you giving us some evidence for "I'm a real bastard to her" here?' I say. 'Want to give me an example or two?'

He surveys the page and writes, 'I am mean to her' in the 'For' column. 'I stay out and don't tell her where I am,' he adds. 'I don't take my meds before meals. I tell her she's a cow.' He's got some good evidence.

'Are you ever nice to her?' I ask.

He considers. He stands up and starts pacing the room again. 'Maybe I'm a terrible person,' he says.

'Maybe you are,' I agree, and he looks startled. 'But I won't believe it without evidence. So far this evidence is something most mothers of teenagers would recognise. Got anything worse?' He shakes his head. 'And what about times when you're not being a bastard?'

'Well, last week she ran out of soap powder so I cycled to the shop for her. It was raining, too!' he says. 'And I wrote her a rap for her birthday, and she liked that. And I always – well I usually say I'm sorry if I've been mean.'

'Write them in,' I say, and he stops pacing and sits down with the pad. 'Can you think of other examples of when you've tried to be kind, or helpful, or patient?'

He underlines 'it was raining' and I realise what a kind act that was for him to cycle in the rain for washing powder. He writes, 'I make her cups of coffee. I help with housework', then adds 'not very often' and I love him for his honesty.

'Right, what do you think now about whether you're a real bastard to her?' I ask.

Christie nods slowly at the piece of paper. 'I can be,' he says. 'But sometimes I'm not.'

'Like she can be overwhelming with her worry, but sometimes she's not?' I ask and he nods more vigorously.

'We're not just one thing, are we?' he observes. A new idea has been born, which he can take away and ponder. We're not Just One Thing.

'Two more statements to assess the evidence about,' I point out. 'Which one shall we do? "I've ruined my mum's life" or "It's not my parents' fault I have CF"?'

'I've already thought about the ruining her life one. I haven't, have I? She says she'd have had me anyway – that's evidence against (he writes it in) – and it's not me, it's me with CF that's the problem, and the CF isn't my fault (writes, 'CF not my fault'), and Dad was a loser when he left us (writes, 'Dad decided to leave = not my fault'), and she loves me . . .' His voice catches. A tear plops onto the pad. He sweeps it away and writes, 'She is lonely' in the 'For' column, followed by 'She loves me' in the 'Against' column. He's got it.

'Now I'd like you to go through those statements again, Christie, and tell me how much you believe them.' He lifts the writing pad and holds it firmly in both hands, surveying our work.

He is quiet as he looks at the page.

'I wonder what you make of that,' I say, and he gives a smile with a shake of his head as if to say, 'So do I'. He takes a breath, and says, 'Well, I still think Dizzee is amazing, and Mum will never agree.'

I laugh aloud and agree he has evidence on both counts. 'Tell me about those other thoughts,' I invite. 'Can you see that I haven't called them "facts"? Why do you think I called them "beliefs"?'

BELIEFS	EVIDENCE	
Dizzee Rascal is amazing	Great rap. Cool rhythm. Style. Stabbed and recovered. Charts	
Mum hates DR	Calls rap 'a racket'. It's not nice music. He's a thug	
Mum must hate me	<u>FOR</u>	<u>AGAINST</u> She worries about me Tries to keep me safe Puts up with my noise Tells aunties she's proud of me Wants me to get a lung transplant
I've ruined Mum's life	she is lonely	she would have had me anyway CF not my fault Dad decided to leave = not my fault she loves me
I'm a real bastard to her	I am mean to her I stay out and don't tell her where I am I don't take my meds B4 meals I tell her she's a cow	Went to get shopping <u>when it was raining</u> I make her coffee Birthday rap I help with housework: not v often

'They are what you think in your head, aren't they?' he says, slowly, wonderingly. 'There's stuff in your head that you think, and you think it's true. And it's *rubbish*!' He laughs, a sheepish and relieved exhalation.

It's great that Christie has worked out this truth from the discussion we have had and the evidence written on the pad. Not everything we believe is actually true, yet when a thought crosses our minds our first instinct is to behave as if it is true. And sometimes it is. But often enough, when we step back, we can notice the thought is not the whole truth.

Christie is in danger of leaping to the opposite extreme: that nothing we believe is true. But we have good evidence that some of the things he was thinking are at least partly true. I point back to the paper. 'Yet it's not *all* rubbish, is it? Look at the page. Some things are true. One belief you have absolutely no evidence for at all. And there's a bit of truth in some, but what was in your mind turns out not to be the whole story once you stop and consider the evidence. Now, I'm thinking about that cousin of yours, who sometimes is your pal and sometimes tells you stuff you don't like to hear. Is there anything in this list that would surprise him?'

'I think he'd be surprised how much I love my mum,' says Christie, face flushing and voice wobbling again. 'He'd be surprised I got my hair wet to go shopping for her. But some of the things he says – they are true, aren't they? Good and bad? I do love rap and I'm good at it and he supports me. And I am mean to Mum and he thinks I should be kinder. And I should.' Christie pauses. 'And I will be,' he finishes, resolutely.

'Thinking about it, do you think he gives you good advice or bad advice?' I ask.

My companion looks at the sheet as though the answer is there. There is a long pause. 'I think he's right,' says Christie, with great reluctance. 'He's a good laugh and he's not mean, and maybe he's just helping me to be a better man. Because he's the closest I've got to a proper dad, a guy to look up to.

'I think I might show him this. I think we can make a rap out of what your head tells you.' Christie jumps out of his seat with a wide smile and starts striding rhythmically around the room, saying*:

Just cos you think it, no need to believe it,
You just gotta test it, to bend it and flex it,
Question yo'self,
Examine yo'self,
Is it truth or a lie? Would you swear it or die?
Your mind's gonna lie,
So question yo'self,
Examine yo'self,
Don't swallow that crap, you're better than that,
You're more than you know, so don't feel low.
Question yo'self,
Examine yo'self,
Your mind is a trap, its jaws might snap
But think, is it true? Am I getting to you?
I sure hope so.
You're more than you know . . .

I love this job every day. But some days, wow – there are moments of pure gold.

Even for well-practised listeners there is something tricky about listening to their own inner voice. All that skill in gathering insight is usually focused outwards on another person's words, voice, body language; on their eyes, their facial expression; their speaking and

---

* With apologies to Christie, whose superb spontaneous rap included these ideas but was far more skilled than I can remember!

their hesitation; their stillness, or earnestness, or tears, or trembling: all these clues add up as we discern another's meaning. But how do we discern our own needs and desires? How do we evaluate ourselves? How can we offer ourselves the same non-judgemental attention that we hope to offer to others?

It can be hard to be completely and trustingly open with another person, yet we struggle even more to be honest with ourselves. Judgement accompanies self-reflection: we may underscore our faults or we may overlook them; we may bask in our gifts or hide them from ourselves; we may be our own worst critic in some areas yet offer ourselves a get-out clause in others. It is very hard indeed to accept ourselves, our skills and our gifts, our ineptitudes and failings, just as we are. We struggle even to understand our full complexity, simplifying ourselves down to two-dimensional labels like 'kind', 'ambitious', 'bad-tempered', 'lucky', 'misunderstood'.

Learning to listen to ourselves is a skill that takes practice and patience. We must allocate time to ourselves in which we can think and reflect, process our experiences, tell our own story and view it with curiosity and wonder. Perhaps this involves talking to a friend or a confidant, or perhaps keeping a journal. Perhaps we talk to strangers on public transport to tell our stories, or we tell them to the sky as we gaze to infinity from a comfortable seat or on a walk outdoors. Whatever method we choose, it is the telling of our story, the focus on what is there and what is missing, the curiosity to fill the gaps and the self-compassion to observe without judging, that enable us to reach an understanding of who we are.

Listening to the voice within with self-acceptance allows us to meet ourselves, to explore our past and to recognise our potential. Like every other person, we are both flawed and yet magnificent individuals, each with capacity to reflect on our experiences in order to grow and flourish. Each of us is capable and worthy of holding a mirror to ourselves to see the non-judgemental truth of our enormous possibility.

Self-care

Our inner voice is a guide to our wellbeing. Self-care is vital when we are using our time, attention and compassion in the service of others. Supporting people requires our energy and commitment, whether we are the go-to friend in our social circle, the supportive relative of a troubled family member, or we have a professional helping role; it can be time-consuming and tiring. Bringing ourselves to sit beside another person's deep distress can make us sad and leave us feeling drained. We are as worthy of our own care and compassion as anyone else.

To be well, we need a sense of adequacy, or 'good-enough-ness', in our physical health, our emotional life, our relationships with other people and our spiritual or existential self. Circumstances are rarely perfect in life, so deciding what is 'good enough' is a personal appraisal for each of us. The more perfectionist our standards, the harder we will find it to meet them and the more we may struggle to stay well.

Physical wellbeing: we need to treat our bodies well. They require enough sleep, enough exercise and the right food to be fit: how fit is 'fit enough' for you is your decision. Some of us are marathon runners; some of us are content if our arthritic knees allow us to walk across the supermarket car park. Our bodies require occasional maintenance checks; access to preventative healthcare (like vaccinations, blood-pressure control, weight management, health screening); and access to recovery time and to responsive health-care that we consult in a timely way when we become unwell.

Emotional wellbeing: we need to respect our own right to emotional wellness and good mental health. Just as with physical wellness, there are actions we can take that promote emotional wellbeing. In addition to sleep we need relaxation time that allows us to unwind: practices as varied as mindfulness, walking in nature, gardening, creative hobbies, reading, listening to music. This kind of 'me time' can be hard to carve out of a busy life, but it is essential for our emotional 'fit-enough-ness'. Like sleep and meals, it may need to be timetabled into our daily routine or it will be crowded out by other things.

Social connection: this is correlated with wellbeing. We may not be able to choose our family or our colleagues, but finding what we have in common with them is conducive to wellbeing. Ensuring we spend time communicating with friends builds up our sense of connection.

Spiritual or existential wellbeing: our sense of selfhood and meaning is an important component of wellbeing. For some people this is a religious faith and practice; for some it is finding transcendence in the wonders of nature, or awe in the presence of great art. Some people strive to serve a cause as a route to finding meaning in their lives. It may be a political belief, a justice issue, an environmental concern or support for a charity or social movement: a way of being connected to something that feels greater than our self, and that gives our lives a sense of purpose and meaning.

Having clear boundaries: this is not a selfish act but a means of self-preservation. Saying no is an important act of self-compassion. Listening to yourself and paying attention to meeting your own needs is just as important as offering that help to other people. It may be necessary to take a break from supporting someone: how can you establish another line of help for them? It may be that rather than taking on all the support for a relative or friend who is in distress, we could help them to set up a support network. This allows us the satisfaction of being their supporter and the relief of knowing that others are co-supporters.

The 'routine maintenance' of our wellbeing includes seeking help and support to remain well. If we leave a conversation feeling emotionally drained by the experience, our self-awareness can prompt us to take a moment for self-care. What restores you best? I know people who go for a five-minute walk in the fresh air, or who take a few minutes to centre themselves in the moment and focus mindfully on their breathing, or who make a cup of tea or coffee (the ritual of making the brew seems to be part of the comfort), or who listen to music on their phone. These are all 'wellbeing first-aid' practices that enable us to carry on with the work of the day.

If a troubling conversation continues to haunt us, something more is needed: now is the time to talk to a colleague or, if the discussion was in a more informal, social context, to find a supporter to talk to without giving away the person's identity. Some people find reflective journal-writing a helpful way to 'write out' the distress and to see it objectively: to move it from 'my distress' to 'someone else's distress that I have been given a glimpse of'. Objectivity helps us to avoid internalising other people's pain. And of course, when we discuss our own distress with another person, we hope to be accorded the same tender concern that this book advocates.

Self-care is the practice that enables us to retain our resilience and wellbeing. I hope that you will look after yourself, for the sake of all of us. It is part of our pact with each other that allows us all to keep on turning up, ready to serve the people who need us.

Building Bridges

Sometimes the situation in which we are holding a tender conversation is complicated. Perhaps the way events may develop is uncertain; perhaps the people involved have different views on the best way to deal with things; maybe unwelcome news must be shared and difficult truths acknowledged.

Disagreement, anger, anxiety and denial of a tough reality can all make conversations more complicated. When trying to build a conversational bridge across a river of difficult emotions, it helps to have some reliable anchor points.

The basic steps of listening well, asking helpful questions and working alongside the other people involved become even more important when there is disagreement or even conflict.

The next few chapters will look at longer interactions, each illustrating some of the complications that arise when the truth is difficult to acknowledge, uncomfortable to tell or unwelcome. How might we support people as they come to a new understanding, as they share or hear unwelcome news? These stories will examine how to remain calmly engaged when emotions run high. How do we bridge disagreement or remain in companionship in the presence of anger? How do we listen when what we hear is breaking our own hearts?

Thresholds: The Courage to Begin

There are times when communication feels both important and daunting. Seeking out sensitive information, giving unwelcome news, broaching a disagreement, making a new acquaintance, asking for a pay rise, inviting someone on a date: each of these may involve forethought and preparation to be ready to begin the task, and yet when the time arrives, or the opportunity arises, it can feel paralysing. Self-doubt and lack of confidence, fear of how the conversation may proceed, anxiety about blame, fear of rejection or concern about causing distress can all conspire to make us miss the moment. There is a 'Threshold Effect' – we require the skill (and courage) not only to conduct the conversation, but also to recognise when and how to begin it.

This holds true for any conversation in which strong emotions may be unleashed: we sense our own reluctance to begin. Sometimes the stars align when a friend offers us an opening or someone asks a question that allows the conversation to get going. Often, though, trepidation about starting to talk leads to a lost opportunity.

Of course, we all want to avoid causing distress. Crossing the threshold is a point of no return. And I understand about missing the moment.

'Am I dying, doctor?'

The exhausted, drowsy woman I have just met on a spring Sunday afternoon has hardly spoken a clear word to me as I've examined her, drawn her blood sample, put up her drip. Her advanced breast cancer is playing havoc with her blood biochemistry: her calcium levels are dangerously high, pushing her towards coma and death. Alone in a tidy hospital room, her husband now returned home to their young daughters, she looks wasted and pale against the white sheets and green NHS bedspread. As the on-call cancer centre doctor, the most junior in the department, I am meeting her for the first time. I put up the drip with a temporary antidote to the calcium problem. But it may already be too late.

'Am I dying, doctor?' she says again, her dry mouth making her lips click.

I am flummoxed. I have never been asked this question before. *Really? Or have I just never heard it so clearly before?* I don't know what to say. She is sick enough to die. But she may pull through. *It's not my role to discuss this. She should talk to the team she knows, tomorrow.*

'Of course not!' I hear myself say. My voice is high; I am gathering my kit; I am rushing from the room. *I am running away.*

By Monday morning, she is dead. She never got to say goodbye to her husband. She didn't have a last cuddle with her daughters. *She was asking me for a truth I found too bitter to acknowledge, and I lied to her. I may never recover from this shame.* Obviously, I tell no one.

More than thirty years later, that shame and guilt are as fresh as ever. Her husband will be a pensioner now; her daughters may have children of their own. They can never have back those hours I stole from them. I wonder how it has affected their lives. I know how it has affected mine.

I have learned to say the D-words. I have rolled them around in my mouth like massive marbles, too huge to articulate, too large to spit out, too painful to swallow. I have chewed them and tasted them and reduced them to a manageable size. Death. Dying. Dead. See? Because talking about death won't make it happen. But not talking about it robs us of choices and moments that will not come again.

I have specialised in palliative care, and I have had honest end-of-life discussions many thousands of times. I have explained the process of dying, whose gentleness consoles people once they know what to expect. I have answered questions with calm clarity: I have seen death many times, and I am not afraid. My voice no longer squeaks. It's safe to talk about dying. It's vital that we do. And it's vital that we talk to each other in families and friendship groups, not only in medical settings, and that we find words with which to cross that threshold.*

Whatever the topic for discussion, anxiety at the threshold is a fear of insufficiency: not enough confidence, experience, time, seniority, knowledge to answer the questions that may arise. And yet we must be able to reach the threshold and then take the step that crosses it. No one can know all the answers; nobody has all the experience required to manage every query on every occasion. There are some important phrases to learn in order to make the threshold feel less daunting.

First of all, a few helpful phrases for when we discover that the threshold has been passed, and we realise that we are already in a conversation about which we may feel more than a little daunted or ill-prepared.

I don't know. Sometimes that is the whole answer to a question. Sometimes the answer is 'I'm not sure, but I will try to help you find an answer.' Being able to say 'I don't know' saves us from fearing being found wanting. Not knowing is part of the human condition. Not needing to know everything is profoundly comforting; the humility to admit not knowing is a virtue. Here we are, together, not knowing.

I'm sorry. 'I am sorry' has more than one possible meaning,

* This story was first published in 2019 as part of a blog for Marie Curie Cancer Care. The full text is at https://www.mariecurie.org.uk/blog/marbles-in-my-mouth-using-the-d-words/225028

and their different inferences has made it a sentence that we are increasingly cautious to use.

In one sense, I'm sorry means 'I feel sorrow'. It is a human-to-human commiseration, an offer to suffer with someone in their sadness. I can be deeply sorry that your dog has died, your firm has made you redundant, your grandchild is sick. It is a kind and heartfelt recognition of someone else's pain.

In its other usual sense, I'm sorry means 'I am penitent'. This is an admission of fault for which we feel an apology is due. I may be apologising for a mistake I made, or that my team or family made and for which I take responsibility, or that my cat has broken your ornament. Apologising is the first step in mitigating a harm.

The difficulty lies in the use of apology as a statement of culpability. If you are my friend and I know how much you love your dog, and I have unfortunately run over your dog with my car, then my 'I'm sorry' will mean both 'I share your sorrow' and 'I apologise for causing your sorrow'. If I run over a stranger's dog, although I will still intend both meanings, the lack of a prior relationship and the suddenness of the news will bring my culpability rather than my sorrow to the fore, even if the dog was running wild, the accident unavoidable and my culpability low.

In medical practice, I see people avoiding apologies in case this means there will be legal action that uses their apology as an admission of wrongdoing, even if no wrongdoing or mistake is involved. Without a sincere expression of sorrow for the pain, the first step in mitigating harm is not taken, and the harm is compounded at that failed threshold. Staff close ranks and do not discuss the events with patient and family; a hospital or practice writes a defensive response instead of acknowledging the sorrow and pain that have been experienced by their patient or family. Instead of leaping to self-defence, a far better start could be the doctor who says 'I am sorry this has all been so upsetting for you.

What can I do now that might help you to deal with it?' or the institution that sends a letter (from a named person whom the patient or family can contact) to say, 'We see how awful this was for you, and we are sorry that it happened. We want to help you to recover [or perhaps 'understand what happened']. We will write to you separately about how your concerns will be investigated, but we want to tell you how deeply sorry we are that you suffered in this way.' It is important to say, 'I feel sorrow.'

I don't know what to say. This is a sentence that helps us when we are lost for words. It is closely related to '*I may need a moment before I can say any more*', when emotions are too high to think and speak calmly, whether from anxiety, anger, sorrow or surprise. Owning our emotions by saying, 'I am too shocked to comment', 'I am too sad to talk', 'I am too angry to think clearly right now', acknowledges that although we have been engaged in a conversation up to this point, we may need a pause to reflect before we continue.

What about deciding to cross that threshold deliberately? If we stand perplexed and anxious at the edge of a possible conversation, useful threshold-crossing statements are variations on '*I have something very important to say/ask*' and include 'This may be an emotional conversation', 'This may be difficult for you to hear', 'I may find this hard to talk about', 'I have unexpected news', 'I am looking for honest answers to some difficult questions.' Each of these conveys that we are about to cross a threshold into a high-stakes conversation.

Making a threshold-crossing statement also allows us to check that the other person or people involved understand that a significant conversation is in prospect, and that they have the right supporters with them before we begin. Preparing them in this way can enable us to share responsibility with them for the way the discussion proceeds. This applies whether it is sharing significant news (good or bad) with family or friends; revealing an unwelcome medical diagnosis; discussing sexual or mental health with someone (theirs or our own); or broaching uncomfortable discussions about violence or abuse.

What advice would I give to that inexperienced and frightened young doctor who ran away from a threshold thirty years ago? I wish I could go back and tell her a few things.

Trust yourself. You don't need to know the answers. Just listen.

'Am I dying, doctor?'

Put all your kit down. Sit down: on a chair, on the bed (this is a once-in-an-illness chance to listen), on the floor. Ask her to repeat her question, to be sure she wants to ask and to be certain you didn't mishear.

'Am I dying, doctor?' she repeats, her dry mouth making her lips click. I am flummoxed. I have never been asked this question before. *Really? Or have I just never heard it so clearly before?*

She has asked twice. She wants to know. She has a young family. You know she may lose consciousness because of the calcium problem. She might like a chance to talk to her family. Trust yourself to step over this threshold alongside her. You are not alone. She is also there, asking her question; she is not just your patient, she is a person. There are wise and kind nurses on this ward; there is a more senior trainee and a consultant on call. You have back-up.

I don't know what to say. She is sick enough to die. But she may pull through. *It's not my role to discuss this. She should talk to the team she knows, tomorrow.*

It *is* your role to discuss this. Today you are her doctor. She has asked you. Twice. You recognise how precarious her situation is. Tomorrow may be too late. Sit here and tell her what truth you can: that you don't know the answer, but that you will try to help her to get answers to her questions.

Start with a question. Help her to tell herself the story so far.

It may help her to recognise how much less well she is becoming. It will begin to answer her question.

'My name is Kathryn and I am the junior doctor on call this weekend. What would you like me to call you?'

Let's call her Myra.

'Myra, it's the first time I've met you, and I've only had a quick look at your notes so far. Tell me how things have been for you over the last few weeks.'

Listen while she tells you how tired she has been; how hard it has been to stay awake. Her mum has come to stay because she is too tired to care for her little girls after school. She's been mainly in bed for the last three weeks. The most recent chemotherapy was cancelled because she wasn't well enough for it. She's worried now that there isn't a plan for more chemo.

Reflect back to her what she has just told you, to be sure you have understood. She's been very tired, mainly in bed, too unwell for her chemo. She has little girls; her mum has come to help. Ask her what worries her the most today.

Listen as she tells you that she thinks she is dying. She's starting to cry. She's struggling to talk because her mouth is so dry. Help her to sip some water. Tell her you'll get some ice for her once she's finished all her questions. Tell her you're not in a hurry, even though you are. Pass her a tissue. Keep listening.

Answer her question: this calcium problem is a sign the cancer is progressing. It does make some people so sick that they might die. Use those words, kindly yet clearly. Pause to let her take it in. Offer her another sip of water. Don't hurry her. You're over the threshold now, you are in the conversation. Keep using questions to gauge what she wants to know, and then answer those she asks.

How old are her girls? She tells you they are ten and seven, and their names. Do they know how serious your illness is? 'No, we didn't want to frighten them.' When did you last see them?

'Last week, before I came into hospital. Children are not allowed to visit this ward.'

You know the ward sister has discretion to allow her children to come in. Ask her whether she would like her girls, their dad, her mum to visit. Tell her that high calcium makes people very sleepy, and although you are giving her an antidote you don't know how successful it will be. If she wants to be awake to see them, to hold them close, she should do it today. Offer more water. Tell her you are sorry to be telling her such unwelcome news. You *are* sorry, and it's fine to say so.

The bad news is not your fault.

This is her bad news. It is her situation. You are simply describing it. You did not make it happen, you are not making it worse by answering her questions, you are treating her like an autonomous person and giving her choices. It is true that the answer is likely to distress her; but perhaps she has guessed the truth and seeks your companionship and consolation there. Perhaps her desire to know is more important to her than her wish to avoid the distress of knowing. Once you have told her the truth, you can begin to support her as she processes it.

Listen to your voice. It was high and squeaky to begin with, but now you have crossed the threshold you are speaking gently, kindly, young woman to young woman. Notice your sadness: it is recognising her sadness. The sadness is in her life, and you cannot suffer for her. If you try to, you will burn yourself out before your time. Be compassionate for her situation, but do not make the mistake of asking yourself how this situation would affect you if she were your sister, your friend, yourself. Your own sorrows will come in good time: don't be in a hurry for them.

But you can be her companion in distress, and later you will weep in the ward sister's office, and she will tell you that all the doctors weep in here, there's no shame, you did a good job. Those children are on their way in with their dad, and one of the nurses will accompany their visit. The senior nurse will advise you that you should check the other patients' IV lines and go home now, it's been a tough weekend for a young doctor. And you will be grateful for her kindness.

And tomorrow you will find that after the visit from her daughters, her mum and her husband, Myra died overnight. Her mum will have taken the girls home and her husband will be beside her when she stops breathing, and you will have learned that we can talk about dying.

If I could go back and help you, I would.

But instead, you learned about opportunities missed and thresholds uncrossed. From this missed opportunity you learned a different wisdom, which took you on a different path. Other families were helped by your reflections on your failure to cross that threshold; but you can never right that wrong, and you will always feel sorry, in both senses of the word.

We limp to wisdom over the hot coals of our mistakes. Bind your feet, now, and keep walking.

Anger

Anger is about unmet expectations. It is an alarm response generated by a gap between what is happening and what someone believes should be happening: a perceived lack of fairness, a breaking of the rules, whether explicit or unspoken. Discussion while one or both parties is feeling angry can make the conversation difficult, and anger can turn a conversation into a confrontation. How best can we navigate discussions when anger is also present?

I'm sitting in an oak-panelled room high above the gardens of the Victorian part of our hospital. The windows are open to cool the air: it's high spring, and a bee buzzes heavily through the room and exits via another window towards the top branches of a heavy-scented magnolia tree beyond. Sitting with me are the complaints manager, Enid, and a retired, eminent professor of surgery, and we are preparing to meet the unhappy family of a patient who has died in the care of our hospital.

We are spaced out around a long, polished conference table. There is a water jug and a collection of glasses on the table, a box of tissues and a tape recorder with a grey microphone. There is an atmosphere of quiet contemplation. The calm before the storm.

Prof Price was a senior surgeon in this organisation for many years. He taught me as a medical student. I found him terrifying. Since retirement he has taken on a conflict-resolution role, and it has been an education for me, as the hospital's end-of-life care lead, to see him in action. The fiery young surgeon I used to fear has been transformed by his life experiences into a wise elder. It is not his glittering career but the challenges, bereavements and personal losses he has weathered that have turned his passion to patience; his once-famous temper has been reduced to a spark that ignites at injustice. When he talks to people making a complaint about care, his palpable sense of their right to fairness sets them at their ease. He can sit with other people's anger and acknowledge their right to feel it. Equally, he brooks no unjustified criticism of the intentions of staff to deliver an excellent service: his is a court of polite listening, generous empathy and clear rules of fairness.

Enid has provided us with bundles of paper: copies of case notes, nursing notes, drug charts, letters from the family, responses from the hospital's senior team. It is all depressingly familiar: an elderly man, beloved of his family, was admitted to hospital for something that seemed routine. In hospital it became clear that he was very much sicker than anyone had previously realised. His surgical procedure went smoothly, but his background health deteriorated and he died before he could get home. His family perceives that, since he was 'not too bad' when he came into hospital, his subsequent deterioration and death must be someone's fault, and that the hospital is failing to tell the truth. Furthermore, on the night before he died, the patient became muddled and called home to say the staff were threatening to kill him. Understandably, his bereaved family was shocked, perplexed and angry.

An extensive investigation at the hospital has identified the reasons for his downward trajectory; it has established that he tried to spare his family concern by not disclosing bad news to them, but once his already-failing kidneys finally stopped working altogether he experienced confusion caused by an accumulation of toxins in his blood. In his confusion, he sensed imminent death, forgot he had forbidden staff to tell his family any bad news and called home to plead for help. What a frightening time he must have experienced, alone in hospital with a sense of unexplained impending doom. What a shocking phone call that must have been for his wife, who came by taxi within minutes of his calling her. How difficult it must have been for this family to make sense of how close this man was to death when they had no idea how sick he had become. No wonder they blame the hospital for his death.

I am also aware that their anger is distorting and complicating their bereavement. Unable to resolve the pattern of events of their beloved's hospital stay, they are trapped in a grief twisted by their belief that his death was avoidable and was caused by a failure of diligence and care at the hospital. This is like a weeping wound, and no healing can begin until the cause of their anger has been resolved – if that is possible.

In preparation for this meeting, I have read and reread all this information, mapping the story out on a piece of paper. Mr Rook was in his eighties, a retired butcher. I know his shop, now run by his son. Mr Rook was known to have breathing problems, and arthritis that limited his walking. Enlargement of his prostate gland, not uncommon in older men, had begun to obstruct his bladder and, unwilling to tolerate a catheter, he had come into hospital to have a simple procedure under anaesthetic to remove part of his prostate and allow urine to flow again.

At the hospital routine blood tests showed kidney damage from the urine blockage was already significant. Mr Rook forbade the team to tell his family. The anaesthetist for his surgery was worried about Mr Rook's combination of lung problems, ageing heart and kidney damage. There is a note about her conversation with him. The anaesthetist warned him about the small possibility of complications of having prostate surgery: heart attack, bleeding from his bladder, breathing difficulties, infection. She notes that 'he accepts these risks and does not want to worry his family about them'.

It is clear from the notes that Mr Rook came through his surgery reasonably well although blood tests showed that his kidneys had deteriorated further, making him sleepy the day after his operation. Mrs Rook came in to visit him that afternoon and assumed his sleepiness was caused by the drugs needed for his surgery. She told the nurses her husband had never wanted a catheter, and they explained that a catheter had become necessary to help them to monitor Mr Rook's poor kidney function. The nurses were concerned that Mrs Rook did not seem to understand the implications of the poor urine output, the suggestion that Mr Rook's kidneys were not recovering. All these conversations are recorded in his notes.

The following day Mr Rook was even more sleepy, a bit short of breath and slightly muddled. His blood tests showed that his kidneys were getting worse.

At visiting time the nursing notes record that 'Mrs Rook was upset to see her husband so sleepy. Mr Rook has forbidden giving medical information to his family. The charge nurse explained that Mr Rook's kidneys have been damaged by the back-pressure from his prostate, and this can take time to recover.'

That night Mr Rook became restless and agitated, and he pulled out his catheter. He used his mobile phone to call his wife at three o'clock in the morning and told her that the hospital staff were trying to kill him. The family came in quickly, and Dr Shah, the gentle Iranian junior doctor, explained that kidney failure was causing Mr Rook to be confused and sleepy. She told them that Mr Rook was becoming increasingly unwell, and that it was possible he was so sick now that he could die. The family protested that Mr Rook had never had anything wrong with his kidneys, he only had prostate trouble. They accused Dr Shah of telling lies, of covering something up. They demanded to see a more senior doctor.

The next day, with his family around him in a state of distressed disbelief, Mr Rook continued to deteriorate. He was too frail for haemodialysis. His kidneys had stopped working completely. He died that evening, his wife at his bedside as she had been since the agitated conversation with Dr Shah.

A bang, as the heavy door of the room slams in the breeze from the open windows, announces the arrival of the surgeon who was looking after Mr Rook. He is dressed in suit and tie rather than the scrubs I usually see him in. He is carrying his bundle of papers provided by Enid, and he looks anxious.

'They have said some very harsh things,' he comments, placing his papers on the table and pouring himself a glass of water. 'My trainees are very distressed. Poor Doctor Shah is distraught. She has never had a complaint against her before.' He sits down and looks at Prof. 'OK, Boss?' he asks, and I realise that Prof Price must have trained Max in the early part of his career.

'Relax, Max,' says Prof. 'Your juniors have nothing to fear. But you'll hear me ask the family their full story, and they may say critical things. The important thing is not to interrupt. They need to feel heard. No matter who else is sad or anxious today, the fact is that they are bereaved. The investigation doesn't seem to indicate that anyone is at fault, but he died in our care and their anger is part of their grief. So, Max,' Prof looks at him sternly, 'I'll give you a chance to speak, but I need you not to get cross. Do you get me?'

Max smiles, and his shoulders relax. Good trainers have an almost parental defensiveness towards their trainees. Prof has had that relationship with Max; Max has it now with Dr Shah. Feathers have been ruffled. Max wants to defend his protégée. Prof's words are important: it is difficult to find our compassion if we feel angry or defensive. Prof is holding this room in balance: today our hospital's representatives must be centred on our compassion for this family. We want to help them to understand what happened to their beloved relative. If there have been faults or mistakes on our part, we must own them with humility and sorrow. We may need to give the family explanations, but we are not here to defend. We are here to listen.

Max recaps the story we have all read; he answers our questions so that all the details are clear to us. Max and I work together regularly to keep his collection of elderly men with prostate cancer comfortable, mobile and symptom free. He is young, an enthusiastic surgeon, and tender as a son with these old men. Like Prof of old, he is passionate: a fervour that can be fanned into anger when operating lists run late or standards of care are not what he demands.

The clock in the hallway outside chimes the half-hour. It is the Rook family's appointment time, and Enid quietly opens the big door to bring them inside. Mrs Rook is short and pale. She walks cautiously with a stick. Beside her are two men of about my age, her sons: I recognise one from the butcher's shop. They are welcomed by Prof, and we all sit down.

Prof asks the family's permission to record the session. They agree, and Prof presses the record button. He always does this with a slightly theatrical flourish. I drop my eyes to my lap. Any sign of amusement would be misplaced in this tense gathering.

'I think you know Mr Max Evans, one of our consultant surgeons and the doctor responsible for Mr Rook's care in our hospital,' Prof begins. Mrs Rook snorts. Her sons nod at Max.

Max says, 'I'm glad to see you again', and Mrs Rook mutters, 'I'm not a fool.' I sense this will be a difficult meeting.

'You won't know Dr Kathryn Mannix, who is our end-of-life lead,' says Prof. 'She has been looking through our investigation report to see whether there is anything we can learn from what happened.

'And I am Professor Eric Price. I was a surgeon in this hospital, and now I am the Chief Executive's representative at family meetings like this one. You are very welcome here. I know the circumstances are very sad for you all, and I appreciate you giving us your time today.

'Enid is taking notes. She will give everybody here a copy of the notes she makes. The tape recording is solely to help her to complete her notes. Is that acceptable to you all?' There is general nodding and murmuring. I wonder why Enid is not accorded a surname or job title. I feel a spark of sisterhood, being frequently introduced differently from my male medical colleagues. *All alike in dignity*, I misquote in my head.

'Now, would you like to introduce yourselves?' asks Prof. The son I recognise speaks.

'I'm George Rook, son of Robert Rook who was your patient,' he says. 'This is my brother, Paul, and he is a pharmacist. He's been giving us medical information while we have been trying to make sense of all this.

'And this is our mum, Robert's wife.'

'Mrs Rook, George, Paul, I'd like to start by saying how very sorry we are that your husband, your father, died in our care,' says Prof. 'I know this is a very difficult time for you all, and we all offer you our sincere condolences. I offer condolences, too, on behalf of our Chief Executive who has asked me to report back personally on the investigation of Mr Rook's death.'

The Rook family make no response. There is a silence.

'I'd like to start by inviting you to tell us what is causing you the most concern. We have all read your letter of complaint, and also your letter responding to our investigation of your complaint. But today let's talk and listen to each other, to try to answer your questions and see whether there were things we could have done differently [I notice his use of *could* rather than *should*] or whether there were things that were outright mistakes.'

Mrs Rook looks across me at Max. 'Your staff failed my husband,' she states. 'He was a well man when he arrived for his op, and a few days later he was dead. That should not have happened. Something went wrong, and we want to know what it was.'

Max holds her gaze and I sit back like a tennis umpire, caught between them.

Prof speaks. 'You feel something went wrong,' he says. 'And you believe we are hiding something?'

'Without a doubt,' says Mrs Rook. 'He was well, then he was dead. And you' – she turns to Max – 'operated on him in the gap between. So what went wrong? What mistake did you make?' Her face quivers. 'He should be alive now. You should be in prison!'

There is a pause. Prof comments, gravely, 'Mrs Rook, we know you are deeply distressed by the loss of your husband. These are strong emotions. But I must ask you to bear with us patiently today, and to try not to shout accusations. We will listen to you carefully, I promise. There will be no need to shout.

'Is there anything else you would like to tell us, or to ask us, about what happened to Mr Rook? About his care, or the treatment, or his surgery?'

'All I know is, he is dead, and a fit man should not have died. I want to know everything, and I want to know now,' says Mrs Rook, her voice quivering with her head.

'In that case, I'd like to ask Dr Mannix to talk us through her understanding of events,' Prof continues. 'She was not involved in his care, so all her remarks are made as a neutral party.'

Mrs Rook snorts again, saying, 'You're all as thick as thieves!' I take a deep breath, conscious of her quietly determined rage for justice simmering beside me, before I begin my summary.

The case notes are in front of me, but instead of using them as a shield, I turn in my seat to face her. I tell her I have gathered this story from reading the clinic letters and blood-test results, ward notes and lab reports, and I'd like her to check that I have understood the details. I start before Mr Rook had ever been seen by Max's team.

'I can see that the prostate problem Mr Rook had was a real nuisance for him. He was struggling to pass urine, and he complained that he needed to get up several times during the night. Have I understood that right, Mrs Rook?' She nods her quivering head. 'I can also see that he had arthritis in his hips and knees, so getting out of bed would have been painful, as well as a nuisance in disturbing his sleep. Even when he got back into bed, I suspect it would take a while for him to get comfortable enough to fall asleep again. Is that a fair comment?'

She nods again and says, 'He complained about his bad nights. But he was always a coper, Bob. He wanted to look after me, not the other way round.'

I tell her that Mr Rook's wish to look after her is clear from the notes: he had mentioned it to several people. She looks me in the eye for the first time.

'Can I move on to talk about the operation?' I ask. She nods.

'I can see that the surgery was planned for two reasons,' I say. 'First, he didn't want to use a catheter, even though that would easily have solved the practical problems of struggling to pass urine and disturbed sleep. He told Mr Evans that he would rather be dead than have a catheter. That's a pretty clear message. Did he ever discuss that with you?' She shakes her head.

One of her sons says: 'We didn't know he had been offered a catheter. We wondered why not.'

'In the referral letter from his GP, the doctor comments that he is *set against using a catheter*,' I reply. 'So both his GP and Mr Evans spoke to him about it, and for his own very important reasons, he turned it down. His doctors respected his choice.'

I pause to let them take in that fact.

'The other reason surgery was planned was that Mr Rook's prostate had got so big it was blocking the flow of his urine and that was causing back-pressure on his kidneys. He had blood tests and X-rays ordered by his GP, do you remember that?' I turn to Mrs Rook.

'He told me there was a bit of a hold-up in his urine,' she says. 'He didn't tell me his kidneys were damaged. I don't think he knew that. The doctor should have told him. Why wasn't he told?'

'The GP letter to refer him for surgery says, *I explained that his kidneys are showing signs of damage, and unless the obstruction is relieved soon, his kidneys will fail altogether. But he still refuses to consider a catheter.* It seems that his GP told him, Mrs Rook.'

She gazes at me, and I cannot read her unblinking expression.

I tell the family that the clinic notes and letters, written by Max's team after assessing Mr Rook in their clinic, emphasise that the operation was a matter of urgency.

'The urgency was to save his kidneys. That's why he was admitted so soon after his clinic assessment. Does that all make sense to you all?'

Paul Rook, the pharmacist, clears his throat. 'May I say something?' he asks.

'Of course,' says Prof.

'Dad was a very private man,' says Paul. 'He never liked a fuss about things. His aim in life was to run his business well so that we could have a good life. After he retired, he wanted Mum to be happy. He felt he had neglected us when he was busy with the shop, with all the paperwork, the accounts and ordering, and early-morning starts. He wanted to make up for all that. Mum was his world.' Through the corner of my eye, I see Mrs Rook's hands begin to shake. 'So it's not unlikely that if he had medical problems, he would have kept them to himself. Dad was like that.'

'Thanks for telling us that,' I say. 'He sounds like a very kind and determined person. If he *was* keeping secrets, it was out of love for you all.' I want to be certain that there is no sense that we are blaming Mr Rook for the effects of his secrecy; rather, it was intended as an act of kindness and protection on his part.

'Can I take us all through what happened from the day Mr Rook came into hospital?' I ask, focusing again on Mrs Rook. 'I can hear that you have concerns that things happened that you didn't know about, and I think that is true. But it isn't because anyone was covering up. It's because Mr Rook asked the staff not to give medical information to his family. He didn't want to worry you. Let me take it day by day—'

'So instead of telling us the truth, you told us *lies?*' interrupts Mrs Rook. 'He was gibbering. He didn't know what he was saying! But you followed his crazy instructions? I am his *wife*. I had a right to *know!*'

The gap between what we expect – what should have been – and what happens is what triggers anger. Anger uses the language of *should*. What the world should be like; how people should behave; what I should have been entitled to expect.

Mrs Rook expected her husband to have a simple, short trip to the hospital. She expected him to be giving her all the information he knew. She expected that, if there were medical concerns, she would be informed. These are her 'shoulds'. Yet the law is clear: every patient has a right to confidentiality, and our contract is with our patient. People can make unwise choices: we may try to dissuade them but in the end it is their right. Declining a catheter was an unwise choice. A few weeks using a catheter could have allowed Mr Rook's kidneys to recover and made surgery safer for him. Their letters show that both his GP and Mr Evans's team discussed this with their patient. Declining the catheter, in the face of deteriorating kidney function, was the first step in a chain of events that led to his death. Mr Rook made decisions that he kept from his family. In retrospect, that was another unwise choice.

I keep all this in my head. I need to choose my words carefully.

'I can see from the notes that he intended to protect you from worry,' I tell Mrs Rook. 'He didn't see it as lying, he saw it as kindness. It sounds as though that fits with what Paul is telling us about his character, too. What do you think about that?'

Her hands clench on her lap. The table is high and she is slightly stooped, so the top of the table is at chest height for her. It's disempowering, and I don't know how to remedy it. The way we arrange our furniture changes the dynamics of a conversation; we need a low, circular table that has no 'head' seat for these meetings. We need comfortable chairs. We need beverages. This Victorian marvel is imposing, but it says that the hospital is in charge. This room is not on the visitors' side.

'They should have told me,' she says, but this time it is a sigh.

'They wished they *could* tell you,' I say, feeling the weight of her bewildered sorrow. 'And in the end, Dr Shah *did* tell you, didn't she? But what a shock it must have been by then. You had no idea how sick he already was when he arrived in hospital, did you?'

Mrs Rook shakes her head sadly, then she lifts her chin resolutely to speak again as another wave of anger buoys her. 'So did the shock of the operation make things worse? Was it a mistake to operate?'

'The only way to protect his kidneys was to operate,' I say. 'There wasn't really a choice. The alternative was kidney failure, and his circulation wasn't strong enough for kidney-failure treatments.'

I look at Max. 'Mr Evans knew it was a risk, and he has written in the notes about discussing the risk with Mr Rook. Do you want to say any more about that, Mr Evans?'

Max leans forward to look past me at Mrs Rook. 'It was all about looking after you, Mrs Rook,' he says. '"I need to be well to look after my wife," your husband told me. He said you'd been diagnosed with Parkinson's Disease, and he needed to be sprightly to look after you.' Mrs Rook holds Max's gaze, her wobbly head demonstrating her Parkinson's.

'I didn't know he had forbidden the ward team to give you updates,' continues Max. 'I always think it's best for families if there are no sudden surprises. Or shocks. If I'd known he'd forbidden them to update you, I would have tried to persuade him.' Max pauses before adding, 'I'm so sorry. That was very tough for you.' This is the tenderness I have seen in him at bedsides. He means it.

There is another silence before I pick up the story: the surgery went smoothly but Mr Rook's kidneys didn't recover as hoped. Fluid was accumulating in his body, settling on his lungs.

Paul leans forward. 'I want to ask about that,' he says. 'His kidneys were already failing, and then someone gave Dad a slug of Furosemide.* That seems to have knackered his kidneys completely. Whose decision was it to give Furosemide, and what do we think about that decision now?'

This has been an important piece of the internal inquiry, and I say so. 'The drug is signed for by Dr Shah, who is a junior surgery trainee,' I reply. 'In the notes she records asking advice from a consultant in the renal team.' I look at Mrs Rook. 'That's a kidney specialist. The best person to get that kind of advice from. The renal team consultant reviewed Mr Rook's blood tests and chest X-ray and advised that, despite the risk of further kidney damage from the Furosemide, the presence of pulmonary oedema – water in his lungs, Mrs Rook – was more life-threatening at that time.

'So it was a calculated risk. A medical judgement. All recorded in his notes.' In my mind I give thanks for Dr Shah's exemplary note-keeping: it is not always so easy to glean the details of medical decisions.

Paul sits back. 'Makes sense,' he says to his family. 'No drug is without a risk. I think I'd have given the same advice, in those circumstances. Hobson's choice.'

'After that, Mr Rook's kidneys just kept deteriorating, and kidney failure makes people muddled,' I say. 'The muddle explains why he phoned you, Mrs Rook. He was frightened because he felt so unwell, and you were always his biggest comfort.' I pause. I ask whether Mr Rook was awake when she arrived.

---

* Furosemide is a drug that acts on the kidneys to increase urine production. It can also be damaging to the kidneys in some circumstances.

She looks at George. 'Yes, I was there in twenty minutes and George was there soon after. He knew it was me, and we were able to sit together while the nurses tucked him back into bed. I couldn't believe the state of him, so muddled and blood on his pyjamas where he'd pulled that catheter out.' She shudders.

'And then that young doctor with the headscarf came to talk to us. She told us he was very sick . . . that he might die. I couldn't believe it. I shouted at her. I made her cry . . .'

'And what do you think about that conversation with Dr Shah now?' I ask. Mrs Rook looks at her sons, then down at her clasped hands. She sighs.

'She was the first person who told me the truth, wasn't she?' says Mrs Rook. 'I had no idea he could get so sick. But knowing he could die made me stay at the hospital. I'm glad she told us. I'm glad I was there. I was so angry with her. But . . . I think she did the right thing . . .

'I'm sorry I made her cry. She was doing her best. She was kind. She wasn't being a bad person.'

'Do you think anyone was a bad person, Mrs Rook?' I ask.

She bends her trembling neck and I see tears drip onto her hands. She takes a long time to answer. Eventually, in a voice that is tired and sad, she says, 'No . . . Everyone did what they hoped was best. Even Bob. Keeping secrets from me. How could he?' and she begins to weep. Max pushes the box of tissues down the table towards her; she nods to him as she takes a tissue, then she sits, twisting it in her fingers.

Prof waits and the silence lengthens. Finally, he says, 'If you feel your concerns have been properly attended to, I will draw our meeting to a close. Does anyone have anything else to add?' He waits again. No one speaks.

'Do you have any concerns that we have not addressed today?' he asks the family directly.

Mrs Rook shakes her head and mops her eyes, and Paul says,

'It's been thorough and professional, Professor Price. Thank you. It's helped me, and I hope it's helped Mum and my brother, too.' George nods. Mrs Rook twists her tissue in her trembling hands.

After they have departed, and Max has expressed relief that the meeting seemed to lift their misapprehensions about covert foul play, Max and Enid leave to pick up their next duties. Alone with Prof, I have one more item to discuss. I am still in awe of him; I have a criticism to offer, and I feel anxious about how he will respond. But just as anger can erupt into conflict and rage, sometimes it provides the energy that sustains people through despair, or it is the spark that ignites a quest for justice. Anger isn't bad, we simply need to use it wisely.

My anger is about Enid's surname. Why were we three doctors given titles and full names, and yet Enid, who has spent hours preparing papers, liaising with staff and getting ready for this meeting, was simply 'Enid' when introduced? At medical conferences, I observe senior doctors introducing each other with titles for men but first names for women of equal or even superior qualifications and experience. This is a lack of fairness. There is a gap between how things are and how I think things should be. And that *should* is the trigger to anger. I must use my anger well. Taking a deep breath, I commit.

'Prof, may I ask you something?'

'Of course, Kathryn,' he replies.

'It's about introductions,' I say. *I'm in now. I have passed the threshold.* He looks quizzical. 'I like the way you introduce everybody in the room to the visitors,' I continue, heart hammering in my chest. 'I particularly appreciate that you give us all our professional titles. That doesn't happen everywhere, and it's important that the visitors know their complaint is being taken seriously by senior people. I'm usually very informal – I know you don't really approve that my patients call me by my first name, but it feels comfortable for us all that way . . .'

I'm drifting. I'm avoiding. Say it!

'I notice, though, that Enid didn't get a title or a surname. I wondered what she makes of that. She's such an important part of the preparation: she isn't just the note-taker. She's a colleague, with a surname and a job title. And she might like to be acknowledged in that way.'

I can tell I'm blushing, which is an infuriating giveaway of my emotions. But I am calling out an injustice, and it is the right thing to do. Anger can feel like a hurricane, a force that overtakes us and leaves us too furious to choose our words or to weigh the consequences of our actions, but it can also be a force that propels us for good. I'm learning to be brave: courage is a sail that catches the wind of anger, using it to set a course for justice.

Prof pauses in the gathering of his papers.

He looks at me, and then away, thoughtfully.

'I'd never even thought about it,' he admits. 'I don't think I noticed I was doing it. But I'll try to do better, Dr Mannix.' He smiles. 'Thank you for saying so. I *will* do better. Do you have time for a coffee before we get back to work?' and holding the door with delightful courtesy for me to leave the room ahead of him, he accepts the feedback.

I am humbled by his quiet grace.

Lessons in Listening

The journey from an invitation into a conversation of listening and wondering, checking and consolidating, understanding and holding silence, to a place of having listened well or having been heard is an essential part of our human experience. These are conversations that flow through our lives as we learn and grow, on our lifetime voyage from innocence to wisdom. Often these are conversations between intimates: between parent and child, between lovers, among friends, between mentor and protégé. Sometimes these are conversations with strangers: I have been held in wisdom and kindness by fellow passengers on trains and in my turn I have offered solace to people I met by chance in airport terminals and cafés.

Whenever they take place, deeply tender conversations are transformational. As the listened to, they allow us to contemplate our reality, to experience our emotions in safety and to move through the process of living with difficulties, grasping opportunities, seeing ourselves and others with sharper clarity; they bring us closer to self-acceptance and to wisdom. Often it is by reflecting on our experience of setbacks, difficulties and unanticipated outcomes that we learn the most.

As the listener, they grant us intimate insights into another person's world, moving us to admiration and profound respect for other people's fortitude and resilience, allowing us to appreciate a situation from an entirely different perspective, challenging us to appreciate the constraints that limit another person's response to their circumstances, enabling us to have a broader grasp of the human condition, and giving us reference points for the challenges, difficulties and joys in our own lives. Listener and listened to are enriched by the experience.

Listening is a skill we can learn. Many of us learn it by trial and error, mistake and reflection. Perhaps it is a skill to include in the transmission of wisdom down the generations. It may even have its place in school curricula.

'Mum, I've been invited to become a peer mediator,' number-one son informs me after school. A vision of a painted booth on a seaside promenade flashes into my mind. *What is this?* 'We get trained during year twelve, and work as mediators for other students for our final year in school,' he adds, helpfully, and the booth on the pier is transposed to the school playground, where it sits incongruously garish against a sea of grey tarmac and black school sweaters.

Over the next six months, I am increasingly impressed as I hear my son and his friends debrief following their weekly after-school training sessions. They learn about listening skills, how to de-escalate arguments, how to create a space for students to be heard in confidence. They learn about confidentiality, how to maintain it, when and how to break it for someone's safety. I hear them discussing drug use, alcohol, safe and unsafe sexual behaviour, peer pressure, consent, contraception. In each session they practise their listening skills. They return home pensive after a session about suicidal thoughts and suicide. Future training asks the students to reflect on and, if they wish, to discuss their own experiences through school: relationships and break-ups, bullying, exam results, performance pressure in sports, performing arts, academic studies. Further sessions discuss parental behaviour: for some students that may be pressure, and for others indifference; family support; family rupture. Bereavement. 'No one has talked about dying, though,' he observes, wryly. 'Shall I put you down as a speaker, Mum?' It never happens, of course.

Peer mediation training in schools, for older children, and peer-to-peer listening training, for younger children, can make a great difference to the self-esteem of the young people involved, and it can change their attitude to listening so that it becomes a skill to be valued for the rest of their lives. The modelling within a school of its belief that students have the capacity to help each other to problem-solve, and that teachers will support but may not be required to intervene or to 'solve' the situations under discussion, changes students' self-efficacy. Instead of help-seeking, they are encouraged to adopt problem-solving as their preferred strategy. Peer helpers are there to enable students to think about their problem, and to flag when the advocacy of an adult is a sensible step. Thus, a few years later, I was relieved when our daughter took another student to find the 'peer listening teacher', after a disclosure from one of her schoolmates suggested that he may not be safe at home. There is growing evidence that the presence of a trained and well-supported peer listening model in a school has whole-school benefits. Students share beliefs like 'We are the people who have agency to change our own lives'; 'Asking for help is a sign of strength and willingness to sort a problem out'; 'Being a listener is a worthwhile contribution.' What a difference those young people will make as they become adults, in their places of work, recreation and homes. Step by step towards a listening society.

This week's session has caused much discussion among the teenagers who routinely gather around our kitchen table after their peer mediation training evenings. The theme was conflict resolution, and I am eavesdropping as I make a pile of pancakes to support the debate around the table.

'I don't think it's the same for girls as for boys,' says a girl. 'Boys get into rages and they fight, and then it's all sorted. Girls freeze each other out, and that's it – friendship over.'

'But it's not always disagreements between friends, is it?' suggests a boy. 'Sometimes we're going to be getting people together for mediation who never liked each other in the first place. We're not trying to get them to be friends. We're trying to get them to draw a line under a disagreement.'

'An *agreed* line,' chips in another boy. '*Listen. Repeat back. Suggest a compromise*,' he narrates the steps.

'What about those freezes?' asks the first boy. 'To be honest, I just don't *get* girls. It must be exhausting to be so . . . *emotional* about everything.'

'Don't boys have emotions, then?' I ask, as I place a tower of pancakes on the table. I should have known pancakes would overwhelm rational discussion. I wink at the girls, who smile back. 'Or do boys just manage their emotions differently?'

'I don't think it's fair to make it a boy–girl thing,' says a boy, chomping pancake as he speaks. 'It's more subtle than that, isn't it?'

There is a hush while the hungry students savour their pancakes. I have provided lemon juice, sugar and maple syrup. There are requests for chocolate nut spread and for cinnamon. Some roll their pancakes and some fold them into quarters; some eat with cutlery and some deal with their pancakes as finger food. Either way, there is an air of contentment and a request for a second batch. I'm happy to oblige.

While I break eggs, spoon flour, pour milk and whisk the batter, the conversation moves on. They agree that aggression can be overt: shouting, fighting, unpleasant text messages, name-calling. The use of phones in disputes and bullying is a phenomenon that is adding to the complexity of teens' emotional lives. They also agree that aggression can be hidden in plain sight: lack of co-operation, sarcasm, sniggering, playing the victim. In school this can degenerate into recruiting allies who will cold-shoulder the 'opponent' and make life miserable for them. They can find examples that include all genders. The boy–girl divide is less clear than they had initially supposed.

'Tell me about the mediation,' I ask, still adding pancakes to the pile beside the stove. 'Did you have to practise? How did it go?'

One of the girls answers. 'It's quite hard to do,' she says. 'The idea is to get each person to listen to their opponent. But like – *really* listen. And then tell it back to them, to show they understood. And to let the other person add things, or correct any details.'

'Yes,' says one of the boys, 'and our job is to make sure they don't interrupt each other, and to make sure when they repeat back they say it in a fair way, not a cross way. We have to get them to say "I heard you say that you think . . ." and whatever it is they think. Or "When I said or did 'x' you felt . . ." and name how that made them feel.'

'It sounds complicated,' I say, impressed by the depth of their model. 'Do you want to show me how it works?'

They look across at me, wondering whether this suggestion will delay their pancakes.

'How about I tell you that I feel aggrieved because a group of people sat in my house, ate all my pancakes and didn't offer me one?' I continue, carrying the second batch of pancakes to the table. They laugh, apart from a girl I haven't met before who must be wondering whether I am genuinely upset about the pancakes.

'Well,' says one boy, 'I would invite you to tell us how you really feel about that situation. You could say how you feel, and then I would invite . . . who's eaten the most pancakes?' There is laughter and fingers point at the girl I know best, who is happily licking her fingers and smiling. 'I would invite Bronnie to listen to you, and then repeat back to you what she's heard you say. Which would give the rest of us a chance with those pancakes!' There is more laughter, and someone points out the passive-aggression of his comment, which makes them all laugh even more.

'Want to give it a go, Bronnie?' I ask. 'We can ask Luke to be our mediator, once he's had another pancake?' They agree. I take a seat at the table.

'I'm having a pancake first,' I inform them. They laugh again.

'OK, Bronnie and Kath,' says Luke. 'I hear you have had a disagreement about the allocation of pancakes. Is that right?'

Bronnie looks at me and nods. 'Kath says she's not happy. But I didn't know anything about it. It's not fair to blame me!' she says in teenage huff manner, very different from the calm and gentle girl I know. She has taken on a role, and her friends nod approvingly.

'Right, here's what I'd like you to agree to,' says Luke, taking another pancake as he speaks. 'I'd like to ask Kath to explain exactly why she feels so upset, and I'd like Bronnie to listen really carefully. Then I'd like Bronnie to say it back to Kath, saying "you said" and "you feel" to show she has understood how it feels from Kath's perspective. Then we'll swap: Bronnie will have her chance to say how she feels about the situation, and Kath will listen, then repeat back to Bronnie. Is that OK?' We nod. 'And I'll butt in if I need to remind you about the rules. OK?' We nod again. Bronnie takes a pancake, grinning mischievously as her friends howl with laughter.

'OK. Thanks for playing along, you two,' I say. 'Now, this evening a group of students came to my house and they were very hungry. I made a big pile of pancakes for them, and I took them across to the table. When I came back only a few moments later all the pancakes were gone and I hadn't even been offered one. The students tell me Bronnie ate my share! I feel sad and disappointed about my pancakes.' I help myself to a second pancake as I finish my speech, causing further guffaws around the table.

'Thank you, Kath,' says Luke. 'Now, Bronnie, what did you hear Kath say?'

'Kath, you said you made a pile of pancakes and when we ate them all you felt sad and disappointed,' says Bronnie.

I feel a pang of uncertainty: I hope they realise I am only playing a role here; I actually love how they use our home as their lounging ground.

'Did Bronnie seem to hear what you said and how you felt?' asks Luke.

I agree that she did, and Luke asks us to swap roles. 'For younger students, they suggested we had a bean bag or a pen or something: whoever holds the item is speaking, and mustn't be interrupted,' adds Luke. 'Maybe Bronnie should hold the frying pan?' suggests the new girl, laughing, and they laugh with her.

Bronnie, still in aggrieved-teen mode, says, 'Well, I came to Kath's house and she made pancakes for everyone. They were delicious and I was starving, and I just piled in. When I looked up I was eating the last one. Kath never said she wanted one. I thought they were just for us! I think it's *mean* to blame me!' She stops, and her smile belies the truculence of her tone. She's a good actor.

'Thank you, Bronnie. Now, Kath, what did you hear Bronnie say?'

'Bronnie said—' I begin, and Luke interrupts. 'Don't tell *me* what Bronnie said, Kath – tell *her*. Say "you said" or "you felt" to show her you were listening.'

Oh, this is powerful. What a good model. I start again.

'Bronnie, you said you were very hungry, and the pancakes were delicious. You said you didn't realise the pancakes were all eaten up until after you'd finished your last one. You think it's mean of everyone to blame you. And you said I didn't say I wanted a pancake, so you didn't know I wanted one.'

'Did Kath seem to hear what you said and how you felt?' Luke asks Bronnie.

'Yes,' she says.

'Kath, how do you feel about the situation now?' he asks.

'I understand now that if I'd wanted a pancake, I should have said so, or nipped in faster to get one!' I laugh.

'And Bronnie,' says Luke, 'how do you feel now?'

Bronnie thinks before saying, 'It was kind of Kath to make pancakes and I wish we had offered her one. But I didn't realise I'd eaten so many!' She smiles.

'So does either of you have something you'd like to say that might build peace?' asks Luke.

I say, 'I can easily make more pancakes, I'm glad you enjoyed them, and you're all welcome any time. And next time I'll make sure I tell you to save some for me!'

Bronnie responds with, 'We love coming here – and it was kind of you to make us pancakes. Next time we'll ask you if you want us to keep you a couple. Or at least one . . .' There is laughter and a round of applause for our role-play, and Bronnie grins happily. I lean across to give her a hug, then I begin to collect the plates.

'We'll do that for you, Mrs W!' shouts one of the boys. 'Shall we make you a cup of tea?' I accept the kind offer and the group clears away, wipes the table, loads the dishwasher and brews seven cups of tea, one each.

I sit at the table watching and thinking as they laugh their way through the task. Even though our dispute was contrived, the emotions were real. I *did* feel Bronnie's hurt at taking the blame, and I heard her penitence that I had been overlooked in the allocation of pancakes. I was glad to have had a chance to say out loud how much I enjoy their visits.

Offering a safe framework for speaking of disappointed expectations, of anger at perceived injustice or of sorrow at needs unmet, and showing disputants how to listen, reflect and repeat back what they have heard is a component of even high-level dispute resolution. These are life skills that can allow disagreement to be named, examined and even resolved before it escalates into regrettable actions by either party. These skills will make school life easier for students, and this 'learning to listen' will stand these young people in good stead for the rest of their lives. I miss those kitchen parliaments.

Those young people are all out in the world now. I hope they are still listeners.

In-Between-Ness

There's a place between Knowing and Not Knowing. I'm calling it 'In-between-ness'. It's an odd place, where the comfort of not knowing is interrupted by the distress of knowing. Not knowing seems kinder, and there are individuals, families and medical advisers who honestly believe that not telling is the right thing to do. The problem is that in-between-ness is not only not knowing. Paroxysms of fright and sadness arise from time to time, visitors from the place of Knowing, and they get progressively harder to suppress, shattering peace of mind. Being in-between is a place without companionship or consolation; it is fragile and brittle, unreliable and lonely.

In-between-ness exists in many situations and occupies the time between first suspecting there might be a problem and having those suspicions confirmed as true. To begin with, not knowing offers a retreat from the emotional discomfort of unwelcome possibilities: my child may not develop like other children do; my firm may be making us all redundant; my healthy-living years may be over. Yet at the same time, any chance to deal with the potential difficulty requires an understanding of what may lie ahead in order to prepare, recruit help, take problem-solving actions and find support.

In-between-ness is a state of looking in both directions: towards the turmoil of knowing a difficult truth and also towards the haven of not yet acknowledging it, the peace of not knowing.

Terry is a nurse consultant in a team looking after people with serious lung diseases. His work involves talking to patients and their families to discuss using oxygen at home, how to modify activities like getting dressed or making meals so that people can remain independent, and how to prepare for the very end of life. His caseload includes older people with degenerative lung diseases and young people with genetic lung diseases. He is used to talking about dying, death and preparation. He is also one of my peer supervision partners for our cognitive therapy practice: a small band of physical health practitioners using CBT skills to support and help our patients. Our meetings take place roughly monthly; we review our practice, talk tactics about specific challenges in therapy, and we feed back about progress from previous case discussions. It maintains our CBT practice and gives us time to pause and reflect with another expert practitioner.

Terry's mum became sick. She had a heart condition and as she reached her seventy-fifth birthday she was struggling more and more with a combination of swollen legs, breathlessness and overwhelming tiredness. Some days she could hardly get out of bed. Terry, his sisters and their husbands all took part in a visiting rota for Mum. Those living close popped in daily; those living further away came for weekends. They cooked and cleaned and encouraged and fed; they talked about 'when you're feeling better'.

But their mum didn't get any better. She became more tired. She grew thinner around her arms and shoulders, although her legs got rounder and tighter with retained fluid. The doctor changed Mum's tablets, so her legs became less swollen but she needed to pass urine so often that the effort exhausted her. She reluctantly accepted a catheter. Her appetite diminished. She sat in bed propped up on multiple pillows, reminding Terry of a sparrow in a plumped-up linen cage. Terry's mum became a regular discussion point at the end of our monthly meetings; he realised that his mum's life expectancy was shortening, and he wanted to do his very best for her.

Terry told me he had spoken to his sisters. 'You do realise that Mum is dying, don't you?' he said to them.

'It was fascinating to see how differently they reacted,' he sighed. 'I think this might be difficult to manage.' He described his sisters' responses.

'Oh, don't say that, Terry! You're wishing her away!' said one.

'I can see her getting smaller and fainter,' said another. 'But I'm glad she doesn't know.'

'Oh, Terry!' sobbed the third, 'I was starting to wonder. It's awful watching her. Do you think she realises?'

'At work I generally find that people have a hunch that things are getting worse,' Terry explained to each sister. 'Giving them an opportunity to talk about their fears and telling them as much as they want to know helps people to cope better and to spend less time worrying.'

'Ridiculous!' snorted the first sister. 'I know our mum. Talking about dying would – well, it would KILL her!'

'I couldn't talk to her about it, Terry,' said his second sister. 'She'd get upset, we'd get upset, and nothing would ever feel normal again. I don't think we should talk about it.'

'She looks frightened sometimes,' said the third sister. 'I worry that she might have guessed. But what if she hasn't? What if we try to talk to her and it makes things worse?

'And anyway,' continued the third sister, 'You know Big Sis would kill us if we ever tried to talk to Mum about it.'

Three sisters. Three different views. This, Terry reflected as we sipped our supervision coffee, is going to be tricky. . .

There is a danger in assuming that everybody wants to know the full details about themselves and their health condition. Some people do, indeed, want chapter and verse: they search online and ask for second opinions and work hard to get as much information as they can about their condition, its patterns and prognosis, the range of treatments available, their efficacy and side-effects. But that attitude is far from universal. Some people want to know 'enough to be going on with'. They don't like the burden of large amounts of information; they prefer to be supported through decision-making with sufficient facts to feel 'informed enough'. There are people who don't want any information at all: I recall a patient who told me, 'If it's bad news, doctor, just tell my wife. I don't want to know.' Using curiosity is the safest way to navigate those conversations.

In addition to what a particular person might want to know, there will be a range of opinions among their nearest and dearest about whether they should be told, and what. It can be fascinating to see how disparate these views are in a family that is close and loving. Terry's family members all want the best for their mum; they all have different opinions on what that is.

In-between-ness is uncomfortable for everybody caught up in it. Nobody is sure what to say or what is off-limits. Nobody wants to cause distress; everybody wants a clear plan. Planning can't be mentioned without moving to knowing, and it's not clear whether we have their permission to go there. In-between-ness is a place without plans or safety, and everybody waits in a sham not-knowing state until the bubble bursts.

Not knowing does not cause distress, tension or questions. For the person who does not know, it is as though the bad thing has not happened. They are calm and at peace. If they begin to suspect, though, they may experience anxious moments of wondering what is wrong.

There are two types of not knowing. In one the person has been told the bad news, and yet sometimes they appear not to know it. Their peace of mind returns for periods of time while they are able to not know. This is a coping device (it's called denial) and it can be very helpful if it prevents someone from being in a constant state of distress about bad news. I had a dear great-uncle who set a place for his dead wife at dinner every evening. The extended family felt anxious that he was 'not coping' with his bereavement. In fact, when I talked to him about it, I discovered that the opposite was true. 'I like the idea that we are still married: that's why I set her a place at the table,' he told me. 'I chat to her, too. It gives me great comfort. Of course, I understand that she is dead. But sometimes I can let myself forget for a while and feel happy.'

The other type of not knowing is more problematic, because it is not by personal choice. The diagnosis of a serious illness has not yet been reached, or the bad news has not yet been told to everyone who needs to know. The person has periods of time when there is no problem, but at other times there are signs that all is not well. They have symptoms that worry them, or the person they are concerned about seems unwell, or perhaps the family seems tense about something but they haven't said what it is. When these intimations of bad news arise, they are accompanied by anxiety and foreboding. Many people describe the period of waiting for bad news as far more difficult than the time after the bad news has been given: many describe a sense of relief, saying, 'At least now I know what I am dealing with.'

The key to recognising this second type of not knowing is to spot the discomfort that the person feels when they move out of not knowing into in-between-ness. The anxiety and sadness they feel when 'what if . . .?' worries arise in their mind might present as moodiness or questions; as panic about symptoms or a disinclination to socialise; as reassurance-seeking; as any manner of changes in the person's usual character or behaviour.

Broaching in-between-ness is often not about confrontation so much as arriving at a shared understanding. This is a gentle conversation that involves mentioning the changes that we have observed in the person and asking them what they signify. It helps us to recognise and understand someone's voluntary escape into not knowing, and it invites them to express their anxieties about the times when they find themselves wondering 'what if . . .?'

My great-uncle who set out dinner for his dead wife was known to us all as 'Unc'. Our conversation about his behaviour went a bit like this:

'Can I help you set the table, Unc?' I am hovering in his tiny kitchen, aware that the Conversation I have come for is rushing towards us both. I feel tense because I know this; he is relaxed and smiling because he is unaware that I am on a family mission.

'The knives and forks are in the top drawer,' he says. 'Give Auntie Al her favourite plate, too, that one with the roses on it.' I take three sets of cutlery from the drawer and carry them through to the dining room; I put three place mats on the table.

'Unc, which seat is yours? Where shall I put Auntie Al's plate?' I ask, holding my voice steady.

'She always sat by the window,' Unc replies from the kitchen, where he is stirring a pan of soup, 'and I sit opposite her.' *Sat, past tense. Sit, present tense.*

'Do you always set her a place?' I ask, innocently, as though the family has not been abuzz with this behaviour. 'Every meal,' he confirms, standing in the doorway. 'It's my way of honouring her. I got her those flowers yesterday,' he continues, nodding towards the vase of roses on the table. 'She always loved yellow roses.' *Loved, past tense.*

'Unc, do you think it's unusual to be setting a place for her after so long?' I ask. He is carrying a tray with two bowls of soup on it towards the table. He sets the tray down, puts one bowl on his plate and one on mine. Auntie Al isn't getting any soup, I note. He straightens his back and turns towards me.

'I miss her every minute of every day,' he says. His voice cracks and he turns to carry the tray back into the kitchen. He reappears carrying pepper and salt mills, and gestures to the chair I am to sit in. As we take our seats, he pours us water and raises his glass to the table. 'Lovely to have you here, Kathryn,' he says. 'Auntie Al and I are very proud of you.' I feel a moment of intense emotion: their love has been a constant for as long as I can remember, and they were both so proud of me getting into medical school. Auntie Al died halfway through my training; and now I have been qualified for two years. I feel his love. And, I realise with a start, I feel *her* love, too. In making her present at this meal, we have opted for a shared not knowing, and a moment of beautiful communion with her. I get it before he explains it to me: the comfort of a short time of not knowing, as an island in the sadness of the truth. He chooses to move between knowing and not knowing. His marriage is his lifelong consolation.

Terry's mum seemed to be in a different situation from Unc's voluntary not knowing. She knew she had a heart condition; her family had observed her increasing frailty and weariness; nobody knew what she thought about this herself. One daughter thought her mum looked afraid sometimes, and maybe had guessed how sick she was; one daughter thought any discussion of dying would kill their mum; one thought talking about dying with their mum would change everything with no way back. Terry's expertise from his work had, interestingly, been discounted by at least one of his sisters. She's Big Sis. Cross her if you dare!

'I've decided to invite Big Sis over next time it's my weekend to look after Mum,' Terry tells me. 'We so rarely get a chance to talk face to face. And I hope I might help her to listen to Mum, instead of bombarding her with relentless cheerfulness. I've advised so many families about telling the truth with gentleness, but I never realised how hard it feels when you are dealing with people you love!' I feel my friend's anxiety. After a long time talking about families: the theory, here he is stuck in families: the practical. We reflect on the situation.

Terry knows that his Big Sis, Ros, loves Mum dearly. Although he doesn't share her conviction that talking about dying would kill their mother, he knows that his sister is speaking from a kind heart and from a lifetime of being the Big Sister, a role she takes very seriously. Terry's years in nursing have given him experience and wisdom about discussions of life and death, but he also knows that confronting his sister directly is more likely to lead to disagreement than to a new, shared understanding. This is a dance they have been joined in for decades.

Ros is also experiencing in-between-ness. By avoiding discussion of their mother's deteriorating health, she is able to not know in front of Mum and preserve cheerful, 'when you feel better' discussion, and yet also to know that Mum is dying and so begin to prepare herself for being Big Sister during the inevitable family bereavement. Choosing in-between-ness is a common tactic in families facing the deterioration and death of a person they love.

The difference is that family members adopting voluntary in-between-ness is not the same as imposing not knowing on the sick person. Terry wants to understand whether Mum is as frightened as his other sister has suggested; he wants Big Sis to be involved in that conversation so that she can observe that Terry is inviting, not demanding, a discussion with Mum. He knows he has the skills to open this conversation with Mum, but he hopes that he can model a style of communicating in front of Big Sis that will be useful for her, too, in Mum's future care. He wants to show her a different way to dance, one he uses every day at work. Let's see how it goes.

'Let's have a cup of coffee with Mum,' says Terry when Big Sis arrives. He has ensured Mum had a morning snooze to be as alert as possible for this conversation. He suggests that Big Sis has the chair beside Mum's bed; he sits at the end of the bed, so he can see both women as he is speaking.

'Hello, Rosalind,' says Mum, who always uses their full names. 'Terence said you were coming. He's cooking something delicious for lunch.' She smiles at her oldest daughter with a wide mouth and sad eyes. Wistfully, she adds, 'I hope I can manage a bit to eat today.'

Big Sis kisses Mum's cheek and sits down. Terry has brought two mugs of coffee and Mum's favourite small cup, and the three-some sip their drinks.

'I'm sure you'll manage a huge bowl of Terry's pot-roast!' says Ros, encouragingly. Mum smiles wanly and shrugs.

'Are you worried about your appetite, Mum?' asks Terry. There is a pause. Ros draws breath to speak, and Terry shakes his head at her. She exhales, deflated, and glares at him over the rim of her mug.

'I find it hard to eat much at all,' says Mum eventually. 'I used to have such a big appetite, too.' Terry nods and sips his coffee. He allows the silence to sit, uninterrupted, for a while.

'A lot of things seem different recently, don't they, Mum?' he says. 'What other changes do you notice?'

Big Sis stiffens but waits in silence until Mum says, 'I am as feeble as a flea. I've got no energy at all. Have you noticed that, Rosalind?' Mum turns her tiny, folded face towards her firstborn.

Ros rushes to say, 'But you'll start to feel better soon, Mum, I'm sure.'

There is another silence before Terry says, 'Does the weariness worry you, Mum?' He fixes a stare on Ros that tells her to stay quiet.

'Well, I can hardly get out of bed at all these days,' says Mum. 'I don't know what will become of me. I don't, really!' She looks down the bed to Terry, and adds, 'Have you seen people as bad as me at work, Terry?'

'Mum!' says Ros, before Terry can draw breath. 'You know Terry doesn't look after people like you! His patients all have bad lungs. It's not the same thing at all.' Terry gently moves up the bed so he can take hold of Mum's hand, sitting closer to Ros's chair. He waits a moment before answering.

'I do see people who run out of energy like this, Mum, yes,' he begins. Ros moves as though to speak again, but Terry reaches out to touch her wrist very gently. 'Some of my patients get quite worried about it. So. . . I wonder whether it worries you, too?'

Mum looks down at her pale, wasted hands, resting on Terry's pink, plump palm.

'I'm getting thinner. I'm getting weaker. I get breathless. I think this can only end one way . . .' and she blinks tears from her eyes.

'What do you mean, Mum?' asks Terry, gently, offering her a tissue then reaching out to take his sister's hand. They are joined like a line of cut-out paper dolls as Mum says, 'I think I might die. I think every night that one of you might find me dead in the morning . . . and I feel bad for whoever it is. I hate to think of upsetting you like that . . .' and she scrunches the tissue to her eyes.

Terry glances at Ros. She is bright pink; she is biting her lip and her brows are creased with the effort of not crying. He squeezes her hand, then turns back to Mum and asks, 'How long have you been worrying about that, Mum?'

'Oh, for months,' she sighs. 'It's obvious to me. But everyone else seems to think things are fine, and I don't want to upset people by talking about dreary things, so we just stay cheerful, don't we?' She looks appealingly at Ros, who sniffs and smiles at her.

Then Ros says, 'Mum, I had no idea you were so frightened!' She leans across to place her hand on Mum's, making a sandwich with Terry's hand beneath. She steadies herself by placing her other hand on Terry's shoulder. A tear runs down her nose and drips onto the bed. 'Why didn't you say?'

Mum's gaze beams back at Ros. 'I was being brave, darling,' she says. 'Like you were. Keep Calm and Carry On. Don't Mention It. It was a way of coping, wasn't it?' Mum rubs Ros's hand and squeezes it. 'I think the other girls might suspect as much,' continues Mum, 'but I didn't think you realised how bad things were, Rosalind, and I didn't want to upset you.'

There is a long pause. Mum leans back into her pillows. She closes her eyes. Terry stands up and lifts Mum's cup of cold coffee off her bedside table. He takes Ros's mug, and says, 'I'm going to check that pot-roast in the kitchen.'

'Mum, thanks for telling us all that. It really helps to understand how you feel. If you want to talk some more later, I'll be happy to. But just now, I think Ros needs a hug.' Mum smiles behind closed eyes and says, 'I feel better already. It was lonely keeping secrets. I kept hoping I was imagining things were worse. I kept hoping we were right when we talked about feeling better soon. But in my heart I knew things were bad, and sometimes at night I get terrified . . .'

Ros kneels beside the bed and gathers Mum towards her. Terry leaves them to be together in the new world of Shared Truth. He knows their love will guide them through these next steps in their new dance. There's more to be done, more to talk about. But that's in the land of Knowing, and there's still time for all that.

Anxiety can be a disabling emotion. In thinking about future possibilities, the mind presents a menu of undesirable options, some less likely than others. The frightening thoughts, whether of illness and death (Terry's mum), loss and distress (Big Sis) or more everyday fears like changes at work, the safety of our family or friends, taking an exam or a job interview, trigger both the emotions of anxiety, fear or dread and bodily responses caused by anxiety-induced hormones: tense muscles leading to stiffness, pain and headaches; rapid heart rate, breathlessness, dry mouth, that familiar 'sinking feeling' in the tummy; and for some of us even nausea, vomiting and diarrhoea. Anxiety is an unpleasant emotional and physical experience: no wonder people try not to entertain their anxious thoughts, retreating into avoidance and inaction.

Enabling someone to spend time thinking about their anxious thoughts allows them to examine the thoughts for what they are: imaginary visions of the future. Just because we think it, does not make it true in every detail. The upsetting thoughts are often images, frequently containing a grain of truth wrapped in a large parcel of conjecture: jumping to the worst possible interpretation, discounting any possibility of coping with an anticipated challenge, mental pictures of future suffering, or humiliation, or of being overwhelmed.

By using helpful questions to allow somebody to identify their anxiety-inducing thoughts and then staying present, curious and supportive while they process those thoughts, we can enable them to separate the conjecture and assumptions from the grain of truth, and to begin formulating their plan for dealing with that truth. Our own impulse to reassure and to rescue someone can feel very strong when we are listening to their fears. This is a time to give away our power: finding their own solution is the only convincing support for someone who is dealing with anxiety. Our reassurance may ease their distress for a few minutes, but understanding how to face their fear and to reason through to their own solutions is a far longer-lasting consolation.

Anxiety is a future-focused emotion, a prediction that something unpleasant is waiting to happen. Attempts not to think about it are rarely successful, leaving the person in a state of 'free-floating anxiety' without the focus of a specific thought to tackle. By helping them to name the thing they are dreading ('What's the worst thing that could happen?' 'What concerns you most about that?' 'Is there something worse than that?') and then looking at the likelihood of it happening, at what resources the person has to cope if it does, at how they could prepare themselves to deal with it, they can move from paralysing anxiety to problem-solving action. Whether that is a plan for tackling exam revision or a family conference to discuss a terminal illness, problem-solving action moves us from anxiety towards coping.

End-of-life Planning

I am frequently asked, 'How do I get my parent [or partner, or older relative] to talk to me about their future wishes? I don't know whether they have even thought about it.' This is then followed by either 'If I try to bring it up, they shut me down' or 'I don't want to make them upset by bringing it up.'

Digging deeper into these questions often brings some helpful insights. The I-don't-want-to-upset-them idea assumes that the person has not contemplated their own mortality, and yet in 2018 a large UK survey found that around 90 per cent of respondents had thought about their own mortality, with those aged over sixty the most comfortable in talking about dying. Many people who ask me about talking to their older relatives are interested to find out that I am just as frequently asked those same questions by older people, or by people with limited life expectancy, but this time about how to engage their younger family members and people likely to outlive them, in conversations they seem keen to avoid. We are all trying not to upset each other, and it's upsetting each other!

There are useful things to bear in mind:

Invite, don't insist: perhaps raise it as something you would like to hear their views about, whether it is your own death and your wishes and preferences you would like to share, or their wishes that you would like to explore. Sometimes news stories or TV shows touch on a subject we can pick up for discussion, or the experience of someone they know offers a way in.

Let parents be parents: older people often feel grateful to have extra support, but they can feel infantilised if their helpers treat them as helpless instead of the wise, experienced if slightly less agile people they are. If parents are avoiding a discussion about illness, dying, funeral wishes and place of care to protect their (adult) children, it can be helpful for those children to share their own worry: no kind parent wants to cause their children concern.

'Dad, there's something troubling me, and I wonder if I could talk to you about it . . . I worry that if you got very sick, the doctors might ask me how you want to be treated and, well . . . to be honest, I wouldn't know what to say. Do you think we could sit and talk it over some time, for my peace of mind?' That is an invitation, the subject is clear, and it is an appeal from a child to their parent. It's up to Dad now.

I have also seen how adult grandchildren can be useful as intermediaries. The bond between youngsters and their grandparents or other venerable family members is precious: once, when we had done something so naughty that we could not tell a parent, we could still rely on a grandparent or other older relative to be our advocate. It turns out that this works just as well in reverse a few decades later: those bonds of affection that are slightly less enmeshed than in a parent-child relationship can be called upon for support.

'Mum, I know it makes you sad to talk about it, but Granny really needs to tell you about her funeral arrangements. Could you help her by just sitting down to listen?'

Of course, for 'parents' here we can use any relationship in which our distress would be a source of concern to the other person. Telling someone who cares about us that we have a worry induces their desire to help us to solve it. It lets them help us, and that helps us to support them in return.

Listen, check, write it down: making plans for the way we would like to be looked after towards the end of our life is sensible and prudent. Only immortals need not bother with this task. The likelihood is that if we become unwell, we may feel too ill to give our views, so planning ahead, telling the people who are closest to us, and writing it down, are all helpful actions. If you discuss your wishes, ask the people you tell to repeat them back to you to be certain that they have understood what matters most to you. Write it down, or ask them to write it down.

No one can speak for you unless you appoint them formally. In the different parts of the UK the laws are slightly different, but most allow us to appoint one or several attorneys who can make decisions about our healthcare or living arrangements on our behalf if we lose the capacity to decide for ourselves. Loss of capacity might be temporary (just too sick to talk, but recovering later) or permanent (after a brain injury or because of dementia, for example). People are often surprised that their next of kin, their spouse or partner of more than sixty years, their dearest friend, has no right to speak on their behalf without this power of attorney. It is not a complicated process, and the forms to apply are available online.* The Citizens Advice Bureau, Age UK and other organisations also offer help and advice about the process.

Our attorneys need to understand what matters most to us. There may be some specific treatments that we would wish to refuse, and circumstances in which we would refuse or accept others: some people will never accept treatments made with animal products; others would not accept a blood transfusion; some would decline the use of a ventilator. That list can be written as an 'Advance Decision to Refuse Treatment' (ADRT),† and if we sign it and ask someone to witness our signature (they don't need to read the ADRT), it will be valid and must be applied in the circumstances we specify. If we would refuse a treatment even

---

* https://www.gov.uk/power-of-attorney for UK.
† https://www.nhs.uk/conditions/end-of-life-care/advance-decision-to-re-fuse-treatment/ for UK.

when that refusal means accepting the risk of dying, we must say so in the ADRT to avoid our wishes being overridden.

It is almost impossible to imagine every potential decision about treatment or care that may face us in the future. We can list the few 'never do this' or 'would only accept this if . . .' wishes in an ADRT, or include them as instructions to our attorney: things they must obey. For everything else, though, it makes it more likely that our attorney(s) can respect our wishes if we explain the values and preferences that make our lives feel worthwhile. Then, if a health or care decision is needed, they can look for the choices that would best help us to live in the way we wish. What our attorneys need is a chance to listen to us talk about what matters most to us: what gives us pleasure, what brings us peace of mind and what makes life feel worth living.*

There is a lot to talk about: a conversation like this may take several sittings. It is worth the time and effort to get the details right for someone's future, including our own. Conversations about the things that matter most to us: these are conversations about the good things in life, and they are exchanges to look forward to.

---

* There is a helpful website about 'What matters to me' conversations at https://www.whatmattersconversations.org/

Unwelcome News

Nobody enjoys breaking news that causes distress. There are times when giving unwelcome news cannot be avoided. It may be a temporary blow or a tragedy, or anywhere in-between. It can be difficult for the bearer of such news to understand what the significance of their tidings might be for the people they tell: sometimes a serious diagnosis is a relief as it makes sense of unexplained symptoms and puts an end to uncertainty; sometimes a seemingly minor setback is perceived as an overwhelming blow to a person's hopes and dreams.

The armed forces and the police have the unenviable task of contacting families with unexpected news of death or injury, dealing with the wretched uncertainty of investigating when someone is missing, and keeping their loved ones apprised of the facts as investigations proceed. Medical staff, paramedics and other clinicians must communicate serious illness and death, often in unexpected circumstances.

People who have received unwelcome news may have the difficult task of passing the news on to family and friends, who may also be distressed in their turn. The news is what the news is: the truth cannot be changed. The tender task, then, is to communicate it in a way that allows the people hearing it to take it in and to understand it, with all the associated distress that it must cause, without causing them to be so shocked that a further brutal injury is added to their experience.

The events of 2020 and the Covid-19 pandemic brought this task home in healthcare in a particularly challenging way. Infection control meant restricting visitors in hospitals. Instead of watching events unfold, with regular updates to confirm their concerns that their beloved person was not doing well, was deteriorating, might be dying, families were absent and patients' progress was communicated by phone or video calls to their loved ones, often by staff who were not used to looking after such sick patients or to talking about dying and death. Families were left distraught; staff were distressed; this was a lose-lose situation.

The NHS in England and Wales asked for help to guide staff through these conversations, and a small band of clinicians pulled together a framework to enable nurses, doctors and other information-givers to manage these most tender conversations with care for the person they were talking to. We used evidence from conversation analysis research,* a discipline that analyses video-taped conversations between clinicians and patients, then dissects the interaction to pinpoint what aspects of the clinician's behaviour, language and communication contributed to the patient finding the encounter safe and illuminating or unsafe and damaging. This resource allowed us to describe a framework for the supportive breaking of unwelcome news.†

There were many barriers to communication for Covid conversations. If one or two family members were permitted to visit a possibly dying patient on compassionate grounds, all parties to a conversation would be wearing masks that covered nose, mouth and most of the face. Professionals would be in personal protective equipment (PPE): aprons, gloves and visors in some areas, full hazmat suits and helmets in others. Most of the cues of facial expression were lost; voices were strained to speak loudly enough through masks; the simple, consoling act of ungloved hand-holding was forbidden.

---

* We received generous and expert help from the Real Talk team at Loughborough University https://www.realtalktraining.co.uk/
† The framework and tools can be accessed at https://www.ahsnnetwork.com/helping-break-unwelcome-news

When medical conversations may be distressing, we usually try to hold them in person. Now the world was different and telephone calls became the main link between families and hospital staff, or between families and the community nursing and medical services that were overwhelmed by the numbers of sick people at home. Families used patients' mobile phones to stay in touch because visiting was limited or banned, but breathless people are unable to speak for long, and the noise of piped oxygen makes it difficult for families to discern the sick person's breathless words. Many people stepped up to become the go-betweens in hospitals, from healthcare students to long-qualified nurses, allied health professionals to receptionists, social workers and psychologists; in residential care homes, this enormous task fell to staff already overwhelmed by the isolation of their residents and without extra pairs of hands to support them. In helping patients to have telephone conversations or video calls, repeating family messages if patients were struggling to hear or repeating patient messages that they were struggling to say, these helpers became witnesses to moments of family tenderness and intimacy that we rarely access: feeling intrusive, awkward and overcome by the necessity of this precious and heartbreaking task.

Staff needed to make phone calls that told families their beloved person was improving, and then a few days later that they were deteriorating again. They needed to explain that their patient was struggling to breathe so much that they were being helped by non-invasive ventilation (a machine providing oxygen-enriched air at high pressure through a tight mask, to 'breathe with' a struggling patient) or to inform a patient's beloveds that, unable to manage alone any longer, the patient was about to be transferred to an intensive care unit (ICU) for sedation, intubation and the support of a mechanical ventilator. They sometimes needed to explain that the patient was unlikely to survive. They needed to tell families that the patient had died. And they were having similar, distressing conversations with many families, many times every day.

Finding a framework for these conversations was important for two reasons. All staff want to do their best for patients and families. Breaking unwelcome news is an important task, and we want to do it as supportively and as well as we can, so that we ensure the family member has understood the news, been able to ask their questions and felt supported in their distress. It is a question of doing a tough and important job well. But the emotional demands on staff of these recurring and emotionally draining conversations were also a big concern: we want to keep our colleagues healthy and avoid burn-out. This was the important second reason for providing a framework for breaking unwelcome news: we wanted staff to feel that they were using an approach that was consistent and helpful to them, guiding their conversation and supporting them, and giving them something to use for reflection and debriefing in supervision and support sessions. Just like this book: principles to guide a discussion, framed in their own words.

The framework we described included some important, but not surprising, components and many are laid out in this book. Compassion, and how to communicate it despite masks or phone calls; use of questions to find out what the person knows and what they might (or might not) be expecting; eliciting their sense of the 'story' of the illness so far, so that the news-breaker brings them towards an understanding that unwelcome news is likely; use of simple language when our latest news is added, in the context of what has already happened; use of silence and short messages of support while the news is absorbed and its implications become apparent; using questions to help the person to decide what to do after our phone call, and giving information as needed; using compassion in ending the call; and taking a moment for self-care afterwards: there were two people in that conversation, and both of them may be hurting at the end of it. Self-compassion seems an indulgence when our teammates are busy, yet we all benefit if we give each other this time for recovery.

I was the only member of the small team not engaged in delivering patient care during Covid-19. My return to the NHS was in a staff-support capacity, and I felt both sad and relieved not to be working at the bedsides, in those dedicated and exhausted teams. Instead my experience and care were being delivered by other people's voices, and as I travelled around the hospital to hear their stories and glean the inside information I needed to be a useful support to them, I was overcome by admiration for a workforce that was frightened and weary, but resolute in compassion and care.

Person after person, team after team, talked about how overwhelming the task was of repeatedly giving unwelcome news, discussing poor prognosis, describing dying. With the palliative care service I had worked in so happily before retirement, we had devised communication skills training for staff aimed specifically at these conversations. The sessions were designed with the least experienced staff in mind: recently qualified nurses, and doctors who had accepted early registration in order to support the Covid-19 effort, having been medical students only weeks before. The response was astonishing: we were overwhelmed by requests, and staff from the least to the most experienced attended, all wanting to share an opportunity to think about how to manage these poignant and tender conversations, to practise the skills in the safety of a socially distanced lecture theatre, to share their experiences and pool their wisdom. Using a skills-practice format, we gave staff a chance to get it right and to feel less anxious, or perhaps more helpfully to get it wrong and to find a way to rescue the situation: with the support of their colleagues in those lecture theatres to practise their skills, and the encouragement of their organisation to take time away from their clinical busyness in order to enhance their skills, they were able to hone the important craft of tender conversations. Just like dancing, learning communications skills requires us to practise the steps, to make mistakes, and to get better as we learn to avoid the trips and to keep our balance when we turn. By offering a compassion-centred framework as the music to this most unwelcome dance, staff were able to focus on providing 'truth with kindness'. That is the core message of breaking unwelcome news.

One of the most disconcerting experiences of walking around the hospital in the summer of 2020 was the silence. As a newly qualified doctor, I used to love the silence of nightshifts: the echoing tap of shoes on parquet floors in the tall, Victorian corridors announcing the approach of the night sister to check the ward; or the long walk to the emergency room from the dimly lit ward, along a corridor illuminated for action yet deserted; the reassuring quiet of a hospital keeping watch. Now, in daylight, the silence was uncanny. No anxiously bewildered visitors looking for directions; no bored out-patients seeking the X-ray department or the sweet shop; no cheery porters chatting to the occupants of wheelchairs as they whizzed them between departments. Very few staff, everyone confined to their individual zones where they now stayed behind the closed doors, wrapped in PPE in the summer heat. Biohazard signs and yellow tape at ward entrances. Silence that was a grim reminder of the danger of simply entering a building full of people who were sick enough to die, their bodies manufacturing millions of virus particles and coughing them into the hospital air.

A woman is approaching from afar along the daylit corridor. She is in scrubs, her face masked, her visor lifted so it decorates her head like a space-age halo. She waves at me – there is no one else in the corridor – but I don't recognise her until she is closer. Megan: I remember her as a student nurse on placement with our palliative care team a few years ago. Now she is qualified and living through what will probably be the most difficult year in her whole career.

'Oh, I'm so glad I've seen you!' she says when we are close enough to converse despite our masks. 'I came to the communication skills training, and I have a question. Have you got a few minutes?' The correct answer is obviously yes, and I change direction to walk with her to the café where she is planning to take her twenty-minute break. 'Sister is making us all leave the ward for breaks,' she explains. 'We're supposed to go in pairs but we're short today, someone's off sick.' In answer to my raised eyebrows (it is hard to read facial expressions behind our masks), she hurriedly assures me that it is not Covid-19, only a bad cold. 'But you can't work with your nose and eyes streaming when you can't take off your mask for hours,' she adds.

The café is not charging staff for beverages and Jane, the counter server who has looked after us all for as long as I can remember, dispensing kindness with every cup, whips up our coffees while we wait by the counter, one metre apart. One at a time we pick up our drinks and head to a table where the chairs have been arranged two metres apart; we slump into our seats and remove our masks. I feel we are too far away from each other: this is anti-social distancing. Megan's nose is blistered by the more rigid mask she must wear when she is fully kitted out in bedside PPE. Damaged skin across nose and cheekbones has become a common sight around the hospital, hidden away while we are at work but declaring itself as staff sniff the outside air, unmasked at last, after they finish their shifts.

'The framework,' Megan says, launching straight into her question. 'It's so helpful to have an order to say things in. But . . . but . . . what if I get upset while I'm talking?' She is gazing at me, and her eyes are swimming with tears.

'In theory?' I ask, but sensing the answer. 'Or did that happen?'

She sips her coffee, then slowly rotates the cardboard cup in front of her on the table, staring at its frothy contents as she speaks.

'We had this patient, about a week ago: a man the same age as my dad, early sixties, worked in the university as a groundsman, helps keep that gorgeous garden in the quad near the high street, you know the one?' I do; it's where my friends and I all posed for our graduation photographs, as graduates have done for a century. It is a public footpath across university grounds, where town and gown meet, and has always been a place of peace: landscaped gardens between red-brick buildings, approached via ornate arches and offering sanctuary from the jostling shops, the frantic university, the traffic noise; rustling branches and birdsong in the heart of the city.

'He had been breathless at home and he came in by ambulance, coughing and sweating and exhausted. He hadn't realised that his wife wasn't allowed to come in the ambulance with him, he must have been too poorly to pay attention as he left home and once he got the oxygen on and came to a bit, he realised he hadn't said goodbye to her. So he got to our ward and he wasn't too bad on high-flow oxygen and I told him once we'd got him settled we could get him on the wi-fi so he could call his wife.'

I nod. Megan continues, 'So he's in bed, and he's got a high-flow mask on, and he's hot but his pulse and blood pressure are OK and his oxygen levels are mid-eighties – you know, some people are way lower than that, but I know it's not great and he'll need a doctor to reassess him, so I get out of my PPE to go and give my report. And then the alarm goes on my pager and he's crashed and the doctors are intubating him and all I can think is, *He still hasn't spoken to his wife.*'

She pauses. The coffee is cooling as she continues to rotate the cup, a restless fidgeting to dissipate her distress. 'So there he goes, up to ICU – which isn't in ICU, it's on the old burns ward because we have so many people on ventilators. And I'm his escort, and when I've handed him over, his ICU nurse asks whether his family knows yet and . . .' Megan stops rotating the cup. She looks up, along the two metres of table, and says, 'I knew it had to be me. I was the one he had told about his wife. About her favourite rose in the quad, about not saying goodbye. So I offered to do it, and the ICU nurse said that would be good, and that he would come with me to answer any ICU questions, and then their doctor would call his wife when they had more news.

'They have the Unwelcome News framework pinned on the wall by their nurses' station,' she continues. 'So they can follow it as they make their call. So we went through it together, and I was going to talk and he was going to support me. We knew we had to tell his wife what had happened, and that there would be more news later. So I called, and I did the Begin bit, you know – said my name, and I was calling from the hospital, and asked if she was his wife and asked her name; she was called Jennifer. He'd been calling her "Jin" but maybe that was a nick-name. Anyway, I usually don't know where to start, but that way of beginning by asking her to say what she already knew really helped. She said she thought he had Covid because he'd had such a bad cough and he was hot and then he just couldn't get his breath and that's when she called an ambulance and . . .' Megan looks back at the cup, as though surprised to discover it there.

'Why not take another swig of that, Meg?' I suggest. This isn't much of a coffee break for her. But we are doing something else, something important, and I don't want to rush her. She sips some coffee and then continues.

'So she's already told me how ill he was. She was worried about him, and she'd told the story up to the ambulance crew saying he'd need to get to the hospital. And then she said . . .' Megan's eyes are brimming again. 'She said . . . one of the paramedics said to her, "Do you want to give him a cuddle before he goes?" and she said he didn't like a fuss so she would just go and get his pyjamas, while they pushed him out of the door on a trolley . . .

and when she got to the front door they were closing the ambulance doors and she realised she hadn't said goodbye.'

Megan sighs, a deep and shuddering breath and her tears are too fast to stem. Resolutely, though, she continues her story, and tells me, 'I knew this was important, and so I told her that he was worried that he hadn't said goodbye either, and he'd been going to phone her, but he'd got more sick and now we had brought him to ICU so a ventilator could help his breathing. And do you know what she said? She said she wasn't surprised, because things looked bad as he left. And then . . .' Megan sniffs loudly, and clears her throat, 'and then she asked me if he was going to die.' There is a long pause. I wait. Megan is rotating the cup again, shaking her head as though in some internal dispute with herself.

'And then . . .?' I ask, cautiously, into the silence.

'And then I started to cry,' she says, 'and I felt really weak and stupid. I'm supposed to be a professional. And I'm sitting with this ICU nurse, who must have to make calls like this all the time. I was just so sad about their story.'

The two metres distance between us is telescoping in two directions at once: like Alice in Wonderland I sense the table extending, pushing us apart as I see her far, far away from me, and at the same time I feel the weight of her sorrow as though it occupies my own heart. I can only sit and wait alongside her, at the permitted distance, aware that the families currently sitting in the car park – because they are not allowed inside the hospital with their loved ones – would accept two metres' proximity in a heartbeat. I know that Megan's sorrow and both our tears are about this enforced separation, this desperate rule that makes medical sense yet rips our hearts apart.

To show her I am listening, not only to her words but to the emotions behind them, I repeat back to Megan, 'You were talking to your patient's wife, and she told you how bad things seemed to her, so bad that she asked you whether he was going to die.

Her question moved you to tears. And then, I think, you felt frustrated with yourself. Have I got that right?'

Megan nods, wiping her eyes and blowing her nose with one of the unforgiving dining-room napkins.

'I apologised for crying,' she says, 'to the wife, I mean. I didn't look at the ICU nurse. But then he passed me a box of tissues, and somehow that made me feel a bit less . . . unprofessional . . . less stupid.'

I nod. I have worked in our ICUs, offering support to patients, families and staff. The emotions are the same, the nursing heart is just as tender. I picture my ICU colleagues, who are used to snatching terribly sick people from the jaws of death, using technology, skill and care to sustain their patients with failing organs for long enough for the miracle of recovery to take place; who have such a reputation for saving lives. Now, during Covid-19, they are seeing deaths in numbers they have never encountered before. Of course there is a box of tissues at the nurses' station.

'I managed to tell her that he seemed safe for now, and that once the ICU team had finished assessing him, another person would call and keep her updated. And then she said . . .' Megan's eyes spill over again, and her face contorts with the effort not to cry. 'She said . . . she was glad there was someone who would cry for them both . . . that she felt reassured that we would *love* him for her . . . oh . . .' And saying *love* finishes her off. She puts her head on her hands on the table and I watch her heaving shoulders as she sobs, at an impossible, unreachable distance. My eyes are filling, too. So often we skate around what is most important. But in the end, what is breaking all our hearts is the familiar love that must be absent from these bedsides, and the love my colleagues are bringing to bridge that gap.

'I'm sorry,' she says, lifting her face briefly. 'This has been going round and round in my head all week. I keep hearing her voice, saying how glad she feels that we will love him for her . . .

'Anyway, I managed to get some deep breaths in while I listened to her, as she just kept saying she loved him, and I said we would do our best, and that the ICU team would stay in touch. And then we said goodbye, and the model says "self-care" after the call, but I still cry every time I think about it.'

'Meg,' I am working hard to hold my voice steady, 'when we started talking, you said you were worried about getting upset when we have to give difficult news. You've just described such a heartbreaking story. May I ask you a couple of questions?'

She fixes a sorrowful gaze on me, pursing her lips as she nods in assent.

'First question: did you tell me the answer to your question as you told me your story?' She rests her chin on her hands as she looks past me towards the café window to consider her answer. As she thinks, I watch her face: eyes flicking and blinking as she unfiles her inner thoughts and re-sequences them. Her back straightens, and she sighs.

'Yes,' she says, at last. 'Yes. His wife told me the answer, didn't she? She was consoled that I cried. She didn't care whether it was unprofessional. She only cared that someone was looking out for her husband. It actually helped her that I cried.'

We leave this idea to lie in the pool of sunlight on the table between us. Our own tenderness is not a weakness: it is a meeting point, a place where we are fully human in relation to someone else's distress. Megan was the bridge between lifelong partners who may never get to say goodbye, and she was discharging an act of love by being a connection between them.

'And that's at least the second time you've used the word unprofessional, Meg, so tell me a bit more about that,' I invite.

She tilts her head sideways on her palm as she blinks towards the sunny window. 'Yeah . . .' she says, slowly. 'Yeah . . . I think I wouldn't have felt so flustered by it on our ward. It was because it was ICU. They always seem so clever and controlled and – well, professional, to me.'

'And the box of tissues?' I ask.

She smiles. 'Yeah . . . turns out they cry, too. The ICU nurse is called Samir, and he's kept me updated after every shift, just to let me know that my patient . . . well, his patient . . . our patient – is still alive. And I know it's early days, and there are no promises. But I'm starting to think that this patient might get back to my ward, and might get back home, after all.'

Megan's coffee break is over and she must head back to the heat of her ward and her PPE. I watch her walk away, lost in her own thoughts between the café and her ward. It sounds to me as though she did a magnificent job: the power of a conversation is not what words Megan said, but what information she communicated, to that distressed wife. By connecting with the wife's hunch that her husband was very ill, they moved straight to a place where the most important things could be discussed. Not pulse rates and oxygen levels, but love.

Revelations

There are times when people need information that may cause them shock or concern. Rather than simply giving unfiltered facts, we help them best if we allow them to build the new information into their 'story so far.' This task requires careful listening in order to understand what they already know, what they want to know and what their concerns are as the bigger picture is built.

Ashley has a question. He isn't sure who to ask. He is fifteen, aspires to be a rock star and has exams next summer. His guitar skills are competent, and his family has been surprised at what a great singing voice he has since his angelic treble broke. A sonorous tenor with a good line in comic falsetto, he is a wow at his Rock School night classes. Everyone wants to know where he got his musical talents from. And so does he.

But who can he ask? Ashley has lived with his foster family since he was almost three years old. The care system is complex and he has been fortunate: the short-term rescue placement he arrived at with only pyjamas and a supply of nappies was with a family on the brink of changing from short-term to long-term fostering, so a stay of three months became one of thirteen years and counting, still safely held in love, and kindness, and those firm boundaries that teenagers appreciate by testing them to destruction. His birth family is forbidden to make contact with him; both his birth parents served time in prison for their failure to care for him. He gets Christmas cards and birthday letters from his maternal grandma, but his family is the mum, dad and brothers, Graham and Malcolm, who welcomed him to their home all those years ago. Although legally the adults he has chosen to call 'Dad' and 'Mum', Ken and Sheila, are foster carers rather than parents, Ashley identifies himself as an integral member of this family. His older brothers are married. They are sporty: one is a semi-professional footballer and the other a long-distance runner. Ashley is averse to sport, to moving too fast, to feeling cold or getting wet, to the Great Outdoors. But music, alone in the family, is his thing.

Like all 'looked-after' children, Ashley has a social worker. Pascal is the latest in a series of them, and Ashley likes him. Pascal comes from a British Caribbean family and he is a musician. It was Pascal who recommended the rock school that Ashley now enjoys so much; Pascal is one of the tutors there. Recently the rock school took over the local concert hall for an exhibition concert, and Ashley's band proved the star turn. His brothers came to support him, and their parents (banned by their teenage Rock Star) sneaked in at the back and were amazed at the power and confidence of his performance.

This evening Ashley is loitering after Rock School, trying to bump into Pascal casually. That is trickier than it sounds: Pascal is in his late twenties, athletic and musical, and surrounded by admirers. Ashley decides to wait by Pascal's car, which he recognises from the social worker's home visits.

'Right, Ash?' asks Pascal cheerfully, opening the boot to swing in his guitar case.

'All right, Pasc,' responds Ashley.

'Can I do something for you?' asks Pascal. 'You OK for getting home?' Ashley nods, and Pascal waits. Silence is his first question when tongue-tied teens are involved.

'Pasc, can I see my fostering files?' asks Ashley in a rush. There. He's said it. He feels relieved and tearful and disloyal and curious and . . . it's hard work being a teenager's emotion system.

'Whoa, that's big!' says Pascal, acknowledging that this is a conversation to be taken very seriously. 'How long have you been thinking about that?'

'For ages,' admits Ashley. 'But more often lately. I just wanna know about who I'm like. I'm not like my family, you know? So . . . who am I like?'

Pascal has had similar conversations many times in his professional life. He cannot carry every client's family history in his head, but Ashley's birth father was convicted of such horrible cruelty that Pascal remembers some of the details. This will be uncomfortable listening for a fifteen-year-old.

'Have you asked your mum and dad,* Ash?' says Pascal. He knows that this conversation will be easier for Ashley if he has support from his loving family while he hears uncomfortable truths about his birth family.

'We talk about it sometimes,' says Ashley. 'It's not a secret. But we did stuff in biology about genetic diseases last term, and I can't get some of it out of my head. How would I know if there was stuff like that in my family? And what if I'm a useless dad when I have my own kids? What if *that's* genetic? Or what if I might get some disease that needs treatment now to save me? And . . . why can I sing?' Pascal lets the questions hover in the air, waiting to see whether any other concerns bubble to the surface. When Ashley simply waits, Pascal says, 'OK, there are some things to find out about, Ash. How about this: you start by talking to Sheila and Ken, and when you're ready they can contact me to get the information out of the files?'

Ashley nods, impatiently. 'Yeah. Cool. So, like, next week, then?'

Pascal laughs. 'Hey, super-keen bean! As soon as I can, but no

---

* The UK's fostering and adoption system officially reserves the term 'parents' for birth family or for adopters. In practice, many fostered children come to regard their foster carers as their parents and they may call them 'Mum' or 'Dad', whether from fondness or to sound like their friends and schoolmates.

promises. And remember that I have to talk to Ken and Sheila, too.' Ashley rolls his eyes and Pascal smiles. 'It's the RULES, Ash. You know? Doing my job the way the law tells me to?'

'Did you want to keep it secret from them?' Pascal adds, serious now.

Ashley shakes his head. 'Nah, they need to know. They know some of it already, don't they? They aren't trying to stop me finding out, but they don't know the genetics answers and they can't say who I'm like.'

'OK,' says Pascal, moving towards the driver's door of his car. 'You chat with them, and then one of them can call me or email to ask for a meeting to talk about your files. OK?'

Ashley suddenly looks very young. 'Thanks, Pasc. Really appreciate it.'

'You are welcome, Ash. And great noise in there tonight, fella – you really rocked that soul number.' Ashley smiles, hoists his guitar case over his shoulder, and sets off to walk home. Pascal watches him leave, pensive. This is going to be a tough ride for Ashley. It's been waiting for him for thirteen years. And now it's time.

Pascal drives home thoughtfully. By holding space and asking simple questions, he has enabled Ashley to show he is serious in his request for answers. Keeping the tone light in a public car park was also important. Pascal skilfully managed the interaction so that the conversation did not accelerate into deep and emotional territory at a time and place that were not appropriate or safe. Pascal has also reminded Ashley that while he is willing to help, there are procedures they are bound to follow. He knows Ashley's foster carers are skilled and kind. They love Ashley, and he loves them. That's a fortunate place to be for a kid whose life started in such unpromising circumstances. But it will be tough for Ashley to discover a birth family history that is marked by neglect and cruelty.

As Pascal expected, it doesn't take long for the email request to arrive, and he reviews Ashley's file. The home visit is arranged, an evening, when Sheila looks anxious and Ken is quiet. Only Ashley is excited.

'OK, Ash, before we start,' Pascal invites, 'tell us what you can remember being told about your birth family. Then we'll check for extra information.'

Ashley recounts the story in the way it was told to him. He has a life-story book, made by Sheila, that tells his story and is updated each year by this devoted mum. For the last few years Ashley has contributed to the updates, providing photos from his phone of moments that he would like to remember. He has been hearing, and later reading or telling, this story since he was nearly three. It rolls off his tongue with familiarity.

'I know I was born in Crowbridge Hospital and my birth mum was only fifteen. To start off with she was going to have me adopted, but then she changed her mind . . . We lived with her mum, the granny who writes to me sometimes, Granny Hilary. I think things were OK for a while. But then my birth dad, who was older than my birth mum, started showing up and asking her to come and live with him. In the end she did.

'They didn't look after me very well. Sometimes that granny used to take me to her house for a few days to give them a break. She thought I was a bit skinny and she took me to the baby clinic. They said I wasn't getting enough food. So then a nurse called a health something . . .'

'Health visitor,' Sheila supplies, quietly.

'Yeah, a health visitor started to visit the flat where my birth parents lived and then they said they weren't looking after me properly, and then I think more people got involved and then I was sent to live with the granny all the time and my birth mum had to visit me there, but my birth dad wasn't allowed to visit the granny. I was very little, so I can't remember any of this.'

'You're doing great, Ash,' says Pascal. 'What else do you know?'

'Then my birth dad went away for a long time, more than a year, I think. I was about one. My birth mum moved back to her mum's house and the three of us lived together and the health visitor and all those people seemed to think that was better.

'But when I was two, my birth dad came back and made us move in with him again. And then lots of people got worried that he wasn't kind to us, and the granny kept telling people that we weren't safe. In the end the health visitor said I couldn't stay with them and I came here to live. I think they thought I would stay for a while until things were better at home. But things didn't get better there. My birth mum didn't know how to look after a kid, and my birth dad said the granny was interfering and then he did something bad. And then they said I would stay here always. And I have.

'I know their names: Jackie and Ross. I have some photos of them in my life-story book. She's only about the age I am now . . . I wouldn't have a clue how to look after a baby. I feel a bit sorry for her, to be honest . . . But he was a proper grown-up. He should have helped her more. So . . . I reckon I was lucky to get a good family here.'

There is a pause. Pascal waits, checking Sheila's and Ken's faces as he has done throughout Ashley's story. They are watching Ashley, nodding encouragingly. They have done a great job. This young man is secure in his new family, but there are details to fill in his back-story if he feels ready.

'That's pretty much the story, Ash. But there are a few gaps, aren't there? Times when your birth dad went away. Things your granny was worried about. Have you thought about what might have been going on there?'

'I thought maybe he got a job far away. I don't know what kind of job he did. Maybe he went abroad somewhere.'

'Do you have a sense of what kind of person Ross was?' asks

Pascal. Sheila clasps her fingers together. Ken purses his lips. Ashley sits, head bowed, and examines his fingernails. He sighs.

'He wasn't a good guy, was he? I mean, he was too old to be having sex with a fifteen-year-old, for a start. And he seems to have wanted things his way. When I was little and Mum used to tell me my story, I used to think he wanted both of us to live with him, but I'm old enough to realise he just wanted Jackie . . . He never wanted me. I must have been an inconvenience.'

Sheila flushes and blinks back tears. Over the last thirteen years she has told Ashley his story, gradually introducing new information when he asked questions and developing a script that has been refined and repeated down the years. She knows that the facts are dreadful, and she has tried to give Ashley an accurate back-story without telling him the extent of his birth father's failings. But she knows what is to be discussed now and she imagines this life-loving lad gradually working out that he was an *inconvenience*. It's a further harm wrought by an irresponsible and wicked man, she thinks angrily, mother-love overwhelming her compassion for Ross's own miserable early life. It is so hard to listen to Ashley working it all out. But listening is the foundation for what must follow. By listening, these adults are enabling Ashley to retell and reformulate his story. Helpful questions will offer him stepping stones towards an uncomfortable truth. Rather than tell him bald facts, they will give Ashley small pieces of truth for him to fill in the blanks in his own story. Ken reaches out to take Sheila's hand. Since the day they cried for joy when Ashley's long-term placement was confirmed and they stepped into the role of being his long-term family rather than short-stay carers, they have known this day would come.

'An inconvenience,' echoes Pascal. 'Is that how it seems to you?'

Ashley nods, and looks squarely at Pascal. 'He had no idea how to be a dad, did he? Not like my dad', and he nods at Ken, 'who is always there for all of us. He always thinks of what's best for us. Me and my brothers. All the same. He's a *real* dad. Someone to rely on. I wish I had *his* genes. I want to be like him.' Ashley is flustered by his public proclamation of admiration for this dad whom he loves and admires and fights against on a daily basis.

Ken simply nods at Ashley and says, 'Thanks, son,' before clenching his jaw to hold back his tears.

'I can see you're starting to read between the lines of the story of your early life, Ash,' says Pascal. 'The story is all true, but you already know it's not the whole truth. What other things have you thought about it?'

Ashley balls his fists. He lifts his face to look around the adults, and asks, 'Did he hurt us? Did Ross hurt Jackie and me?'

There is silence. Pascal asks, 'What makes you wonder, Ash?'

'Those people thought we weren't safe,' says Ash. 'When I was little, I thought it was because the flat was high in the air somewhere and it wasn't safe for a baby to crawl around a flat where he could fall out of the windows. But "not safe" doesn't mean that, does it? It's . . . it's about domestic abuse, isn't it?'

Ashley waits, and Pascal says simply, 'Yes, Ash. It is. Do you remember anything?'

Ashley shakes his head. 'I can't remember them at all. Even the photos don't remind me of them, really. I remember Granny Hilary, though. I remember she had a cat statue by her door, like a doorstop, I suppose. I used to talk to it and pretend it was real. I can remember she had a sandpit in her garden, too. I got sand in my eyes once and she sang to me while she poured water in my eyes to make them better. She always sang to me . . .

'Oh . . .

'*She always sang to me* . . .' and a new piece of Ashley's jigsaw slips into place. The singing. It comes from somewhere.

'That sounds like a happy memory, Ash. Do you have other memories?'

'Not of Ross or Jackie. Nothing at all.'

'When you first came here, Ash, you were afraid of the dark,' says Sheila. 'Granny Hilary sent that little night-light, the one with the mice in, because you liked it when you stayed at her house. Do you remember that?'

Ashley smiles and nods. 'I forgot it came from Granny Hilary,' he says. 'But I loved it when I was little, didn't I?'

'You talked about domestic abuse, Ash. But you don't remember any incidents, or feeling afraid?' asks Pascal.

Ashley cannot find any memories at all of the flat, of Ross's face or voice.

'You talked about Ross going away for a year, Ash. Any other ideas where he might have gone?'

Ashley heaves a deep sigh. 'Was he in prison?' he asks.

'Yes, Ash,' says Pascal. 'He was. He was on remand for three months because he hurt Jackie, and then he served nine more months. That's when you and Jackie moved back in with her mum.'

'And when he came out, he came and forced her to go back to him?' asks Ashley.

'Exactly. And that made people very worried, about your safety and Jackie's. Because he had a very bad temper, and when he got angry he was violent. He hit Jackie. And the health visitors think he squeezed your legs to hurt you when you cried. He gave you bruises. That's when you were taken away and brought here, to keep you safe.'

'Did she stay with him?' asks Ashley.

'For a while,' replies Pascal. 'But when the investigation showed he had hurt both of you, and that she had lied about it when the health visitors came to do their checks, he went back to jail.' Pascal pauses. 'And Jackie went to jail for a while, too. Not a long sentence, because she acted partly out of fear. But while you were safe here, they were both arrested. A case conference decided that, for your safety, you needed to be kept away from them. And you deserved a loving family. You *do* deserve a loving family, Ash.'

Ashley has his face in his hands. He sits still and quiet. His parents watch, silent and anxious. This must be hard to hear.

'Who else knows all this?' asks Ashley.

His mum speaks. 'Just Dad and me. We didn't know details: I knew they were sent to jail, but that's all. But the case was in the papers, so we got to know more then. It was hard to believe anyone could hurt you.

'Your brothers only knew you were a baby who needed a family. That's all they ever needed to know. They wanted to keep you. We wanted to keep you. And we will always keep you, Ash. You are ours, and I feel you always have been, even though you were nearly three when you joined us. We all love you and I feel very lucky that you are our son.'

Ashley stirs his long body from his seat and leans to embrace his mum. 'I know, Mum. I love you all, too. Even when I'm grumpy . . .' He laughs nervously as he steps back and sits down.

'Grumpy is nothing,' says Ken. 'We practised on grumpy teen-agers with your brothers. You're a pussy cat in comparison to Grumpy Graham!' They all laugh: Ashley's elder brother is famously incapable of anything but a frown before his breakfast.

Pascal picks up his bag and unzips it. 'Right, Ash. There are no more surprises in your file. Obviously the file can't be removed from the office but I have copies of relevant information in here . . . Do you want to ask anything else that we might need to look into?' He places a thin cardboard folder on his knee.

'Is that all you've got about me?' asks Ashley, incredulously.

'This isn't your file, Ash, this is just copies of information I am allowed to share,' says Pascal. 'Now, what are your questions? Do you need a break first?'

'Shall I make us coffee?' asks Sheila. Everyone approves. Ashley goes into the garden for some fresh air and thinking time, and Ken sits quietly with Pascal.

'Great job, Ken,' says the social worker. 'That's some man you've raised.'

'I'd give my life for him,' says Ken, and they sit together in thoughtful silence. Pascal reflects on the highs of his job, the care and diligence of foster carers, the turning around of damaged children's lives. There are awful days; there is harm that can never be resolved. But there are days like today, when the whole thing makes sense. Ken contemplates that declaration from Ashley, *He's a real dad. . . I want to be like him.* Some fathers might never hear those words in a lifetime. There's a glow in his heart.

They regroup around coffee. Ashley opts for cola. He likes his caffeine cold and fizzy. Pascal points at the folder on the table between them all, and asks again about Ashley's unanswered questions.

'It's medical things, mainly,' says Ashley. 'We learned this thing in biology about Huntington's Disease,* and if you get the gene you get the disease, and I don't know whether I might have the gene. How can we find out?'

Pascal takes a deep breath. He sits back in his chair, and says to the room in general, 'I knew you were going to ask that! It must be on the school curriculum because every person we talk to about family history is terrified of it. Here's the thing: first, it's very, very rare. Second, we have some family medical information, but we rely on birth families contacting us if health issues crop up that they think their birth children should know about. When a child is taken into care, we know they may end up brought up by another family so we gather all the medical information we can. Right . . . here's what we know.' Pascal opens the folder.

---

* Huntington's Disease is a rare genetic disorder that causes early-onset dementia, problems with coordination of movements and premature death.

There are photocopies of preprinted forms with handwritten answers; of printed forms, boxes neatly ticked; there are copies of faded photocopies of forms. There is a sheet of photocopied photographs: Ash recognises them, the same photos are in his life-story book. And there is the information he is looking for: Ash sees a medical history sheet.

'Jackie's brother has diabetes,' reads Pascal. Immediately he realises he has dropped a piece of information Ashley was not prepared to hear. They have not discussed any extended family. Pascal is annoyed with himself for giving information without checking first.

'Jackie has a *brother*?' says Ashley, just as Pascal feared he would. 'I have an *uncle*?' He pauses, brow wrinkled. 'Are there . . . are there any other family members I don't know about? Do . . . has . . . did . . . have I got brothers or sisters in that family?'

Sheila looks immensely relieved when Pascal says that there are no siblings the fostering team is aware of, although it's always possible that in the time since last contact Jackie or Ross may have gone into new relationships and had children. 'Do you want me to try to find out, Ash?' asks Pascal.

Ashley reflects. 'No. Not now, anyway. I have a family. I have brothers. There's no room for new people. No. Leave them alone. Don't let's get involved with them now.'

'So, back at the medical history, Ash, there's a relative with diabetes, and Jackie's granddad had a stroke when he was an old man. We haven't got much information about Ross's family. He doesn't seem to have had much contact with them.'

'I wonder whether he lost contact because he was angry and mean,' muses Ashley. 'Or whether he was angry and mean because he didn't have a good family. It makes a difference, doesn't it?'

'Yeah, Ash, it does. Good men show boys how to be good men. Maybe Ross had no good men in his life.'

'And I've got loads,' says Ashley. 'There's Dad, and Graham and

Malc. There's Grandpa and Uncle Reg. And there's you, Pasc, too. You're all very different, but you're all good men.'

'Thanks, Ash, that means a lot,' says Pascal, gathering the papers into the folder. 'We didn't find your music genes, did we?'

'Granny Hilary,' says Ashley. 'She was a singer. When I send her a photo this Christmas, I'm gonna send a Rock School photo and tell her I'm a singer, too. So I got one good thing from her family. But most good things came from here, didn't they? I'm sad for them, they had a hard life and they didn't get much of a chance.

'And look, I know who I'm like: I'm like Dad, and Malc and Graham. I know they can't sing like I do, and I can't play football like them, but we're all grumpy and we all can't wake up in the mornings and we all laugh at the same stupid jokes. This is my family. This is who I'm like. It would be good to find someone else who looks like me, but that's not as important as what I feel like. I feel like this family . . .' Sheila smiles at him and can't quite reach to take his hand.

'Yeah, so are we done here?' Ashley has heard enough, said enough, has big ideas to process. He is beginning to understand who he is. And he's been helped by people who have listened to him, provided information in digestible chunks and checked how he was processing it, not just today but for the last thirteen years. Listening to him making sense of himself, like all young people must. Building the jigsaw, one piece at a time.

Cross-Purposes

Tending to our differences is an important part of maintaining a relationship. When misunderstandings and disagreements arise, we can let them pass or we can bring them for discussion. Sometimes letting them pass can allow them to be forgotten but sometimes they sit within us like silent companions, pinpricks of hurt or rage, slowly and subtly changing our relationship with the other person. It is as though our steps are out of time: the dance continues but now we bump into one another when we used to anticipate and accommodate each other's every move. We become careful, guarded; despite yearning to re-establish that old, easy partnership we find ourselves always slightly at odds.

The longer the misalignment goes on, the harder it feels to mention it. We often use distancing tactics to prevent the need to discuss the change in our relationship, either holding ourselves aloof within our shared circle or even moving apart, avoiding contact in our attempts not to misstep, not to trip into exacerbating the hurt.

It is an act of courage and determination to come back to the disagreement and to seek to resolve it. Doing so is a declaration that this relationship merits retrieving, that continuing with new understanding is worth the effort of re-encountering an old wound to begin healing. Whether that is with a work colleague, a family member, the estranged co-parent of our children or a long-lost friend, the work of resolving a difference can allow a relationship to move back into a shared rhythm of understanding, cooperation and mutual appreciation.

Sally and Fiona are at odds about the best way to care for their mum, my dear friend Wendy. They propose different solutions, each trying their best for their mum and for each other, and yet each tripping over the same misstep that has put their relationship out of rhythm for more than a decade. Until they recognise and address the misunderstanding that has pulled them apart, they will not be able to re-synchronise their relationship. The stakes could not be higher: the care of their mother, and the future of their lifelong love for each other.

Wendy has been living alone in her farmhouse since her husband died more than ten years ago. She feels his presence there, a comfort and balm, as she runs the farm and maintains the wildlife habitats they created and protected together. Wendy and I stay in touch by text messages and calls between my occasional weekend visits, and I have observed the changes in my friend that are causing her daughters such concern. As their mum's mobility becomes increasingly restricted by arthritis, both her daughters fear for her safety. But that is where their agreement ceases. Their proposed solutions are very different, and this is made harder to discuss because one of them lives in a different time zone on another continent.

Wendy and I shared a flat at university; she was a mature student at least ten years my senior. We bonded over music, nature and tea. She met and married her husband while we were still students. They were not expecting to be able to have children; their shock and delight when Wendy realised she was pregnant was followed a few weeks later by further surprise: 'Twins!' Wendy exclaimed down the phone.

Fiona and Sally are those twins. 'We've always been twins,' Sally used to explain when they were small and I went round to their flat to babysit.

'I know, I met you the week you were born,' I would say, and then they would beg me to tell the story of meeting them and trying to work out which twin was which, 'Because we're identical,' Fiona would remind me, 'apart from Just One Thing . . .' Then they would giggle and put their hands over their heads to make it impossible to tell them apart: only their hair partings, running along opposite sides of their heads, were discernibly different.

And so I would tell the tale of coming to meet them for the first time, and how their dad opened the front door of their flat, carrying one baby with a tuft of black hair standing up on her head, and led me through to the lounge where their mum was nursing another baby with an apparently identical hairdo. My dear friends, with their unexpected pregnancy and even more unexpected twinning, their joy as wild as their exhaustion.

'Which was which?' the girls would sing with delight, both hopping excitedly from foot to foot like a four-legged, two-headed, fabulous beast. 'Which was which? Who did you see first?'

And I would say, 'Oh, it's hard to remember, but I think it was . . .' and they would shriek with delight until I said, 'Clockwise!' Then they would turn their backs to me, showing the crowns of their heads on which Fiona's hair spirals out clockwise while Sally's mirror-image hair is arranged anti-clockwise around her crown. Fiona, the Big Sister by twelve minutes, was the baby at the front door. This ritual went on until the girls were nine or ten years old. They loved to be mistaken for each other; very few people could tell them apart, and although I could usually name them correctly, it is hard to describe what I see that says 'Fiona' or 'Sally' when I meet one of them alone.

When the twins were ten years old, Wendy and her husband took over his family farm in Norfolk, where they began a rewilding project, farming for wildlife long before the current interest in conservation took hold. It was wonderful to visit and watch the small plantations flourish; the sound of grasshoppers, by then a distant memory of my childhood, whirred across the glowing wildflower margins in high summer; the orchard outside the kitchen scattered confetti petals in spring, and then we helped to unburden the bowing branches of their glowing fruit in the autumn. I missed seeing them all regularly after their move, but we basked in the pleasure of week-long visits to maintain our bonds. I am an honorary godmother to the twins, and I have watched these girls grow from babies to young women, and now one of them has children of her own. We feel like family. The girls even call me 'Auntie', later shortened to 'AK'.

As adults the twins have supported each other through life's whirling fortunes: Sally is a researcher in a marine biology centre off the coast of Alaska; Fiona is a music teacher with a young family. After their dad died, Fiona worried about their mum living alone; Sally told her that mum had choices, and that by remaining at the farm she could stay in touch with the land and with their dad's memory. Both stepped up visits and phone calls home, and they leaned in to support each other in their own grief, friends and confidantes in that unique and unfathomable closeness enjoyed by twins.

They had the first great test of their relationship a few years after their dad died. I was invited for 'urgent coffee' by Fiona, who lives a short drive from my home.

'Auntie Kath, I don't know what to do. I'm so glad you could come today. It's Sally . . .' and Fiona flushes, her eyes latched on to my face for a response. I imagine all the possible trouble Sally could be in, because whenever there has been trouble, Sally was there relishing it. Sally who cut her own hair with the nail scissors at the age of six so she could look more like Daddy; Sally who ran away from home after school one day at the age of ten and got lost, until a kind shopkeeper offered to phone her parents who drove across town to retrieve her; Sally who wanted to be a dairy farmer aged twelve and had to shout for help when she was cornered in a field by a herd of inquisitive cows; Sally who changed university courses twice before settling into training as a marine biologist. Sally was the Danger Mouse to Fiona's Captain Sensible. I wonder what it is this time.

'Sally wants to go and live in Alaska,' says Fiona. 'She's been offered a job there, some kind of research position, and it's for *five years!*'

I let this sink in. I feel very proud of intrepid Sally, and not a bit surprised. But Fiona is clearly both surprised and perplexed.

'How do you feel about that, Fi?' I ask.

Fiona draws breath and blinks at me, then sighs. 'It's not about how I feel, is it?' she says. 'It's about Mum. She will be devastated! Sally shouldn't even be *thinking* about going so far away for so long. It's just . . . selfish!'

Wow. Usually whatever hot water Sally may be in, Fiona is her advocate and supporter. Fiona is governed by kindness: her inner guide seeks whatever will maximise everyone's happiness, sometimes at the expense of her own. Fiona is placid, thoughtful, yet determined. Sally's inner compass is fairness: she will never take more than her share, and injustice inflames her. She is an environmentalist, a feminist, a champion for the overlooked. She is fiery, focused, demanding. I have never heard either twin criticise the other, apart from their taste in clothing or boyfriends, and even then there is a loving undertone to even their most sarcastic comments. They are each other's champions. This is their first crisis of disagreement.

Fiona's kindness overrode her desire to rebuke Sally; Sally's sense of fairness ensured that she took care to visit home from the USA twice each year. Instead of airing their difference of opinion in curiosity and mutual trust, they left it unspoken. The disagreement was buried, the troubling emotions suppressed and the conversation avoided. Perhaps it felt too difficult, too emotionally laden, perhaps too risky to their lifelong partnership. I regret that lost opportunity, for their current impasse is built on the same invisible foundations. This time it cannot be avoided.

Their suppressed differences were not unfelt. Living in Alaska, Sally worried that Fiona was exhausting herself with long trips to Norfolk at least once a month. Fiona simply saw this as the right thing to do, a kindness to their lonely mum. Fiona felt disloyal to name her unease that Sally's choice to live abroad was unkind. Sally extended her contract in the USA, but she felt frustrated that Fiona's need to support their mum was undermining Fiona's own home life and happiness. 'It's not fair on Fi,' Sally told me during one of her Christmas visits to the UK. 'She should be able to relax, and let Mum visit her if she's lonely. Mum's only come out to see me once, too. She used to have such a sense of adventure; I can't understand why she's become such a home-body.'

I've reflected often on this impasse, with its layers and subtleties, that I have seen played out in families throughout my medical career. I've observed the burden of discomfort borne by people whose love is expressed differently, each believing their way is the only way and so feeling surprised, disappointed, aggrieved by the other. The foundation of the predicament is often the mismatch of expectations between people of loving intent whose values default to different principles either of fairness or of kindness, each a worthy principle and each sincerely held, and yet each in subtle opposition in particular circumstances. The kind/fair dichotomy can blow into a storm of disagreement when conditions align, when life deals people a hand that exposes their differences while conspiring to disguise their mutual concern.

So, kindness-motivated Fiona disrupted her family life for long trips to see her mum, visiting twice as often as she would have done had Sally been in the UK, to make up for her twin's absence. Although this decision was made by Fiona alone, never accusing Sally of 'not doing her share', it silently fed a gnawing sense of abandonment that hurt Fiona too much to examine. Meanwhile, fairness-motivated Sally spent her tiny annual research stipend on trips to the UK; she sensed the increasing coolness in her twin's affections but found herself unable to understand or ask about it, all the while worrying about Fiona using so much of her time travelling to and from the remote family farm. Sally's UK visits were islands of precious shared time, not to be wasted on raising disagreements or airing differences of opinion. The un-named struggle was buried deeper as resentments grew stronger.

In many families I have also met hierarchies of relationship: the local family, embroiled in a relative's health and social challenges and wanting to ensure sufficient support is provided, sometimes over-providing and occasionally even smothering, although always motivated by good intentions; and the far-away family, no less loving yet far less aware of the day-to-day difficulties of living. Often it is the visiting family members who discern changes that have crept imperceptibly past the local family, but their enquiries can be misperceived as criticism of the home team, as a reproach for lack of diligence. Home-based Fiona saw their mum pull out all the stops for Sally's twice-yearly visits to show how well and happy she was, while between these stays Fiona saw Wendy at her lowest, accompanying her to appointments with the farm's account-ants at which the annual money worries were pondered, and on hospital visits during which Wendy's arthritic joints were examined and new treatments proposed to maintain her mobility and inde-pendence. Sally was horrified when she heard that Fiona had ordered a chair-lift for the farmhouse staircase so that Wendy could safely get upstairs at night-time, but on her next visit home Sally was shocked at the change she found in her mum.

This was Sally's summer visit. She had been invited to give a lecture at the twins' alma mater, the same university where I met their parents, so there was great excitement at a visit to stay in Fiona's home near by for a weekend. Wendy had explained she had seasonal workers at the farm and did not want to stay away. I understood this was Wendy's excuse to avoid the discomfort of travel, and with her blessing I gladly accepted the twins' invitation to join them for the weekend, in Wendy's place. After spending a few days with her mum, Sally drove up to our city and we had a couple of hours to chat in my house before Fiona finished work and we could join her with her family for the evening.

'When did you last see Mum?' Sally asks me, straight to the point, as soon as she is in my living room. My most recent visit had been January, a quiet time on the farm and a chance for Wendy and me to enjoy long chats beside the kitchen stove. Wendy's mobility was undeniably reduced: she stooped, she limped, her hands and feet were distorted by a ruthless, painful arthritis. But her humour and determination were undimmed.

'I think she needs residential care,' says Sally. 'She's got fruit pickers living in one of the barns, but she needs personal help. She's struggling to make meals, she uses a seat in her shower and using the toilet is difficult. She tells me it's all fine – she always tells me that – but I'm worried if she falls on those stone farmhouse floors she'll break a hip and end up in hospital!'

I ask Sally if she has talked to Fiona about their mum. 'Oh, AK, Mum thinks Fi is a saint! She's worried that Fi might move in to look after her if she realises how bad things are, and so Mum's thinking of moving out into some kind of residential care. And I think that could be a great solution – but Fi won't hear of it. She says that after having all that space, and all that land, to live in a single room with a view of houses and streets would kill Mum.'

'So your mum is worried about being a burden to Fiona,' I say.

Sally swallows hard before saying, 'I worry about Fi, too, you know. I mean, she takes on too much, far more than her fair share. Mum could afford carers but Fi won't hear of it if she can give more help herself, says Mum. I know Fi worries a lot, and travelling to visit Mum so regularly must exhaust her – but it also reassures her.' She sighs. I let the silence hang, waiting.

'Even if I lived here, I don't think I'd visit as often as Fi does,' she says eventually. 'It all seems a bit . . . over the top, I suppose . . . like Mum is an invalid . . . Which maybe she is now, maybe she *does* need all that help now, but . . . well, Fi's been doing it for twelve years!'

I wait. Sally is quiet.

'Sal, what do you think Fiona would say?'

'Oh, something saintly,' sighs Sally. She looks away from me as she talks about her sister. 'She's such a good person: far nicer than I am. She makes herself miss out to do things for other people. She was always that way. I used to fight people in school who took things off her; they would say they had no lunch or no coloured pencils and Fi would share hers, and they were just *using* her!'

I smile at the idea of a tiny, feisty Sally sticking up for her sister, battling for the fairness that Fiona herself never demanded. 'Did she stick up for you, too?' I ask.

'She wasn't a fighter,' replies Sally, 'but she used to console me when I was upset about things. One time I got dropped from the netball team and I was really mad because it was an important game, and Fi explained that I was so good they needed to give other players a turn, and that I should go along and cheer for them even though I wasn't playing. She said it was the kind thing to do. But it wasn't fair, was it? Even as an adult, I think it wasn't fair to that little girl who trained so hard.'

'Did the others not train hard, Sal?'

'Well, yes, but . . . but I was the best goal shooter *by a mile*!' The mature woman opposite me laughs as she hears the nine-year-old hurt in her own voice.

'And I guess that's the top and bottom of it, isn't it?' says Sally, eventually. She catches my eye. 'You know, AK, my main worry about going abroad was that Fi would exhaust herself for Mum, and she has, hasn't she? She's kind, and she will accept being not at the front of the queue so someone else can benefit. But I'm not like that: I'll fight for their right to be in the queue, but they should be in the *right place* in the queue!' She laughs.

'It's been the same since you were very small,' I say as we settle ourselves back into our long, comfortable relationship. 'Kind or fair; fair or kind. Both important. Both morally right. But not both the same. You loved each other too much to let it be a barrier, but now you need to support your mum together, you may notice that you're coming from different directions . . .'

'You're a wise old auntie, AK,' smiles Sally. 'Do you think Fi understands that difference?'

'I don't know, Sal. I reckon she'll have an interpretation of the last twelve years that's her own, just like you have. Yours is that Fi has taken on too much, because she's more kind to others than fair to herself. I wonder what her view is.' I watch as Sally looks pensive. 'You could ask her,' I suggest.

Sally gathers our teacups and heads towards the teapot for a refill. 'I think I will,' she says.

'And if you do,' I say, gently, 'here's a wise-old-auntie suggestion: do it tenderly, and listen to what she doesn't say as much as to what she says.'

Sally drives us across town to the tall, stone townhouse where Fiona lives with her husband and two children. Sally is excited to be here, shouting greetings to the children waving from the upstairs windows as she unloads a bag full of gifts for them. There is hugging and tears, laughter, and a lot of running up and down stairs to settle Sally into the guest room, up in the attic with a fantastic view over the rooftops towards the river and the bridges that span it, gleaming in the afternoon sunshine. The twins head downstairs with the chatting children; I hover at the view from the attic for a while, to give them time with one another. I come downstairs to find the twins relaxed and smiling, sitting side by side on a sofa, feet tucked under them in symmetrically opposite poses. The children are in the garden with their new American frisbee.

'I was reminding Fi of when she made me do the kind thing and support the netball team after they dropped me,' smiles Sally as I take a seat. 'I thought she was crazy!'

'They lost horribly without Sal,' laughs Fiona. 'And she couldn't help herself smiling when the girl in her place missed shots at goal. I felt so sorry for them all I wanted to cry. And I was really upset that Sally was happy about their humiliation!'

'Did you ever realise that you approach the world in a different way?' I ask them, and they look at me, and then at each other, and then back at me.

'I only realised it as my children were getting older,' says Fiona. 'Gregor is just like me. I know what he's thinking and how he will react to things. Sometimes I even feel frustrated that he won't stick up for himself a bit more. But I used to find his sister so unpredictable, always fighting: just like Sally was. And then one day I got it: it's not unpredictable at all – it's just a different view. My Flora is always *fair*. She sticks up for the underdog, even when that's her big brother. She argues and pushes back when things don't feel right to her, but it's because she can't bear to see people cheat at games, or tell a lie. And that's exactly like you, Sally – you're always going to make things fair. Justice matters to you. I think Gregor and I will give in to make people happy, and we get a kick out of doing that just like you get a kick out of winning a point in an argument or getting someone to keep a promise.

'When we were younger I didn't understand that. I couldn't fathom how you could be so brave and stand your ground the way you did. I wanted to be like you, but I didn't know how.' They smile at each other, Fiona's smile tinged with sadness.

'And I was so sad when you left us and went to America . . .'

'I know, Fi. I knew you thought it was too far and too long, but for me it was such a great opportunity. I hoped you would follow your own opportunities, too, with your music. I wouldn't have asked *you* not to, so it was fair that you didn't ask *me* not to, even though I think you wanted to.' She looks sideways at her twin, and Fiona nods sadly.

Sally continues, 'You have always been kind to everyone, even people who didn't deserve it. I would boil inside when I heard people take you for granted, knowing you would just step up and help them when they never helped you back!'

I watch this conversation of love and reconciliation: taking turns, testing the water, saying what each appreciates as well as what each finds challenging about the other's way of dealing with the world. I realise that they are naming behaviours, 'what you do' (how you fight for justice; how you are always kind), rather than saying 'what you are' (bad, good, selfish, anxious), and they are listening as well as speaking. How I wish I had pushed harder all those years ago to get them to air their silent differences. But who knows: perhaps they needed that time and distance to reflect on what was left unsaid.

Over a thoughtful weekend, we listen to Sally's lecture and we attend a youth orchestra performance conducted by Fiona. We watch Flora and Gregor compete in a swimming gala at which Flora is outraged after one of Gregor's competitors' false start is not disallowed, costing Gregor a medal. Gregor seems unperturbed. 'I won last time,' he says, 'and everyone knows he cheated today. He won't enjoy his medal. I feel a bit sorry for him, to be honest.' Flora stomps off to find ice creams, infuriated that Gregor won't join her in fuming at the injustice he has endured, and the twins smile at each other over Gregor's blue-capped head.

'It's so familiar!' laughs Sally. 'I'm with Flora on this. But look how that chilled attitude has saved Gregor's day.' Gregor looks up at his aunt, who smiles at him and says, 'I'm really proud of you, Greg. Not just your swimming. Your calm. Your poise. You are a good man.' He blushes and heads off to shower and change. 'He's just like you, Fi,' observes Sally as Gregor drips his way towards the changing rooms. 'And I should have realised that you would never stand in my way when I was offered the Alaska post, even if it was killing you inside. I wonder how much I hurt you, without ever meaning to.' Fiona smiles at her twin, a tear sliding down one cheek. They are finding their way back into a shared rhythm again, step by courageous step: love in action. Even the decision to love is an act of bravery; forgiveness is a choice, based on love and hope. The twins are reclaiming their lost comfort in a mutual, unconditional trust.

This is our last evening together. The children call Grandma Wendy to tell her about the swimming, and then go off to their rooms. Their dad takes himself out of our way. It's time to talk.

The twins are back on their sofa, a matching pair in mirror-image poses.

'If Mum needs a carer, I can move down there,' says Fiona, just as Sally had predicted.

'You can't move there permanently, Fi, the children need you here,' she says. 'You could be there while we scope a long-term solution, but we do need to work out what that could be.'

'She'd be miserable living in some tiny room somewhere, Sally. She's a *farmer*!'

'Have you *asked* your mum?' I enquire. There is a long pause.

'I'd hate her to feel she's a burden,' says Fiona. 'She could live here with us.' I think about Wendy's painful joints and the steep stairs in this four-storey townhouse. It would be a huge challenge without a lift, modified bathrooms, a downstairs toilet.

'She has to be realistic about the risks,' says Sally. 'She could have carers to help at home.'

'We can't afford care unless she sells the farm,' sighs Fiona, 'and I think that might break her heart. The only care we have is . . . us . . . well, me.'

'But that's too much to ask of you, Fi! That's not fair on you, or on your family!' says Sally. 'Mum will need to accept she can't take all your time and energy. Anyway, I'm the free spirit here.

Maybe it's time for me to come back and move in with Mum.'

'Sally, your research! Your birds! Your life in Alaska! You can't possibly give it all up!' says Fiona, agitated and tearful. 'I mean, that's such a generous offer, but it means you'll give up your whole life!'

'And what have you been doing for the last twelve years, Fi? Twelve trips a year, hours on the road, sorting out and supporting Mum's finances and medical visits – yes, I know you do all that, she tells me when I call her. I know you've given up the chance to play in an orchestra and to travel the world. You've supported Mum, while I've had a whole career without any ties.' Sally is tearful. 'I've had it all, Fi, and you've let me. It's not fair to ask any more of you. It's my turn now.'

There is a silence. Again, I ask, 'Have you asked your mum what *she* wants?'

Fiona looks across at me, tucking her fringe behind her left ear. 'We can't ask her. She can't make a decision like this. How would she choose which twin to live with? It will break her heart!'

Sally shakes her head and tucks her fringe behind her right ear. 'It's not fair to decide without her. It's her decision.'

There they sit, identical yet not. But the difference is not just the direction of their hair, the famous Just One Thing different of their childhood. Here we are on the horns of their other difference: kindness versus fairness. Two right choices, sitting in opposition. Two rights that somehow confound their good intentions and produce a wrong.

'I wonder how you would feel if two people who love you very much got together to make decisions about your future,' I say. They look startled. Their eyebrows furrow and their nostrils flare, with such similarity it is almost comical, then on the same beat they object, 'But it's not the *same*!'. And that moment of twin-speak breaks the tension. We all laugh.

'I'm speaking as the wise old auntie now,' I say. 'I can hear how much you love your mum and how you want to protect her. I can hear you both offering your most loving suggestions: you want to stop everyone else suffering, Fi, even if it's hard for you; and Sally, you want to take on new responsibilities, because that feels a fair solution that will pay back all Fi's efforts while you've been in Alaska. If you keep listening and working together, I'm sure you'll find a solution that works for both of you. But . . . is that really the issue here?' They blink at me, perplexed. 'Shouldn't this be about what works for your mum?'

And that is how all three of us end up in Wendy's farmhouse kitchen a few days later, mugs of coffee on the table and Wendy at her own fireside for a family conference. It is clear that she is struggling to live here alone, but she has ideas of her own, and is explaining the home modifications the occupational therapist has suggested to maintain her independence: grab rails, raised toilet seats, a tall stool to lean on in the kitchen as she prepares meals.

'And if that doesn't work, I have a plan B,' she announces mysteriously, rummaging in a drawer in the sideboard. 'Look!' she declares. 'This could be perfect!' It is a brochure for a care village, not in Norfolk but near our city, with bungalows for those able to care for themselves and a care home facility that offers support to the bungalow residents, too. 'It looks out over the university farm,' she explains. 'Where your dad and I first met. That's a view to die for!'

'But Mum, how would we afford it?' asks Fi, aghast.

'We'd sell the farm, of course!' says Wendy. 'It's been our happy home, but I won't have it become my prison!'

Sally looks at Fiona; Fiona looks at Sally. In unison, they fold their fringes behind opposite ears. They smile at their mum.

'Will that make you happy, Mum?' asks Fi.

'Well, that sounds like a fair exchange, Mum,' says Sally. They turn to each other, then to me and burst into laughter. *They've got it.*

On the way down in Sally's car, we have discussed how best to explore any disagreements that may arise once discussion of Wendy's future begins. They acknowledge that their desire to keep the peace stopped them from discussing Sally's departure to Alaska as thoroughly as they might have done, and how their misunderstanding of each other has subtly undermined their relationship. This time, no mind games: each will try to understand the other's viewpoint, listening and repeating back to check their understanding. They will notice what they agree about: discussions can get bogged down in peripheral issues when there is agreement in principle on the things that really matter. They will value each other's contributions, even the parts they don't agree with. Both are committed to finding a way forward for their mum, so Fiona will stay engaged when emotions run high instead of rushing to soothe and help, and Sally will listen patiently when Fiona or Wendy express emotions that seem like unnecessary diversions. Above all, they will think before they speak, to avoid speaking in anger or distress. They will look for solutions, not problems. They will look for agreement, opportunities to collaborate, new possibilities that may not previously have occurred to them. They will name their emotions: 'I feel . . .' is a simple statement of fact, devoid of blame, very different from 'You make me feel . . .' This time, they will show their working out instead of just giving their answers.

And yes, they will listen in the same way to their mum. They are going to support her in looking at options and in finding a solution that she can be contented with. Their discussion of the choreography of collaboration warms my heart.

We also sing to the radio, wave at children on bridges and stop for coffee and cake on a regular basis. The twins are rebuilding their shared faith in each other, and it is palpable as we head south and turn east towards the shimmering plain of Norfolk. From the back seat I look at the beloved, mirror-image heads in front of me and doze off to the sound of their identical voices and shared laughter.

Learning to disagree is a life skill. The ability to express dissent while not escalating a disagreement into a fight requires curiosity, patience and listening combined with a focus on the subject under discussion rather than the people discussing it; and, of course, the courage to step over the threshold into that discussion by saying, 'I don't agree'.

Resolving Disagreement

Few of us relish conflict. Many people find it awkward or emotionally disturbing. Finding ourselves in disagreement leaves us in a quandary: do we voice dissent and risk causing offence? Do we stay silent, and be assumed to agree? If we voice our disagreement, will that lead to a fight? And how would that impact the people we know in common, our family, friends or colleagues? How might our disagreement affect our friendship or working relationship, and what might the long-term outcomes be on my career progression, my ability to mentor you, your trust for me as your carer?

Sound familiar? Welcome to conversations with other human beings.

Disagreement cannot be resolved unless it is named, and there are ways to manage disagreement without escalating it into conflict.

It helps to bear in mind that disagreement is usually *about something*: an option to be chosen, a decision to be made, an approach to be adopted. If we **voice our disagreement as 'seeing the situation differently'**, it is usually possible to disagree about the issue under discussion without making it an attack on the person holding a different view. Resolving disagreement is about working together, the approach advocated throughout this book.

Using curiosity and questions to **listen carefully to each other** can help us **seek to understand each other's viewpoint**. We can then check our understanding as we **repeat the other perspective back** with an intention to present it in the best light we can. If we **point out what is good in the other's contribution to the discussion**, this helps us to examine the merits of their viewpoint, and it enables us to **look for what we agree about**. This is not the time to sabotage the other party's view: we are collaborating to find our way forward together, despite our difference of opinion or viewpoint. A curious, collaborative examination of our differences ensures that there is an honourable retreat available, if required, to all participants in the discussion.

This collaborative approach requires all parties to **be committed to the process**, willing to stick with the exploration of different views, in order to reach a compromise or to accept a final difference of opinion with good grace. It is always wise to **avoid letting our emotions speak**: if we cannot speak calmly, we might ask to resume the conversation later.

Curiosity is a versatile tool: it accepts that there can be different ways of interpreting a matter under discussion, and that our own position is as worthy of interrogation as any other.

Last Conversations

My postbag includes many messages about conversations at the end of a life. Some are about the relief of being forgiven, of expressing appreciation, of sharing love. Every week, though, also brings new messages about words left unsaid, conversations not completed, regret about closing down discussions for fear of either party 'getting upset'. And then there was Covid-19. It turns out that, although many people spend a whole lifetime avoiding the idea of mortality, they still live with an unspoken assumption that at the end of our lives we will get a chance to say what matters most to us. Infection-control measures robbed people of those last moments together, and that additional loss showed us how precious the time of last conversations can be. Can we take courage to cross the self-doubt threshold, and tell our beloveds what they mean to us? Do we need to wait until one of us is dying to say those things?

What would it feel like to say it now?

Deathbeds. Some thoughts.

Most of us haven't seen somebody die in real life. We get our mental pictures from TV dramas, cinema screens, media stories. We've had more of those media stories than usual during Covid-19. But most of us haven't been there for real.

Worse: for some of us, our beloved person died and we weren't allowed to be there. We have pictures in our minds of how it might have been, but no way of knowing for sure.

Some of us work in health or social care. We're more likely to have been alongside a dying person. But unless we recognise and understand the dying process, we may not understand what we are witnessing. Even experienced workers in hospitals and care homes haven't known that there are similarities between most deaths; that there are things we can recognise that help us to ensure the process is running as comfortably as possible for the dying person; that there are things we can tell their beloveds to look and listen out for that help them to know their loved one is 'dying safely', or when to summon help because their loved one is unnecessarily distressed.

And further: I have discovered from accompanying my own friends and family that until we've been at the bedside of a person we love, our own beloved instead of a patient or a resident in our care, and until we have applied what we know about the process of dying to the death of a person we love deeply and know well, we can't really understand the experience of those families, whether related by kinship or by choice, who are accompanying their beloved to their final breath.

So I want to say this about deathbeds.

They are inevitable. The day will come for all of us. For a few, it won't be a bed, but perhaps a motorway or a shopping centre or an ambulance trolley. But for most of us, death will approach gradually, and we will have a chance to recognise and to reflect on the situation.

A lifetime among dying people has taught me some helpful things. First, although no one usually feels keen about dying, those on their deathbeds are often more concerned about their beloveds than about themselves. They have things to say. And their dearest people can help by listening. This is a precious task, to listen to the messages of people reaching the end of their life.

If they want to say sorry, don't bat it away. This is their conscience speaking. Listen to their sorrow and recognise it. Accept that apology. Say thank you. Tell them your love is constant. Let them know you heard.

If they want to thank you, don't pretend it was nothing. This is their heart speaking. Listen to their gratitude; recognise that you are being thanked. Accept the thanks. Tell them you are glad, that you would do it all again, that it was your pleasure or your honour or your grim-faced determination to provide that thing for which they are grateful. Let them feel heard.

If they want to forgive you, you may feel embarrassed, ashamed, unworthy, overwhelmed, uncomfortable. Sit with it. Let them speak. This is their soul speaking, and their making peace with you now will give their soul ease. Accepting their forgiveness is a gift you can bestow. Thank them. Ask for their blessing. They are laying down their burdens of fear and sadness, and you don't need to pick them up. Leave them there, those past mistakes. They are in both your pasts, and this is a new present at the edge of their life. Hear, acknowledge, accept that forgiveness.

If they want to speak of love – oh, join in. Let your souls rejoice for all that you have meant to one another. Now is not a time to be coy, to be embarrassed about emotions. Here, at the end of things for your beloved person, it's time to live in the truth that your relationship is made of love. Whether it's marriage, parenthood, friendship, a fondness for a work colleague or a neighbour: it's all love. Listen: hear that love. Let them feel heard.

Next, my lifetime of deathbeds has taught me that the process of dying is peaceful, provided two important things are in place. The first is good management of the symptoms of whatever condition is causing the death. Just because we're dying doesn't mean we must tolerate pain, struggle to breathe, experience nausea, or other symptoms. Let's insist that the best symptom management is in place, whether that's from their GP, or their specialist cancer/respiratory/cardiology/whatever team, or whether those usual professionals are reinforced by expert help from palliative care specialists.

Without uncomfortable symptoms to divert the process, dying people simply become more weary over time. They do less. They sleep more. That sleep helps them to have renewed, but short, bursts of energy: perhaps enough to have a conversation, or to listen to their favourite music, or to clean their teeth. Gradually they begin to dip into unconsciousness, into a coma that becomes deeper until they are unconscious all the time. I've written in detail about this elsewhere.*

The second important thing is peace of mind. It's about feeling prepared; that the things they want to sort out are complete, that relationships are healed, that their life was worth something. Achieving this is often helped by conversations in the preceding days, weeks, months, even years; by recognising our mortality and working with it instead of fighting against it. Just like writing a will or taking out life insurance, doing our end-of-life preparation won't make us die any sooner. But it certainly helps people to die more peacefully. So when people ask us to speak of things that will soothe their minds, let us listen. Let them feel heard.

Here's the thing about deathbeds: each one is a chance for us to get better acquainted with dying. To see how it happens. To witness the gradual change from alive to no longer alive. To learn how to have those precious conversations. To be companions as, in our own turn, we will be accompanied.

So as we take our turns at the bedside, or the virtual bedside, of our beloved dying person, we are giving them the gift of our companionship and attention, and they are giving us the gift of

* www.withtheendinmind.co.uk

showing us how to die. It's not like on TV. It's usually not dramatic. It's memorable and profound. It is life-changing. It is our privilege to be there for each other as we learn the lessons of the deathbed. Listening, with ears and eyes and hearts.

Listen

Grief. Even the word discomforts me. The unalterable fact of loss. The helplessness. The hopelessness. I'm an optimist. I'm a hope-monger. I find satisfaction in excavating hope on barren plains of despair, in discovering ways to make unalterable threat bearable, in finding crumbs of comfort. That's how I was able to spend decades in the service of people who were learning how to live while they were dying: because there were problems to solve, solutions to be devised, things to do. And then, during their dying, there are explanations to be provided to loved ones, symptoms to be managed, watching to be accompanied. More things to do. Then, after the death, the bereaved bid a sorrowful farewell and leave us, their erstwhile companions at the deathbed.

Now it is done, and their next task is one of enduring their loss. There are no things left to do. That sounds unbearable. Please don't make me face that. I have nothing to offer. Or so I thought. Here's how I learned differently.

I have a confession to make. Although I have spent a long time in the presence of dying people, I never understood how to behave in the presence of bereaved people. There is a lot to do in end-of-life care: actions to be taken, explanations to be provided, care to be delivered. After the death, though, there is an odd vacuum. Bereaved families comment on the strange transition they experience as all the bustle of care fades to an unfamiliar silence. That silence, that place of utmost sorrow without jobs to do, unnerved me. And so, although I was kind when I was in the presence of bereaved people, I did not seek their company. I think it's fair to say I avoided them.

I know I am not alone in this. Bereaved people report this consistently: avoidance by others, being invisible in plain sight, becoming ghosts themselves. The loss of their person is compounded by the loss of contact with friends, family and neighbours; the loss of the old life; the loss of the planned future. Even after I experienced my own bereavements, I still felt helpless in the presence of other bereaved people. In fact, now that I understood some part of their devastation, my helplessness felt even worse.

My understanding of how to 'be', by which I mean how to behave, be present and be a companion to bereaved people, came from two unforeseen directions. First of all, my view of myself as a person 'too inexperienced to help' bereaved people was shifted when, after writing a book about dying – the useful, things-to-plan-for and what-you-might-expect practicalities I have learned from a career at deathbeds – I began to receive messages from readers.

Bereaved people contacted me. First only one or two, then a trickle, and then a flood. Tens, hundreds, I have lost count. Letters and cards sent to newspapers that had carried book reviews or interviews; social media messages; emails from friends forwarding messages from people unknown to me; letters to my agent and publisher. Bereaved people, the very people I have spent a career hiding from, were looking for me. All of them saying the same two things: *thank you for explaining what I saw and heard at that deathbed*, and *this is my story*. Story after story after story, sent in confidence and kindness, and each a tale of one life lost and other lives changed for ever. Stories of love and remembrance, loss and sorrow, gratitude and trust, anger and ambivalence. I read them, and thought about them, and tried to respond if there was a way to do so.

Initially it was overwhelming, and in the early days I told each correspondent that I was not a person with lots of experience of working with bereaved people, in case they mistook me for an expert in dealing with grief. Yet with each message I received, a truth became increasingly clear. Stories are the way we make sense of death and loss. Didn't I already know that? This overpowering tide of personal witness of final moments and living on with grief began to change my sense of what I knew. I began to understand that I knew bereavement, too. I had suffered enough personal bereavements to recognise the core pattern and its individual variations each time. And now, thanks to the trust of these many correspondents, I was developing an eyewitness familiarity with grief. I was no longer an imposter when I talked about bereavement.

Still my sense of helplessness overwhelmed me, but reading so many grief stories taught me about the cause of my avoidance: in the presence of the dying, I knew what my role was but in the presence of the bereaved, I did not know how to be. Is this the feeling that leads people to cross the road when they see their bereaved neighbour approach? Bereaved people attribute this common experience to people feeling awkward, to not knowing what to say, and it is partly that. But I realised that it is more than that: before we can speak, we must become present. And we are reluctant to be present when we don't know 'how to be'.

Life delivers lessons in wisdom, whether we feel ready or not. My next lesson was delivered unexpectedly. I attended a film screening at a book festival: a film that I had tried to avoid, because it was a documentary about bereaved parents made by filmmakers who were bereaved parents themselves. They had travelled and lived with and interviewed other bereaved parents to make a film that explores this most unbearable of bereavements, the death of a child. The process was the more insightful not only because of the shared experience of the filmmakers and their interviewees, but because one of them is also a psychotherapist. They called their film *A Love That Never Dies.* *

I knew about this film because the filmmakers had approached me with a request to help them to promote it as a service to other bereaved parents. They were looking for people who could talk about death as panellists for question-and-answer sessions at cinema screenings of their film. I was horrified. *I don't do bereavement. I don't know how to be in its presence.* I wrote back to explain that I was not a grief expert. They were undaunted. 'It's not what you are expecting,' they said.

They sent me a link to watch their film at home. It was beautiful, of course. Heartbreaking, soul-wounding, life-changing. Here are parents of all walks of life dealing with the death of their child: accidents, illness, murder, suicide. Living on with a part of their soul missing. Parenting the surviving siblings. Making meals, doing the school run, bearing the unbearable. Trying to make sense of it all. Living through it. Telling their stories. I know I cannot sit on a stage and talk about this. It takes me days to watch the whole film. I am restless, I cannot sit still, I get up for drinks, I discover that I must bake or write a letter or walk through the woods to the shops for milk. I take the film in twenty-minute snatches, sometimes less. I can barely sleep for the next few nights, waking with the faces and voices of those grieving people in my mind; startling to distant traffic noise and imagining one of my children is hurt.

The screening of the film following on from my session about dying at the same arts festival meant that I was unable to wriggle free. After walking to the screening with the filmmakers, Jane and Jimmy, I selected an inconspicuous place to sit, and I prepared

---

* Their website is at https://thegoodgriefproject.co.uk/ and the film is available worldwide at https://thegoodgriefproject.co.uk/watch-a-love-that-never-dies-now/

myself to endure sorrow. What happened next was as surprising as it was overwhelming, and even as I recall it I feel myself sliding back into that seat, my coat hanging over the backrest and my shawl around my face in an attempt to seek a private place in which to suffer the next hour.

The film begins. Stories are told, one by one, strung together by stunning footage of Jane and Jimmy's travels. We are standing beside the road in Vietnam where their son Josh died, witnesses gathering to greet and support us, to give us their own versions of Josh's final moments. These new details to the story feel like going back to add illustrations to a book previously composed of bullet points. We are watching this family grieve, moment by moment, as they support the mourning of Josh's shocked young friends, plan their funeral and memorial ceremonies, attend to the needs of everyone who loved Josh. I am held in my seat by their generosity.

Their trip, our trip, to meet other bereaved families begins, Josh's ashes with us on our journey: we are taking him to complete his travels. Cinematic skies and beautiful landscapes contrast with intimate and heart-rending close-shot conversations with grieving parents recounting their loss and the impact of bereavement. The faces of other grieving parents and families fill the screen and when my sorrow and agitation become too great to bear I close my eyes in the darkness. But the voices are all around us, inescapable. Each family reeling from their loss, and each seeking their way to face their forever-altered futures.

When I open my eyes, I notice people nodding as the onscreen families speak. People are sitting forward in their seats to be as close to those on the screen as they can be, just as I lean backwards holding a mental shield in front of me. Sitting here as a member of this audience I am drawn into an experience that I had been unable to bear alone. I can hear occasional sobs all around me, blowing of noses, clearing of throats. People in the audience are hearing echoes of their own stories. 'This is what loss of a precious person is like. Like this. And this. And this.' 'This is how we minimise our expressions of grief,' say these bereft parents, 'to fit in with non-grieving people – yes, that is what we do.' Yes, the audience nods, leaning forward. Yes, it is. Yes, I hear you. I hear your story and in it I hear my story, too. Yes, yes, yes.

This is a room suspended in time, filled with grief. But not only grief. There are memories, and tears, and sorrow, for sure. But each family talks of the enduring power of their love for these dead children, lost to them for ever and yet held safe within them for the rest of their lives. It is unthinkable not to say their names, not to remember their lives, not to re-encounter the pain of the loss, because that is the gateway to the joy of their having lived, the ever-present sense of belonging that these families describe. This grief is the touchstone to their continuing relationship with their beloved and lost child, brother, sister. The alternative would be forgetting, or even never having known, and none of them would wish for that. Their grief is a price worth paying for love.

In every story on the screen, I encounter my inadequacy in the face of grief. My helplessness. My not knowing how to be. And I hear those bereaved voices describe people who probably feel just like me: they name their sense of abandonment by friends and neighbours in their grief and describe how those who don't know what to say avoid saying anything, even avoiding contact, turning away, not returning calls. My sliver of consolation is that I don't turn away, but in meeting bereaved people I always feel that in some way I am letting them down, that I should not be here, that somebody who knows what to do should be here in my place. If only I could discover how to be what they need at that time.

The film plays on and I am suspended in not knowing, in moving between my own sorrows and the sorrows of the families who are speaking. As Jane and Jimmy's campervan streams across a red American desert beneath unbroken blue skies, something happens inside me. The hole I have been trying not to fall into swallows me, and I am lost. I am weeping. I am part of this communal sense of impermanence and the painful, inevitable consequences of love. By sitting alongside so many grieving families, one after another, I have finally come to understand that there is nothing we can do or say that can ease this kind of grief, but *that is not what we are required to do.* Our supportive role is simply to be willing to be present, to witness, to use the dead person's name and to hold them in memory. This grief cannot be 'made better'. But simply by turning up, powerless, lost for words yet willing to be present, we can hold a space for their grieving and mark our sense of shared humanity.

As the film ends, there is a long, still silence before the applause begins. People turn to each other and compare stories, they share tissues and embraces and there is a prolonged hubbub before the panel can find the hush they need for the Q&A session to begin. Witness stories are told: the same stories I hear in my correspondence are told over and over by this audience.

Now, though, I am looking from a different vantage point. I watch Jane and Jimmy acknowledging that we are powerless, and that simply being is the only way to survive. It is a masterclass in holding others' sorrow without trying to fix it, or hurry it, or justify it.

I *do* know how to be. I've been doing it all along. It is to feel this sense of utter powerlessness, and to recognise its truth, and to turn up anyway. All we can do, at times like this, is listen.

Advice from Bereaved People About Making Contact

And what of bereavement support? This is another rich vein in my postbag, and there is advice here that all of us can benefit from. Grief is the natural process that enables us to live with loss. It is emotional and physical, overwhelming and exhausting. Bereaved people discover that their attention is fractured and their memory unreliable. There are moments of calm and moments of immense disruption of life-view: not just emotional distress but even a sense of being dislocated in time, in space, in how to draw the next breath or take the next step. Simply getting through the day is tiring; sleep is disturbed; hormones released in stress cause physical tiredness. Making contact, therefore, should replenish rather than drain their remaining energy and attention.

Grief is not an illness, it is a response to loss. The grief will last as long as the loss does, and after a death the loss will last for ever. The loss permeates a bereaved person's present, their memories of the past and their expectations of their future. Although they will eventually find their pain is a smaller component of their everyday life, it is not going to leave them completely. They will not 'get over it' despite encountering many people who tell them that they should. Grief is a process that will eventually enable them to live alongside the loss. It will take the time it takes.

Our sense of awkwardness can paralyse us into not making contact with our bereaved friends and neighbours, and yet that is the very opposite of what they need. There are recurring messages from bereaved people about how best to support them; here are a few principles they would like us all to consider.

Please don't avoid us. We have no energy to reach out to you but we feel abandoned when you remain absent and silent.

You don't have to 'cheer us up'. That is not possible. We appreciate your contact as an act of support, and we don't expect you to know what to do or to say. Often we don't know, either. Try 'I'm sorry', 'I'm thinking of you', 'It's good to see you', even 'I don't know what to say'.

Say their name. You won't make us sadder by mentioning the person who died. We love to hear your memories and stories, it feels like being given another little glimpse of them.

'How are you?' is too big to answer. Every day, sometimes every hour, is different. 'How are you right now?' 'Do you feel up to a chat?' or even simply 'Hello' can be easier greetings to respond to. Sometimes we don't really know how we are, or we think we should tell you we feel better than we do.

Practical help can be welcome. If you ask us what we need, we may feel too overwhelmed to say. Offers of specific help that we can accept or decline are easier for us: 'I'm going to the shops: what do you need?' 'Can I walk your dog/help with the school run/put your bins out/mow your lawn?' 'Here's a meal for your freezer.'

Remembering to check in is supportive, but don't require us to respond. Think about sending text messages, notes or cards. 'Thinking of you.' 'I'm here if I can help.' 'I'm free all evening if you'd like company.' 'Sending love.' 'No need to text back.' Please don't give up reaching out after a week, a month, a year. There's no time limit on grief.

Instead of platitudes, just express kindness. Please don't try to justify this death with 'He's in a better place', 'Her suffering is over', 'The good die young', 'At least . . .' Instead, just say that you recognise our pain, that you remember our dead person. 'This is hard. I'm sorry it's hurting you.' 'I can't imagine how sad this is for you, but I'm here if you'd like company.' 'I am so sorry they died. I'm sending all my love to you.' 'I've been remembering that time when . . .' 'I loved him, and I'll miss him.' 'She was such a special friend to me.'

It's awkward. We get that. But please don't let awkwardness get in the way of making contact. If we weep, it's not because you did something wrong. It's often because you have listened to us and allowed us to express our loss, and we appreciate that kindness.

Help us return to work and social circles by contacting us to ask how we would like you to deal with our return. Some of us are glad to come back to familiar routines without ceremony; some of us will appreciate a card or flowers to welcome us back; most of us appreciate colleagues or friends who tell us they are sorry our dear person died; a few of us don't want it mentioned. Some of us would like a companion for our first outings as we return to socialising. Don't try to guess: ask us in advance.

Listen to us. Let us remember, tell stories, retell our memories. By listening, you create a space where we can feel past happiness as well as current sadness. There is a lot of laughter at funerals because that is an occasion when everyone talks with fondness about the dead person. Can we do that more often?

Towards Connection

We looked at pity, sympathy, empathy and compassion in 'Getting Alongside' on page 63. On an individual scale, we have examined how to create a compassionate space to be alongside someone in deep distress without trying to fix or advise, or to minimise or dismiss their emotions.

We have looked at how we can enable people to review their difficulties in safety, to feel heard. We have considered how to help them to find possibilities for coping with or solving their difficulties while offering them a secure base to return to. We have contemplated the difficulties of holding calm discussions when emotions run high. We have counted the cost to ourselves as compassionate helpers, and recognised the need for self-care and self-compassion to maintain our own wellbeing.

So far we have looked into acts of individual compassion and care. Yet we are more than individuals: we belong to one another. We are members of friendship groups, families, work teams; we are neighbours in our streets, villages, towns and cities; we are members of shared-interest groups, societies and clubs: all communities of one kind or another. We are social beings, and our collective self is Society. To finish, let us turn our attention briefly to the bigger picture and our human need for connection, to be able to tell our stories, to be heard. Where are the listening spaces in our communities?

Where Are the Listening Spaces?

The world is busy. People are caught up in their own affairs. We move between tasks and places distractedly, rarely living in the present moment, largely preparing for (and often worrying about) what may lie ahead, and sometimes remembering about (and perhaps reproaching ourselves for) what has already passed. When life suddenly brings us up short through an event that is sad or shocking, we are tipped out of our distraction into the present moment. The world moves past us, unaware or uninterested; we are islands of presence in a distracted world.

Where is the space for sorrow and reflection in the busyness of the world? Who will listen to us as we formulate our sadness and make sense of our disappointments? Where can we express grief, explore anxieties or be consoled in our loneliness?

We are social animals. We are hard-wired for connection to one another. Yet community living becomes lost in urban anonymity and rural distance; it has become harder to make meaningful relationships; a loneliness epidemic has been recognised. Loneliness is not about lack of company but lack of connection. Surrounded by people but with no one to hear us can be a place lonelier than isolation.

How can we recreate connection? Where and how can we provide compassionate spaces in which people can meet and communicate, to reflect and recover equilibrium? Where are the spaces in which we can speak, where we will find ourselves heard, where we can experience connection, compassion and care?

Valerie's ear is hot and sore. She has been holding the phone for twenty minutes, listening to tinny music interrupted by the insurance company's recorded announcements about how much her call matters. She has a list of tasks and a cup of tea, grown grey and scummy as it has cooled. She tries not to think about things cooling. Irvin's hand had been cold as she said goodbye. How can he be dead? The panic rises again, and she shakes her head as the music shifts, mid-phrase, from Mozart to Albinoni. Or not Albinoni, as she has recently discovered. She sighs.

Widow. What a word. How can she think of herself as a widow? She stares at the list before her, typed by Irvin as he was dying, listing all the things that would need attention after his death. The bank; the car insurance; the house insurance; the phone and power companies; the credit card; the library: all these organisations need to be told to cancel Irvin out of life. The charities they supported together will need to replace his name with hers, if she can afford to keep supporting them. First there is the matter of rearranging the bank account. The lady at the bank told her she cannot withdraw money from their joint account or use her bank card now Irvin has died: she should have taken out some cash before telling the bank. *How would anybody know that?* wonders Valerie. *This is the first time my husband has died.*

'Ponchester Insurance, thank you for waiting, my name is Maxine. Please tell me your name,' a perky voice suddenly interrupts Albinoni.

'Valerie,' she says.

'And your surname?' trills Maxine.

'Anover,' says Valerie. 'A-N-O-V-E-R.' No one has ever heard of Anover. She has spent her married life spelling her husband's family name.

'Is that Miss, Mrs or Ms?' Maxine intones in a voice that could ask these questions in its sleep.

Valerie can't think. Is she still Mrs? Is there a different title that says 'My husband is dead'? She hesitates.

'Sorreee,' drawls Maxine. 'Perhaps it's Lady, Doctor or Reverend?' Valerie is perplexed. How has it become so hard simply to state who she is? But who is she, now?

'My husband just died,' Valerie stutters into the phone. 'I used to be Mrs. I don't know whether that changes when a husband dies. What would you call me now?'

'Oh, that's still Mrs then,' trills Maxine without a change in pace or breezy tone. 'And what can I do for you today, Valerie. May I call you Valerie?'

'I just told you. My husband has died,' replies Valerie.

'Yes, Valerie. You did tell me. And I told *you* that you would still be known as Mrs. Now, why are you calling me today?'

'To tell you,' says Valerie. 'To tell you that Irvin has died. For the insurance. For the name on the policy.'

'Oh-kay,' sings Maxine. 'And do you want to know the value of the policy? Do you have probate? Are you the executor?'

'I beg your pardon?' asks Valerie. What is this language? What do all these words mean? Is Maxine real, or is there a tiny silver robot at the other end of this phone, babbling words at her?

'Do you have a policy number for me?' the robot asks, cheerily. As it happens, Irvin has typed the policy numbers beside each company name. And the telephone numbers. He is so methodical. Was. He *was* so methodical. Valerie reads out the policy number and the inanely chirpy Maxine repeats each digit. Valerie can hear her typing them.

'Oh, this isn't *life* insurance, Valerie! This is your *house* insurance. Is that the right policy?'

'Yes, it's our house insurance,' says Valerie. 'That's why I'm calling. Because it's my house now. It's not our house. Well, it is still our house . . . the house we lived in . . . but Irvin's not . . . Irvin's no longer . . . it's his name and my house now, you see?'

Her voice is pleading *please understand me* but Maxine is still trilling.

'Do you have a copy of the death certificate?' she asks, cheerfully. 'You'll need to upload it on our website. Once you've done that we can change the names over. Got a pen? I'll tell you the website.'

'Upload?' repeats Valerie. That sounds like a computer thing. Valerie doesn't do computer things. She'll have to get Irvin to do it. Except . . .

This scenario is both tragic and common. People like Valerie will encounter any number of telephone voices that work through their algorithms without regard for the story they are being told. People who listen without hearing, taking in information but screening out context. This is function and effectiveness without compassion. All bereaved people encounter it. Similar indifference to their difficult experience is reported by people notifying employers or statutory bodies about disability or illness, redundancy, mental health problems, legal issues, divorce and separation. There are noble exceptions, with companies who train their public-facing staff to notice the context and to express empathy when appropriate, but largely the business remains transactional rather than supportive.

Irvin, Valerie's recently-dead husband, was an amateur motor mechanic. He loved playing with engines and machines, he built a computer from a kit, he liked hot chilli sauce, he was a tone-deaf but enthusiastic singer. There is nobody now to smile about these things. Since he retired from teaching, he had happily taken old engines apart and repaired them: sewing machines, washing machines, motorbikes, anything not too modern. 'Nothing with a chip in it, except a chip butty,' he used to joke. He had been a tech teacher at the local high school, and that is Valerie's next call.

She is surprised to hear an automated voice on the school

number. Her heart sinks. 'For notifying student absence, press 1. For the exams office, press 2. For the lower-school admin team, press 3. For the upper-school admin team, press 4. For the library, press 5. For the pastoral team or special educational needs, press 6. For sixth-form enquiries, press 7. For all other matters, please hold . . .' She holds. The music is better than the insurance company's. It's young people singing something about 'Once in a Lifetime'.

'Southside High School. How can I help?' says a woman's voice. Valerie has not prepared anything to say. After hours of being asked questions, she is surprised to be given space to say an original sentence.

'This is Valerie Anover. I'm—'

'Oh, Mrs Anover! I'm Gillian in the Big Office. We are all so, so sorry . . . We heard this morning. We all loved Irvin . . . I'm . . . we . . . oh . . . How are you?'

The relief of talking to a person who sounds sad, who uses Irvin's name, who cares, is overwhelming. Valerie feels herself sinking from her brittle state of spiky anxiety into a formless puddle of sorrow. She is unable to speak.

'I'm sorry, that's a stupid question,' says Gillian. 'You must be really sad and shocked. We all don't know what to say. But I'm glad you rang us. Mr Burton the new head, he didn't know Irvin, but most of Irv's old colleagues are still here and we are all very sad. Can we do anything to help you? Would you like the school to print any orders of service? Or to send musicians to Irvin's funeral? We've done that for other people, and we like to help when we can . . .' Gillian stops talking. Valerie takes a breath.

'I don't really know what I need just now,' she says. 'I was ringing to make sure you knew. I haven't thought about the funeral yet. Thank you for those ideas, I hadn't thought about orders of service, but Irvin's left a list of the music. I think he'd like the school to be involved.'

'Of course,' says Gillian, kindly. 'Give me your number and I'll ask Mrs Green to phone you. You remember Amanda Green, the music teacher? She runs the school choir. They are very good. And the sixth formers will remember Irvin. They'll like to help.'

Well done, Gillian in the Big Office. She isn't following an algorithm. She isn't sure what to say. But she is expressing compassion and concern, offering practical help and talking about relationships. These are hallmarks of connectedness, and although Valerie is sad, she is also consoled by this response. Compassion by telephone is possible.

The school had been told about Irvin's death by his friend Albie, who was pastoral care lead when Irvin was the tech teacher. In emergencies they were a troubleshooting twosome. Albie came to the rescue when students fell apart, and Irvin when equipment failed. Their students referred to them as 'The AA – emergency response team'* with fondness. After retirement Irvin missed access to some of the larger tools that had been available in the school tech department, and Albie just missed company. That is how they found their way to an organisation called Men's Sheds, where men (and a few women) who like to make or mend things gather to use the organisation's tools, to make and mend and ponder, and to chat or ignore each other in a companionable way.† It's not about the tools, of course: it's about connection. Men's Sheds welcome those who want to use their resources to become members. Some come because they have heard on the grapevine that it's friendly and there's a lathe or a jigsaw or some other piece of desirable kit to be used. Irvin and Albie have met men who were referred to the Shed by their GP, too, as part of a social prescribing

---

* In the UK, the AA is the Automobile Association and its workforce attend broken-down vehicles.
† You can find more information about Men's Sheds here https://menssheds.org.uk/

move in the NHS that helps people to become connected and active to enhance their wellbeing. Social prescribing is a national programme to connect people with other people in a life-enhancing way, and it includes referring people of all ages to outdoor gyms (exercise by working to maintain public outdoor spaces), walking groups, choirs, knitting circles, community gardening groups, sports clubs and many other activities. Social prescribing recognises that we are social beings, and that connection is good for us, boosts our mood and keeps us healthy.

What all these activities offer is Compassionate Space: a place to belong to, to connect with people, to tell our stories and to hear theirs, or to create new stories together. The rise in emotional ill-health during the Covid-19 pandemic was partly related to fear or sadness and bereavement, but mainly it was the impact of social isolation. Watching social groups reinventing themselves in a virtual setting has been fascinating: online choirs, quizzes, mutual interest groups; social media forums for people with shared interests or similar challenges in life; uptake of online yoga, meditation, dance or fitness training, with members discussing their classes online in much the same way they previously chatted in the car park after using the gym.

As a relative newcomer to social media, I have been astonished by the compassionate communities I have found online. There are communities of interest ranging from book clubs to charity supporters, grief circles to pet photos, locality residents' groups, groups coordinating volunteers to shop for the house-bound; crafters and nature lovers and recipe swaps. A single comment from a stranger on my Twitter or Facebook accounts about feeling lost in grief will attract many responses from kind people willing to empathise, offer virtual companionship, answer questions or offer resources, often hours or days before I find the comment. These are self-sustaining communities and, despite the widely reported presence of some less positive influences in the social media world, my heart has been warmed by the compassion and willingness to listen to each other's stories that I have found there.

What about our public spaces? Not everyone has the means or the interest to be online; where can people meet and connect in a physical space? There are public spaces in our hospitals, town halls, libraries: do they offer space for connection? There are some inspiring developments out there, as well as a need for more thought. We met Laura and Alan on page 70, when they had just discovered Laura's miscarriage. The compassionate team caring for them provided a room away from the other expectant parents to gather themselves and to begin to mourn their lost baby and expectations.

The privacy of the grieving parents' lounge in Pete's service represents an unusual resource in hospitals: a place to retire to away from the clamour and the discomfiting presence of other patients who may trigger, or be distressed by, another patient's distress. Currently there are hospitals where newly bereaved people sit with other visitors in anonymous waiting areas when they arrive to collect their dear, dead person's belongings and all the death-related paperwork; where women attending clinics for infertility investigations sit alongside other women there for termination of a pregnancy, each sensitised by the other's suffering; where parents anxiously carrying a baby who will be born to struggle with physical and cognitive difficulties attend antenatal clinics with excited families carrying healthy pregnancies.

Sometimes hearing unwelcome news at the hospital is made more difficult because urgent decisions need to be made. For example, when someone is given a new diagnosis of cancer, an empathic recognition that this is a life-changing conversation is essential. The patient will have a deep, individual response to the news, no matter how much they may have been expecting it. The possibilities of a changed life or shortened life, of a future with an altered body, of shifts in the balance of personal relationships and roles: all these potential changes may open up in the mind of a person sitting on an uncomfortable plastic chair in a clinic room. And yet there are pressing decisions to make. How can they possibly apply their mind to matters like dates for surgery, treatment options, nutritional advice, the need for staging investigations? A pause is necessary: a time, and a space, to experience the shock, sadness and grief of the news. Only then is it possible to begin to converse rationally about the practicalities. And yet there is no space: we press them for decisions as they struggle to take in the news.

How can we design our clinics so that there is a safe space to feel overwhelmed? Because that is what is required. Our clinical spaces currently reproach expression of emotion: public waiting rooms, brightly lit and sparsely furnished; no room to sit and think or weep, apart from a toilet cubicle; hospital cafés without booths or screens. The absence of a space in which to cry is part of a public denial of the possibility of bad news. The Compassionate Hospital would offer time, calm spaces and trained, willing companions as a basic right for anyone receiving life-changing news, either of death or of an unwelcome change to their own or their dear one's expectations in life.

This lack of access to private spaces in our hospitals applies not only to patients and their families or companions, but also to staff. After delivering unwelcome news or participating in stressful incidents in their work, there is nowhere for a distressed doctor or nurse to retire to for a few moments' quiet. The same is true for porters who encounter upset patients and families, or who companionably transport patients around a hospital only to meet them for the last time as dead bodies to be unloaded at the mortuary; for housekeepers encountering messy and perhaps heart-rending scenes for cleaning; for administration staff who handle emotional phone calls from families or who type discharge letters describing tragedies. We weep in the sluice, we sit on the floor of the linen cupboard, we are invited into the ward manager's office only to find it is full of staff having a handover report or a meeting. At least as staff we know where the more spacious cupboards are: for in-patients, there is breaking of bad news behind curtains and nowhere to weep but the en-suite facilities. Hospitals are not designed for the heartbreak that takes place within their walls.

Yet it is known that the 'therapeutic environment' in hospital affects recovery. Research has shown that simple yet profound changes in environment, like the view from the bed, a window that looks on to greenery rather than a wall, exposure to natural daylight with its circadian rhythms of length and intensity, and the presence or absence of intrusive noise will all affect wellbeing, mood and even rates of recovery from surgery. Of all our public spaces, hospitals are places that deal most frequently with the breaking of bad news; with grasping the truth of an unwanted new reality; with illness and injury, heartache and sorrow; with death and grief. There is an overwhelming need for the design of compassionate spaces in hospitals, to support patients and their loved ones, and for the wellbeing of staff.

Valerie has to register Irvin's death. He died in hospital, fairly suddenly in the end. His prostate cancer had spread to his back, and he lost the use of his legs. He had asked Valerie to bring his laptop and files into the hospital, where he typed out all the instructions for his funeral music and preferences ('Shoot me into space in a rocket. Or do what makes you happy if that's easier'); a list of all the tasks Valerie would need to tackle once he had died, which he emailed to Albie for printing because Valerie had never liked computers; and he emailed their solicitor to say he was dying and please be kind to Val when she needs help with the will. He was hoping for a few more months, and was learning to be independent in a wheelchair, when he had a sudden attack of breathlessness and he was unconscious by the time Valerie arrived at the hospital. She might have found him awake if it hadn't taken her forty minutes to find a space in the hospital car park. Irvin never regained consciousness. We need Compassionate Car Parks, too.

The medical certificate says, 'Pulmonary embolism'. It's in her handbag. She is parking at the town hall car park, which has an impenetrable one-way system that goes anti-clockwise and confuses her completely. She can't work out whether or not she is supposed to pay and display, and she's got no change, and everything seems terribly difficult. The bereavement officer at the hospital very kindly made this appointment for her with the registrar. 'Don't go on Monday,' he'd said. 'Monday the waiting room is full of new dads. All those weekend babies. Leave it until Tuesday.' Now here she is, following signs through the Victorian building, a gothic masterpiece, to 'Registrar for Births, Marriages and Deaths'. She remembers being a bride in this very building, but the signs are pointing away from the corridor where she and Irvin took their vows and she realises she must climb the ornate stairs: third floor.

'Lift's on the right, pet,' says a cleaning lady who is dusting the intricate banister. Valerie thinks she may have posed for photos in her wedding dress on the wide turn in those stairs. It all seems vague, somehow. 'You OK, pet?' asks the cleaner. 'Are you looking for the Registrar's Office? Somebody died, darlin'?' Valerie nods, feebly she feels. She wishes she could be more present, but since Irvin died everything feels strange and far away.

'Over here,' says the cleaner, kindly, leading her to the lift and pressing the call button. 'Press number three when you get in. Turn left when you get out. It's straight ahead.

'You'll be all right, pet. We all get used to it in the end. Got to, haven't we?' She squeezes Valerie's hand and Valerie realises that nobody has touched her for days. She steps into the lift, alone. The cleaner watches as the door closes on the pale woman wearing mismatched shoes. She's seen it all before.

As predicted, the door to the Registrar's Office is on the left and straight ahead. Valerie hasn't remembered the instructions, it's just that turning left is the only option when the lift doors open. She pushes the polished wooden door and peeps around. There is a reception desk. The receptionist looks up and smiles at her. 'Mrs Hanover?' she asks.

'Anover. A-N-O-V-E-R,' says Valerie as she approaches.

'Take a seat around the corner, we'll call you when it's your turn,' says the receptionist.

Illness, accidents, bereavement, lockdown during a pandemic: these are all disorienting, disconnecting experiences. Although social connection is vital for our wellbeing, it needs to be a connection that we can control: the principles of invitation and acceptance, mutual responsibility, conversations by consent all apply as much in our families and friendships as they do when we seek or offer support or advice elsewhere. We require contact on our own terms, in spaces that are conducive to meeting and the enabling of privacy: choice is the key. There are times when we need company, and there are times when we are alone and content to know that company would be available should we choose it.

Since earliest times, people have lived in communities. We know that loneliness and isolation deprive humans of wellbeing, and we have learned that overcrowding and lack of privacy are damaging, too. As urban slums were cleared and new housing solutions were developed in the second half of the twentieth century, the rush to provide 'accommodation' sometimes failed to provide 'homes', with neighbourhoods, neighbourliness and community identity being lost to social experiments of high-rise living or isolating suburban housing estates. We have learned that housing developments need to be planned on a neighbourhood scale to create connected communities: neighbours need to be able to meet and greet each other, to have access to their own personal space and still be able to connect with other households as they choose. Estates designed with only motorists in mind force pedestrians to walk circuitous routes to shops or schools, without pathways on which they can pass each other and connect; social housing complexes can make residents feel corralled, resenting those shared areas that are overcrowded, belong to everyone and yet no one, and so become unkempt and inhospitable. Housing development requires good architecture and careful social design to create and nurture communities; in the UK, bodies like the Design Council work with central and local government, and with residents and communities, to promote integration, connection and accessibility in spaces ranging from individual public buildings to projects for social integration across whole cities. There is still much work to be done.

Municipal hubs are also necessary to ensure social connection. Where once communities might have gathered regularly at a place of worship, in a more diverse and increasingly secular society new places of gathering are needed. Libraries often serve this function, providing access to public information and advice, as well as to training in business skills or IT literacy, and offering computing facilities that some citizens do not have at home; running groups for particular interests that include reading and story events for children that also generate social opportunities for parents and grandparents; dementia-friendly events that offer opportunities for community connection both for people with dementia who may be losing their social independence and for family carers who benefit from the mutual support; 'chat cafés' and similar events that encourage strangers to strike up conversations, some open to all and others dedicated to people wanting to speak of ideas they struggle to engage their families in discussing, like grief chat spaces and Death Cafes. The loss of public libraries is a backwards step. Connection enhances wellbeing, reducing health-care costs down the line. Compassionate towns, cities and rural communities need accessible social hubs for the wellbeing of their citizens.

Valerie sits in the registrar's waiting area, handbag on her knees and chin up. She has Irvin's list in her bag. After she has the death certificate, she will need copies to send to many agencies. Irvin has typed it all out. She cannot imagine how she will find all these people: the pensions agency, the disability parking permit office, the passport office, on and on. Her reverie is interrupted by a voice.

'Mrs Anover? Hello, I am Derek Jennings, I am the Registrar. I am sorry to hear you are with us to register a death. Would you like to come with me to this office?' He is holding a door open, and Valerie walks through to an office overlooking the car park. She can't remember whether she paid and displayed. She worries how she would explain the fine to Irvin. Except . . .

'Please take a seat, Mrs Anover,' says the registrar. 'I'm going to take some details from you, and I'll explain some things. I'm going to give you all the information in writing, too, with a folder you can keep it in. I know it can be hard to remember everything at a time like this.' He smiles reassuringly and she feels slightly less frightened. She is surprised she feels so anxious all the time. *Shouldn't I feel sad?* she wonders. *Not just mixed up and afraid. Sad. Maybe that comes later.*

She opens her bag and brings out two envelopes, a brown one from the hospital, containing the medical certificate, and a large white one that holds all the couple's documents: birth and marriage certificates, national insurance cards, NHS cards, passports, driving licences. Irvin was good at keeping tabs on things. She feels she is already losing tabs. *Is that a thing, losing tabs? I can't quite tell.* She also lifts out Irvin's list. It feels like having him there to guide her.

The registrar asks for Irvin's full name, as registered on his birth certificate. Thankfully, Valerie empties the contents of the certificates envelope onto the wide desk. The registrar beams at her. 'Thank you, Mrs Anover. This is everything I need. Many people have no idea where all this information is. I hope it wasn't a lot of trouble to find it all.'

'Oh, not at all. My husband is very organised. Was. Was very organised.' She sniffs.

'I'm sorry, I know this is a hard time,' says the registrar. 'Excuse me not speaking for a moment, but I just want to put all of this information into my records here.' He knits his brows and taps notes into his computer: name, date and place of birth, birth certificate number, NHS number, all the details in Valerie's envelope.

'I am going to print out the death certificate now,' says the registrar. 'I know that you are likely to need a few copies, for your bank and for insurance policies. There are some official offices that need to know your husband has died, too, and I can sort that out for you. It's called "Tell Us Once", and it lets me notify all the government agencies on your behalf. I can see you have a list . . .' He gestures towards the paper in Valerie's hand.

'Yes, Irvin made it for me. All the people I need to notify,' she says.

'Shall I tick off the ones I can do for you?' offers the registrar, and Valerie pushes the paper across the desk to him. 'Right,' he says. 'Excellent list, Mrs Anover. Your husband was very organised, wasn't he? Let's see . . . OK, I can tell the Passport Office . . . the pensions agency about his Old Age pension, but not his private pension . . . I'll need to tell them your national insurance number, too, in case they need to recalculate your pension now. They will write to you to explain what will happen next, and they will stop his pension.' The registrar looks up to check she has heard. Valerie nods, and he goes back to the list. 'The driving licence people, and also the road tax people . . . the NHS . . . the library . . . the disability parking permit office.' He ticks them neatly, and Valerie thinks Irvin would like the neat ticks. 'All the government agencies, in one go. We hope it helps to ease a little bit of the load. It's taken a chunk off your list, see?'

'Tell Us Once' is a compassionate response to the administrative burden of the bereaved: an action by the state in response to distressed feedback from bereaved people about NHS appointments, road tax renewals and government agency letters sent to deceased people, causing heartache and confusion. It is a sign that the state can listen, and it can respond well. We need more of this. Listening can enable individuals, organisations and the state to offer compassionate responses that ease the burden of difficult times.

But listening is even more powerful than that: listening can save lives. Listening services for people who are experiencing thoughts of self-harm or suicide can make the difference between acting and waiting, between isolation and connection, between being alone and being heard. Samaritans is a national charity with a vision of reducing deaths by suicide. They offer free telephone, email and face-to-face support across the United Kingdom and the Republic of Ireland.* The service is staffed all day and night, every day of the year, by thousands of volunteers who are carefully selected and then trained as listeners. Their training teaches all volunteers the power of supporting someone to tell their story. Over the last five years alone, they estimate that they have taken

---

* Contact Samaritans by dialling 116 123. For other ways to get in touch, see https://www.samaritans.org/

a call for help every seven seconds. Their work has had a major impact on millions of lives, and yet they offer no advice or intervention: instead, they listen; they use helpful, curious questions to enable the full story to be explored, and they offer a space in which their callers can speak of their distress and helplessness. The power of telling the story and considering how to respond to their own difficulties allows callers to examine options other than suicide. Some callers are on the brink of taking action to end their lives, others call in the midst of sorrow, panic, self-doubt or loneliness. There is no judgement, there is simply calm and compassionate listening, focused on hearing the story, exploring what the caller is thinking and feeling in the moment, using silence and short messages of support to encourage them to speak, and checking understanding to show that the story is being carefully attended to. Listening as a lifeline.

In a highly successful campaign to reduce suicide deaths on railways, Samaritans trained more than fifteen thousand railway employees in conversation skills to approach people who look distressed at stations, beside railway crossings and on trains. There was a measurable impact on the reduction of railway suicides. A campaign to engage the public to act followed, funded by Network Rail, called *Small Talk Saves Lives*. Simply by striking up a conversation, lives have been saved as a person's suicidal thoughts were interrupted by a concerned member of the public mentioning the weather, asking about train times, asking their name or asking, very simply, 'Are you OK?' It is estimated that, thanks to this awareness-raising, for every death by suicide on a railway six lives are saved by a member of the public striking up a conversation. This is the power of human connection.

The mental health campaign Time to Change encourages everyone to 'ask twice'. This is another reminder of the power of showing willingness to listen. When we ask someone whether they are all right, their almost automatic response is to say, 'Yes, I'm fine.' *Ask Twice* reminds us that by showing sufficient interest to ask again, we are signalling that our question goes beyond mere politeness. A second enquiry is far more likely to evoke an admission of distress, struggle or difficulties, and to begin a helpful conversation. Asking twice says, 'I am willing to listen.'

There are suicide prevention or crisis listening services all over the world.*

Valerie waits for the lift back to entrance level in the town hall. She cannot remember whether she has anything in the house for Irv's evening meal. Perhaps she should pick something up on the way home. The shock of remembering makes her jump as the lift bell dings and the doors slide open. She peruses the list of departments and floors in the building to distract herself. 'Coroner's Court' is on level one. Valerie remembers the Coroner's Court, because she and Irv had to attend the inquest into Irv's dad's death there. That must be a long time ago, now, she reflects. *I wonder whether they have anywhere to sit these days.* She remembers how Irv wanted to catch a quiet word with the pathologist after the verdict was announced, as expected, as 'industrial disease'. Irv's dad had worked in the shipyards, and asbestos exposure caused lung diseases that affected many workers. A quiet word was impossible: the only place to talk was standing in the corridor among the families waiting for the next case and the bustle of staff moving to and fro. There was some kind of disagreement among the members of one family waiting, and a lot of shouting, she remembers. The lift doors open, and she is back at the foot of the grand staircase. The kindly cleaner has gone, and Valerie retraces her earlier steps to the foyer, past the scale model of this

---

* There are several websites offering crisis call numbers, including www. suicidestop.com/call_a_hotline.html

very town hall made by a local school, and out into the car park. She thinks Irv might have talked about that model. She'll ask him later.

The Courts and Tribunals Service (HMCTS), like the NHS, owns or leases buildings around the country to serve the population, in this case to provide venues where justice is served. Again like the NHS, the premises available comprise a mix of older buildings, built to serve a function that has changed over the passing years, and newer facilities, some of which are new enough to have benefited from a recent HMCTS review of their estates and the resulting recommendations for the design and fitting of courts and tribunals buildings. In these places, where judgements are made after intense scrutiny, there is sorrow, blame and shame for some and vindication after long waiting for others; as Justice is played out families can be created or broken, reputations and businesses may be saved or ruined, family disputes over the care or medical treatment of people without capacity to decide for themselves may be resolved to the satisfaction of some family members and the despair of others; and in the coroner's courts, as experienced by Valerie and Irvin, causes of death will be ascertained to the best of the coroner's ability, with verdicts that may ease or compound the grief of the bereaved. These are theatres of high-stakes decisions and deep emotion. Surely here is a need for compassionate spaces?

Sadly, as for hospitals, the professionals and the users of these services describe the paucity of protected spaces for quiet, sensitive conversations. The system is too busy, the attendees too numerous for waiting spaces to be conducive or private; the need to maintain order and safety takes priority over providing space for the tender conversations that might yet save a family from rupture or individuals from anguish. In the criminal justice system, jurors may hear and see highly disturbing information yet find themselves unable to discuss their distress with their closest supporters; after a sentence is pronounced, families may leave a convicted loved one in custody and have no moment of farewell; in the family courts, adversaries may have to wait for their hearing in the same communal waiting area.

Official guidance about the design of HMCTS buildings emphasises the need to ensure that users of the premises are safe and that they feel their needs for access and dignity are understood and addressed, but there is rather more guidance about ensuring the dignity and authority of the courts and tribunals than the tender consolation of the service users; the guidance acknowledges that open waiting areas, as well as any consultation rooms that may be available, are the spaces in which users prepare for their hearings. The corridor conversation will live on, it seems.

Although HMCTS is a service that is predicated on establishing the truth, or on deciding the right action to take in difficult circumstances, courts are not designed or intended to provide space for reflection, consideration and discussion between people affected by a specific case. By the time a matter has escalated to court, the time for reflection is usually past. Like our hospitals, our justice buildings are not designed for tenderness, but for the processing of their essential business. Although crisis can often be a catalyst for human connection and reconciliation, the often adversarial processes and unforgiving buildings of the justice system mitigate against that possibility.

Valerie will arrive home and find her house quiet and empty. Over the next few days, arrangements for Irvin's funeral will keep her occupied; friends and family will rally, apart from those so incapacitated by their inability to speak to her for fear of saying the wrong thing that they will avoid her completely and compound her pain. Loss of connection begins invisibly: people mean to make contact but find themselves distracted; invitations are not offered; cards sit, unwritten by their would-be, could-be, won't-be sender. Loneliness is not a choice; it is a sentence imposed by circumstances that sever our connections. There will be days when Valerie will relish solitude; there will be days when she longs for company. Most of all, though, she will miss the easy conversation of people who knew Irvin and who still have memories of him to share. She will miss the chance to say his name, and to hear it said in return.

One of her cherished moments will be a parcel sent by Southside High School, containing messages of condolence from staff and students. 'Mr A' retired five years ago, but the older students and most staff remember him with fondness. Messages, cards and notes from students recall how Mr A gave them faith in themselves; how the tech room was a haven for unhappy students, a safe space in the mayhem of a busy school; how Mr A always had a listening ear or a job that he 'just needed a hand with' the very moment he bumped into a distressed-looking student. Schools, too, are communities, where compassionate spaces are needed and where the experiments of designating quiet rooms or outdoor spaces, in which students can study quietly or withdraw from the commotion of their peers to reflect or to connect, are being evaluated. Intuitively, Irvin Anover had provided the 'quiet space' in the high school, where all were welcome at times when no class was in progress and after school, whether to work on a construction project or just to find a welcoming space for quiet reflection. There is a reason that Mr A was the favourite teacher for students like Jake: he wore his compassion on his overalls sleeve and used listening as a tool of his trade.

The wet and windy pavements of Britain and Ireland do not readily lend themselves to café culture. Despite this, a new type of space for conversations is growing and spreading, albeit mainly indoors, as chat cafés of various types become established. Some welcome people with specific life challenges, like dementia cafés and carer cafés. Some are set up to offer spaces for personal connection for the elderly, or for the bereaved. Some are for carers with their pre-school children; some cater for teens. Some are held in actual cafés, and some are ad hoc affairs that borrow rooms in libraries, village halls and schools. Since the Covid-19 pandemic, many chat cafés that began in physical spaces have added an online dimension. Moving online has made chat spaces more accessible for some people, although others who lack the requisite technology or know-how find themselves excluded; in the future, both real and virtual spaces will be needed to allow people to choose their routes to connection.

Death Cafes are gatherings to talk about dying and death. The Death Cafe movement is nearly ten years old and its aim is *to increase awareness of death with a view to helping people make the most of their (finite) lives*. There is no specific agenda apart from that of offering a welcoming and compassionate space in which people who may be strangers to each other can speak and be listened to, a space to share their ideas and experiences. A social franchise that has spread by reputation, offering advice about running meetings on its website,* Death Cafe has recorded more than twelve thousand events in seventy-eight countries. People gather to reflect on many matters related to death. It may be to discuss their own mortality or to prepare for the death of a beloved person, or to think about and rehearse for the conversations they would like to have with their own closest people, about their wishes and preferences when they are dying. The rules of the movement are few and simple, and they are there to ensure the space is supportive and free from any external agenda. Recommendations for running a Death Cafe include advice to provide refreshments for participants that include, as a recommendation by Death Cafe's founder, Jon

---

* https://deathcafe.com/

Underwood, tea and delicious cake. This combination of the mundanity of cake and the profundity of death offers an invitation into a thoughtful and shared listening space. With the right support, we can talk about anything. We just need people who are willing to listen.

The UK had declared a 'loneliness epidemic' two years before the Covid-19 pandemic, with a government minister appointed to oversee efforts to reduce loneliness in society. Lockdown during the pandemic introduced many more people to the experience of being alone, and it increased discussion of loneliness, but it is important to distinguish between the states of lonely longing for better and more frequent communication, or of sorrowful resignation to loss of meaningful connections in life – both of which might describe real loneliness – and a state of simply being alone. The state of loneliness is partly about the perceived gap between what connection people wish for and what they have, and partly about how they interpret that gap.

A busy home life may leave some people craving time alone: this voluntary and elusive aloneness is viewed as a positive experience, as 'me time'. The experience of taking a retreat, originally a spiritual practice of withdrawal into solitude for contemplation and prayer and more recently also describing a non-religious well-being exercise, might involve the experience of loneliness but here it is interpreted as purposeful, a useful part of the retreat's benefit.

Loneliness is complex, and 'providing company' is not a panacea. Any strategy to tackle loneliness will need to be multi-faceted to address its various interconnected and confounding causes, recognising that loneliness disproportionately affects older people, people on low incomes, people with disabilities and those living with long-term ill-health. Loneliness is more likely to be reported by women than by men, and a large minority of teenagers and young adults report frequent loneliness, despite their electronic connection via screens and phones. The gap between young people's expectations and reality may, perhaps, be found on their screens as they watch others post about their 'perfect' social lives while observing the relative poverty of real connection in their own.

Loneliness, in turn, affects people's health, being associated with both physical harms such as cardiovascular disease and premature mortality, and mental health harms such as depression. Treating loneliness like a health problem, though, is unlikely to be the solution on its own. A nuanced and widespread social change will be needed that tackles poverty, design of multi-occupant accommodation, neighbourhood connectedness, availability of social events and the practical and emotional support needed to attend them. Good design of neighbourhoods means that people can meet and greet each other in spaces that are accessible to all and feel safe and welcoming, such as pedestrianised areas, parks, local shops, markets and high streets; or spend time together in cafés, libraries, village halls, locality hubs, leisure facilities or places of worship.

Neighbourliness is something that can happen by chance, or that might be encouraged by social policy, but it cannot happen unless we embrace it. We are each other's neighbours. While we watch local and national politicians and campaign groups implement anti-loneliness strategies, perhaps it is worth asking ourselves what our role is as individuals in tackling social isolation and loneliness.

What would it take for us to incorporate the skills of tender conversations into our society? What could be the benefits of becoming a Conversation Nation? In the end, this is not about other people. Those people with dilemmas and anxieties and stuckness; those people who don't know what to say or where to start the conversation; those people who need connection for their health and wellbeing: they are us. We are all participants on the dancefloor of humanity.

Sometimes change happens, not when we wait for a leader and the development of innovative strategies, but when we act on what we already know. The need for connection affects all of us, change can begin with any of us, and we can all act on this truth: compassion shared transforms lives, and listening is a good place to start.

Listening: a Style Guide

Skills *and intention*	Keep in mind
Invite, don't insist *The other person has control*	Right time, right place? Reduce any power imbalance
Listen to understand *The other person feels understood*	Accept without judging Check your understanding Accept that the solution is not simple Accept that emotions are high You don't need to know what to say: trust yourself Value the silences
Remain curious *The other person feels listened to*	Be open-minded Meet as equals You don't know the answer, and that's OK
Helpful questions **1. Current situation** *The other person is enabled to examine their situation* **2. Looking for ways forward** *The other person is enabled to examine their options*	Use open questions Explore together Don't give advice

Useful phrases

Please may we talk about . . .?

Where would you like to start?

What do I need to know?

I'll listen

Tell me the story

Can I check: do you mean . . .?

What you've told me so far is . . . Have I got that right?

It sounds as though you feel sad/angry/afraid/. . . about this . . .

. . . Silence . . .

Would you tell me about . . .

I'd like to hear more about . . .

How . . .? What . . .? When . . .? Where . . .?

Tell me more about . . .

How do you feel about that?

What else did you think/say/do/feel?

What do you think about/make of all that now?

Could we be missing anything here?

Could there be a different way to interpret this?

What have you considered so far?

Is there something that could easily be changed?

What previous experience could you apply here?

What would you advise a friend in a similar situation?

Skills *and intention*	Keep in mind
Sit with distress *The other person feels their distress is acknowledged*	Don't try to fix it Acknowledge the distress
Let silence do its work *The other person has space to think*	Don't fill the silences Use simple expressions to show you are still present
Finish safely *The other person is not left feeling exposed or more vulnerable*	Share the timekeeping Closing doesn't mean it's finished Watch for tiredness or loss of privacy Mutual agreement
Self-care *You are able to remain healthy*	You deserve care, too Keeping well is important Boundaries matter

Useful phrases

This is hard

I am sorry this is so sad/frightening/. . . for you

I am here

I will try to support you

Hmmm

Take your time

There's no rush

Yes . . .

It's hard, it's tough, it's OK to take your time

There's lots to think about

It's time to finish soon, but we can come back to this

Thank you for listening/talking to me

Would it be all right to leave this for now?

I'm sorry that I can't take this on

I wish I could, but . . .

. . . I don't have the time this needs right now

. . . I need to recharge my batteries first

No (repeated if necessary)

Acknowledgements

This book has had a long gestation. I am deeply indebted to all the patients, families and colleagues I have worked with in hospitals, hospices, the community and universities for four decades, for your wisdom and example. You have shown me the importance of tenderness in our conversations and fuelled my curiosity about how we might develop our listening skills. Thank you to all the readers of my previous book, *With the End In Mind*, who made contact to tell me about the impact of tenderness, or the lack of it, on your own experiences, and for the huge correspondence about how we might approach tender conversations in the future.

Reflection on readers' feedback with my agent, Andrew Gordon, and my editor, Arabella Pike, prompted the possibility of condensing my understanding of tender conversations into a book. My beloved family then had to live with me while it was being written: thank you for your patience, your encouragement and for providing the gallons of tea that have fuelled this endeavour. I'm sorry that recently I've been more invested in writing about listening than in being a listener for you all: I hope I can do better from now on.

During the writing I have consulted a variety of experts to make sure I was describing their work accurately. I am grateful to you all for your time and your willingly shared wisdom: Brigid

Russell and Charlie Jones, for welcoming me into your #SpacesForListening and for mulling over the importance of being listened to; Becky Whittaker and Gemma Chady, for insights into dance as a metaphor for listening skills; Ruth Parry and Becky Whittaker, for sharing your vast knowledge of conversation analysis; Tom King, David Leat and Rachel Lofthouse, for discussion of pupil peer support and teaching of curiosity in schools; Jane Harris and Jimmy Edmonds, for teaching me how to be a companion in grief; Jools Barsky and Jon Underwood, for Death Cafe; Damian Cooper, Joe Cooper, Gary Rycroft and Alex Ruck Keene, for discussion of spaces for compassion within different parts of HM Courts and Tribunals Service; Julie Bentley, Lucia Capobianco and Clare Lemon of Samaritans, for insights into your campaigns and the vital work of your volunteers; Anita Luby and her colleagues in the Death-Positive Libraries movement, for insights into development of compassionate spaces in public libraries; Margaret Stafford, for discussion of conversations with looked-after children and young people. I'm also indebted to the much-missed Ian Clark, and his colleagues at JDDH Architects, for awakening my interest in providing compassionate spaces in public buildings, an idea they have championed for decades.

I am grateful for the many companions on social media who have included me in thoughtful conversations about the way we discuss those hard-to-broach topics. Your honesty and your confidence in me are deeply appreciated, and I have learned much from our conversations there. I also appreciate the tenderness in which you hold each other in that virtual world, sharing each other's sorrows and walking alongside each other in dark times.

My first readers: Chris, Josie, Tom and Jaclyn Wright, Denis and John Mannix, for your insights and patience. The Reading Group: Kathy Burn, Julia Byrne, Alison Conner, Lindsay Crack, Julie Ellis, Sam Genders, Beda Higgins, Ros and Geoff Hoskin, Lilias Huxham, Terri Lydiard, Christine Milton, Ruth Parry, Jane

Peutrell, Margaret Price, Fiona Rawlinson, Lynette Snowden, Margaret Stafford. Thank you for your love, time and support.

During the writing I have been grateful for supportive contact from David Evans, and from Alice Howe and her colleagues in the translation department, at David Higham Associates. Thank you all for your efforts to get these ideas out into the world.

I am forever grateful for the wise counsel of my agent, Andrew Gordon, and for the encouragement and expertise of the team at William Collins. In a year unlike any other, you have remained positive and enthusiastic supporters. Special thanks to Arabella Pike, Katherine Patrick, Jo Thompson, Liv Marsden, Matt Clacher and Shoaib Rokadiya for your undimmable energy and wise counsel, to Iain Hunt for your detailed and supportive copy-editing that sharpened the clarity of my writing, to Katy Archer for keeping editing on track and to Ellie Game for your inspiring cover design.

In the end, human wellbeing is rooted in community and nurtured by being listened to and understood. Thank you, all of you, for being my community.

Kathryn Mannix
Northumberland
July 2021